EARLY PRAISE *for* BEHIND THE DRIVE

"A great read! This book contains much wisdom as well as practical lessons about business as well as life. Kenney Moore is a man who loves people – and he gets the fact that the business of business is people."

— **JAMES C. HUNTER**, international bestselling author of *The Servant*

"I can't say enough about this book. *Behind the Drive* is a brilliant reminder of what really matters in both business and life. Kenney Moore bares his soul, flaws and failures and all, with a stark honesty that makes this one of the bravest and most refreshing books I've read in a long time. And on top of all that, it's a beautifully written, simply thrilling story full of high drama, a gripping read from start to finish. This is an essential book for anybody — of any generation — who wants more out of life."

— **PAT WILLIAMS**, Orlando Magic Senior Vice President and bestselling author of more than 95 books, including *Coach Wooden, The Mission Is Remission,* and *How To Be Like Walt*

"Kenney Moore is a rebel with a heart of gold — and with a story that our world needs right now. As you read about his excruciating battle with the banks — and with himself — to save his business, you're not just learning from him, but you find yourself rooting for him harder and harder with every page. Whoever you are, whatever your story, whatever your politics or your beliefs, whatever your lot in life, *Behind the Drive* is a must-read for anybody with a dream."

— **KENNAN BURCH**, President and Founder of Brand Catalyst Partners

"'Genuine best' describes Kenney's story and Kenney's approach to life and people. I have had the pleasure to know Kenney for 15 years, personally and professionally. We have a shared passion for helping others identify and activate their American Dream. This book is a vivid example of how and why it is still alive. Kenney is truly driven to excel and inspired to pay it forward. He has lived an inspirational life, reflected perfectly in this book."

— **SAMIR GUPTE**, Senior Vice President of Human Resources at OTG Management, former Senior Vice President of Culture at Darden Restaurants

BEHIND THE DRIVE

A STORY OF PASSION, DREAMS, DEMONS, AND HWY 55,
THE WORLD'S NEXT FAVORITE BURGER JOINT

BRANDON SNEED AND
KENNEY MOORE

TEN22
PUBLISHING
www.ten22publishing.com

Published in Greenville, North Carolina, by Ten22 Publishing.

For permissions and other information, contact
Ten22 Publishing at ten22publishing@gmail.com.

ISBN: 9780986119101

Library of Congress Number: 2015901618

Book design by Katie Sneed | www.katiesneed.com

Cover photography by Amanda Holloman of
Millie Holloman Photography | www.millieholloman.com

First Edition 2015

Printed and bound in the United States of America

Ten22 Publishing
www.ten22publishing.com

1 2 3 4 5 6 7 8 9 10

KENNEY MOORE
*To my wife of almost 30 years, Karen — you've been
by my side and loved me, sometimes in spite of me,
while raising four amazing kids and always keeping
the home fires burning.*

*Oh, and also, to Van Halen, for getting me through my
teenage years.*

BRANDON SNEED
*To Jonah — you showed up right when I started on
this book, you grew into a tiny human along the
way, and you make your mom and me happier than
anything else ever has. Love you, kid. Dream big.*

CONTENTS

AUTHOR'S NOTE

We set out to tell a good and honest story. To that end, a brief breakdown of our process: Kenney and I spent countless hundreds of hours talking, and I also interviewed more than 300 people and read and/or consumed countless articles, television stories, and other media sources about Moore, Hwy 55, and others related to this story. In other words: This *is* a collaboration between Kenney and me, yes, but he was wonderfully gracious and transparent about his story.

We also decided that others in this book may not be quite as excited as Kenney about sharing their worst moments. Thus, we have changed some names in order to protect the innocent, have mercy on the guilty, and give grace to those who were probably just having a bad day.

For more information, contact me at www.brandonsneed.com or our publisher at www.ten22publishing.com.

—— BRANDON SNEED

"I remember seeing a presidential campaign commercial in 1984 that said, 'It's morning again in America,' and being inspired by it. I believed that I could do or be whatever I wanted. And I just don't hear that anymore. I don't hear our leaders talking about, 'Go get the American Dream.' That's the sad part. Most of what comes out of Washington, D.C. — and from either party — is incredibly negative. The rhetoric you often hear from politicians and you get from the media now, it's almost like that American Dream is dead. And it's not. And if anyone can call B.S. on that, I can."

—— KENNEY MOORE

1

THE FUTURE, WHICH
ALMOST WASN'T

He had to go a long way to get here, and really, he should have never made it. There's no *way* he should have made it, not if you look at things like destiny and fate and statistics, not to mention good logic and common sense, but here he is.

His name is Kenney Moore. (He spells it *-ey* because he likes to be different.) It's March 2014, and he is standing in a restaurant called Hwy 55 Burgers, Shakes & Fries that looks like something straight out of the 1950s. White tables with silver piping and silver chairs with teal and maroon seat cushions are scattered throughout the center of the restaurant, with vivid teal and maroon booths lining the walls. The floor is shiny black and white squares. Vinyl records and vintage-style murals cover the walls — men driving '57 Chevys, couples wearing classic '50s outfits eating in booths that look like the ones on the floor, and Elvis, Marilyn Monroe, and their peers performing. It's the newest Hwy 55, and while Moore can't make it to every store the first week it opens, he sure tries, and no way was he missing this one.

Moore just turned 51. He started the chain back in 1991,

when he was 28 years old and broke and desperate. After a year and a half, he was tens of thousands of dollars in debt and struggling. He hoped to, maybe one day, open 20 restaurants in eastern North Carolina, maybe do a few million a year in sales, make a nice little dent in the area, maybe even give some money away to people who could put it to good use, that sort of thing. That's aspirational enough for a kid who grew up broke, and who was a terrible student, and whose greatest ambition heading into college was to make it as a baseball player or maybe even as an actor. Twenty stores wouldn't be too shabby a legacy, and it would provide for his family, and he figured he couldn't handle much more than that, anyway.

Moore's been here all day, talking with his newest business partners, handsome young men in their twenties with manicured beards, and dark skin, and Lamborghinis. Moore's eyes are big and blue and alive, crackling with electricity, and he has a strong voice, one cultivated over years of practice. He has a goatee, mostly gray, and he has thick hair, almost shaggy but not quite, parted on the left and hanging over the sides of his forehead, over his ears, dirty blonde and gray. He wears dark blue jeans with brown loafers and a black v-neck t-shirt. His arms and chest are strong and thick, and his shoulders broad, like a man who works out, yeah, but who also just plain *works*.

The Hwy 55 he's standing in now could be anywhere in North Carolina, with a few minor exceptions. The telephone number on the glass door is a little strange, and there's Arabic on the menus, and a lot of the guys hanging out in here wear white *thobe*s, tailored shirt-like tunics that reach to the ankles, and white *shora*s, scarves worn on the head and held in place by an *egal,* a black rope-like headband.

These are his newest business partners.

Moore steps outside to take a breath. He opens the glass doors and walks across the black marble threshold and down black marble steps. Rising before him are skyscrapers, many of them, all around. He's in Abu Dhabi, capital of the United Arab Emirates, where more than half a million people live, richest city in the world, miles upon miles upon miles away from home in every figurative and literal sense — 7,268 miles and a day in a plane around the planet from Mount Olive, North Carolina, population 5,000, the place he calls home, and even further from his past. This Hwy 55 is number 107 to open in the world, and just the first of dozens coming to the Middle East, and the next in a long, long line of what should one day be thousands more.

Moore flew out of Raleigh on his birthday, March 15, with his family and Guy Guthrie, the Hwy 55 Vice President of Franchise Sales. They spent a day in London with Moore's family, and then he and Guthrie hopped a flight to Abu Dhabi.

Once he arrived, he was astounded. Fifty years ago, Abu Dhabi's streets were lined with shanties. Earlier today he saw 11 new skyscrapers under construction on the same street. The city is full of breathtaking buildings — some that look like they are waving, some that look like perfect circles, some that look like pineapples. It's a city wild with human creativity and ambition, a place stretching all of its limits, a place growing and growing and growing — a good place for Moore and Hwy 55.

Moore looks up. It's a perfect and clear night. He can see all of the stars for millions of miles. He takes a deep breath, and then another. *I am halfway around the world.* He's in one of the most inspiring cities on the planet, in the middle of a booming epicenter of modern architecture — and right here, right behind him, in the middle of it all, is his restaurant, his modest little slice of North Carolina. And not only that, but back home, there are Hwy 55s in a dozen states, and there are nearly a thousand more to come, all around the world. It's a safe bet that before long they'll hit sales of $1 billion. The *Franchise Business Review* just ranked Hwy 55 as one of the best food franchises in the United States, and Hwy 55 also recently won a nationwide contest for the best burger.

This all hits Moore hard as he stands here on the Abu Dhabi sidewalk, humbling him, bringing tears to his eyes and nearly driving him to his knees as he thanks God.

■ ■ ■

The next day he flies to Paris — *Paris* — where his wife of 29 years, Karen, and three of his four kids are waiting for him: Emma, 21, a student at St. Andrews in Scotland; Isabelle, 13; and Dylan, 11. His fourth, Andy, the oldest at 24, is back in the States, where he graduated from Duke two years ago and now lives in New York City, an editor for a big website.

When Karen married Kenney way back when, the idea of *Kenney Moore* flying her to *Paris* was ridiculous. She didn't know she was marrying a guy who'd become the owner and CEO of a multinational company and be *flying her to Paris.* (For that matter, neither did he.) Karen grew up in a swanky private school where her father was the principal, and she came of age around trust fund babies who aspired to things like joining exclusive country clubs and, well, flying to Paris. She never wanted any part of that. She had no clue this is where she'd be at this point in her life, that her husband would be this type of guy.

Of course, Kenney is not *that* type of guy — he's a man who on any given day will wear T-shirts into the office that say "da fuq?" and "Libertarians: Quietly plotting to take over the world and leave you alone" (a joke on good days, a little less so on bad). He drives too fast, and he still has a weakness for dip, and he still cusses more than he wants to. The cussing bothers him so much that one of his New Year's resolutions was to stop. He broke it on January 2.

■ ■ ■

After a few days in Europe, Kenney is back in Mount Olive at 7:30 on Sunday evening. After a turbulent childhood spent all over the world as the stepson of a Marine, this is home. Mount Olive is about an hour west of Wilmington, 50 minutes south of Raleigh, and Kenney has lived here for the last 20 years. There are no skyscrapers. There isn't even a bar. It's small-town America at its finest: a small local college, a tiny downtown, the whole town taking up just over two square miles, surrounded by miles and miles of sprawling fields and farmland. His house is a two-story Colonial with wood siding painted olive green. A white fence surrounds the property and a gate blocks the driveway. That's new, and Kenney would rather do without it, but people kept breaking in. They're just a few blocks from Karen's parents, and they've renovated and added onto the house, building up their home over many years. There's a pool on the side and chickens in the yard — Karen likes fresh eggs — and four dogs runing around, all different breeds and sizes.

Kenney's in his chair in the living room by 7:45, and by 8, he's asleep.

The next morning, he's up around 8. He puts on sweatpants and a t-shirt and meditates for half an hour. Then he puts on a golf hat and running shoes, gets into his black Tesla Model S, and drives to the Hwy 55 Burgers, Shakes & Fries corporate office building, about five minutes from his house. (Cars are all he really splurges on, and even then, while he buys expensive ones, he keeps just one at a time.) Kenney arrives at the office around nine and does his morning workout in the office gym — yoga today, working out the kinks from all the time in planes. After a shower, he changes into a v-neck t-shirt, jeans, and loafers, and he works until lunch, a few minutes before noon.

Lunch, as always, is in the conference room down the hall from his office, and, as always, the conference table is surrounded by about a dozen of Kenney's executive staff. They all eat lunch together almost every day. Today, they all buzz and gush about Kenney's Abu Dhabi trip. Most of them, anyway. The in-house attorney, Keith Moore — Kenney's younger half-brother — eats fast and silent at the end of the table, as he often does, and he's the first to leave, as he often is.

The room is lit by the sunlight pouring in through the window. Outside is a cool, clear spring day. There's also a parking lot with a maroon Trailblazer, an older, black Hummer H2, a black Camry, an old, white Jeep Cherokee, and a few other such modest cars, along with about a dozen bright teal Ford Fiestas wrapped with the Hwy 55 logo. Beyond the parking lot, three acres of fresh-cut grass stretch to the road, and beyond the road, and all around the office building, are acres upon acres of flat eastern North Carolina fields, stretching for miles interspersed with groves of green pine trees.

Kenney works until 7, and then he stays for a managers' meeting. Several dozen men and women of all ages fill the first floor meeting room. Kenney tells them about his trip, about the Abu Dhabi staff, about how hard they are working. He tells them about walking out of the restaurant and looking up at the night sky going on forever, and how he'd almost cried, overwhelmed by gratitude. And then he tells them how he almost didn't make it there.

He almost didn't make it to Abu Dhabi, or Paris, or this office, as the head of one of the best franchises in America, for a multitude of reasons. Personal, professional, spiritual, existential — in many ways, he could have ended up going down a different and darker road.

Today, he tells his managers a simpler story. He's achieved remarkable things in his life, and he considers getting on a plane again as remarkable as anything else he's done. He is afraid of flying.

When Kenney started franchising outside of North Carolina a few years ago, he knew he should probably get over it at some point, but he still avoided it as long as he could. When he went to New York for a national television interview in October 2013, he took the train. That same month, Kenney's wife and two youngest kids, Isabelle and Dylan, flew to London to visit Emma, who flew down from Scotland. Kenney couldn't make himself go with them.

When he'd last flown — two decades prior — he nearly had a panic attack. He couldn't talk. He had cottonmouth. He couldn't eat his complimentary peanuts. He spent the whole flight squeezing his armrests so hard his hands cramped. He didn't mind the takeoff and landing, even though those were technically the most dangerous parts. It was flight itself that terrified him. Flight is, after all, a war against gravity, and a war that, when you're sitting in a seat in a metal tube in the sky, you can't help fight. It was a real fear borne out of his complete lack of control, and in many ways, Kenney Moore's entire life has been a fight for control.

But with his family an ocean away, "I was absolutely beating myself up for it," Kenney says. "One, for not going.

For letting that fear get to me. And then, here I had my wife and my kids in another country, in a big city, and I'm not even there with them. You know, to protect them as a husband and a dad, and to share that experience with them."

So it wasn't Abu Dhabi and becoming an international restaurant mogul that made Kenney overcome his fear of flying — the sweeter, almost saccharine truth is that it was for his family.

Karen gave Kenney a book called *Soar: The Breakthrough Treatment for Fear of Flying,* by Tom Bunn, a pilot of 31 years and licensed psychologist.

Kenney devoured it.

Every November, he and several of his old baseball buddies make a trip down to Kenney's house in Orlando, and they always take an RV. That November, though, after Karen and the kids' great London adventure, Kenney determined to fly down to Florida, beat this fear. He told few people — he didn't even tell Karen. "I didn't want her to talk to me the whole week leading up, and saying, 'How are you doing?' all the time, and all that," he says. "I was so bad that even if we talked about flying, I would get anxious. Just *discussing* flying."

His friend Billy Godwin, an old college baseball teammate who was going to drive the RV to Orlando, offered to go with him, but Kenney said, "No, this is something I have to do by myself."

He wore jeans and a T-shirt and a blazer. He checked his bags and his golf clubs and made his way through the security line, making sure to take his laptop out of his carry-on. He took off his blazer and his belt and his watch and dropped his wallet in the bin, and he headed for the metal detector. The only anxiety he felt was when a TSA agent yelled at him because he forgot to take off his shoes.

While waiting to board, he didn't take a tranquilizer or a Xanax. He didn't even drink. He wanted to *feel* the bumps, feel everything that scared him.

He had a window seat. When they took off, he didn't squeeze the armrests or get cottonmouth. He looked out the window, watching as they left the ground, and he smiled. *Whoa. I'm doing it.* When they descended toward the Orlando runway, and the plane passed over the ocean and then some lakes and ponds, he didn't worry about crashing into them. He admired the beauty, and he thought about how nice it was to fly to Orlando in two hours instead driving for nine, and he looked for alligators.

To make up for missing October, Kenney made the Abu Dhabi trip into a whole big thing, with the weeklong stay in London and Paris for his wife and kids, so they could all hang out, so they could do what they should've done the year before, together. And then that night in Abu Dhabi, looking up at the stars, he felt that moment with God. Worth it, a million times over.

After telling his managers that story, Kenney said, "Look, I practice what I preach: You decide who and what you're going to be every day. I'm so glad that I overcame my fear of flying so that I got to experience that. I made a decision that this fear was all in my head. That fear was based on nothing real. It was all me. And I overcame it. So I'm practicing what I tell you all to do: Do not worry about your past. Do not worry about where you come from. It's not who you are that matters, it's who you aspire to become, and how hard you are willing to work to get there. You wake up every day, and you decide who and what you're going to be."

Good and inspirational words, a good talk from a good CEO. Leaders everywhere and throughout history have given speeches like it, and probably several times over. But Kenney feels like people are forgetting it — and not just everyday people like himself whose mission (or plight) it is to find a way in this world. He feels like even the world's leaders seem to be losing hope. Soon after his Abu Dhabi trip, Kenney tells a writer, "I remember seeing a presidential campaign commercial in 1984 that said, *'It's morning again in America,'* and being inspired by it. I believed that I could do or be whatever I wanted. And I just don't hear that anymore. I don't hear our leaders talking about, *'Go get the American Dream.'* That's the sad part. Most of what comes out of Washington, D.C. — and from either party — is incredibly negative. The rhetoric you often hear from politicians and you get from the media now, it's almost like that American Dream is dead. And it's not. And if anyone can call B.S. on that, I can."

■ ■ ■

Kenney has become what he's become and built the company he's built and helped the people he's helped not only because he's learned how to be a great businessman and a great leader, but also because he's had to learn how to be a decent man. And that was much harder — *still is* much harder — than being a great businessman, and that's as much if not more a part of his story than any of the ways he built his business. Kenney hasn't just wanted to build a great business and do great things for the world and live the American Dream. His whole life has been an exercise in getting control, not only of his business but also of himself.

One thing Kenney loved about flying to and from Abu Dhabi: the in-flight entertainment, a movie buffet. He watched *12 Years A Slave, Jobs, Nebraska* — and one in particular that his travel buddy, Guy Guthrie, remembers with horror: *August: Osage County.*

It's about a dysfunctional, vicious Southern family. One scene goes on for more than 10 minutes with everyone yelling and swearing and saying the worst things to each other, all while sharing a meal. Guthrie was recoiling and squirming in his seat, not believing people could speak to each other like that. Kenney, however, was all too comfortable. Watching the scene didn't feel *good,* but it was familiar, the way an ex-con might feel visiting a prison.

Kenney grew up in one such metaphorical prison, its bars and locks and guards all so much yelling and swearing and chaos. He also thought he'd long ago broken free, only to discover, not so long ago, that he was wrong. Over the past few years, he's found himself fighting to break free all over again in order to save all he's built from being laid to waste.

2

THE DEVIL STIRS
The Bank Saga, Part 1

Big challenges require all of who we are, and Kenney faced a big challenge in 2008. Hwy 55 Burgers, Shakes & Fries was called Andy's Cheesesteaks and Cheeseburgers back then, and it was only found in North Carolina. The Andy's corporate office started getting one phone call after another, from customers and employees alike, from all over the state, all asking, "What happened to our Andy's?"

The total came to 15. Fifteen stores, nearly 15 percent of the company, had just shut down. Their owners and managers were even missing. And nobody knew why.

All too quickly, Kenney solved the mystery: With the economy hurting, Andy's sales were down more than 20 percent. "When that happens, you gotta get in there and strap your boots on and get after it," Kenney says. "And they didn't want to do that, so they walked out." Between the economy and various personal matters, those stores' owners decided to lock up and walk away.

Kenney could have left it at that and let the company's bank deal with it. That would have been simple, clean, and easy, and Kenney needed simple, clean, and easy. The economic crash of 2008 was hurting him like it was hurting everyone else, but on top of that, he was also in the process of buying — and acquiring the debt of — 10 stores from his former Chief Operating Officer, Dan Jones, who left the company in late 2007, and 16 more stores from Neal and April Dennis, two longtime franchise owners whom he had recently brought onto the corporate staff. He already had plenty of financial stress to handle, and he didn't need to add another 15 stores going bankrupt onto that.

But all the bank had in collateral was used restaurant equipment, so the bank would have lost millions. That bothered Kenney. He'd had a relationship with the bank almost since he started the company. "I didn't want to let that happen to them," he says. "I didn't think that was the right thing to do, because I think character matters. I wanted to make good."

Kenney decided to take over the failing stores and pay their debts, keeping them from going bankrupt. He paid their employees, he kept their food stocked, and he kept the stores up and running. This wasn't unusual for Kenney — he'd taken over failing restaurants plenty of times before. Neal Dennis, his Chief Operating Officer, says, "He goes out of his way to help people, and give people chances, and second chances, and third chances. He's taken over a ton of stores for people in the past if a franchisee is having trouble, because they either change their mind, or they are struggling, or they want to move and be in this location, and this one's not as good."

Gordon Douglas, Kenney's longtime CPA at Dixon Hughes Goodman, says, "He did it for a couple of reasons. One was because he felt responsible for the bank's position of lending them money. But also, he wanted the stores to keep running, and he felt like the stores needed to be successful and look successful, so he would assume that responsibility, and make it work."

In the span of about six months, between taking on Dan's and Neal and April's stores, plus the bad franchisees' failing stores, Kenney went from zero debt to nearly $7 million. When Kenney called Douglas to update him, Douglas said, "I'm not sure I'd have done that if I were you."

Dennis says, "Kenney is very astute, and he's got great business instincts, but sometimes that's outweighed by his willingness and desire to help people."

But nobody had any idea just how badly this whole thing was about to go.

■ ■ ■

Kenney was paying the bank $136,000 a month. With sales slipping, the stores were not supporting that. In the meantime, he tried and tried to get the bank to meet with him. The bank kept telling him they would meet and work something out, but they never did. Kenney began dipping into a personal $1 million savings account to cover the payments. "And I was *begging* them to come in," he says. "Saying, '*Hey, I'm paying other people's notes here. Please come in and refinance this, get it under my name. It's better for you, it's better for me, let's come together and do this.*'"

This went on for a *year.*

And even then, instead of coming in to refinance the loans, the bank sent Kenney two insurance salesmen.

"So now I'm starting to get mad," Kenney says. "I've basically lost a million dollars of my own money that I had saved, keeping things afloat, trying to get the banker on the phone, trying to get him to come in and refinance this thing. And the way I wanted to refinance made perfect sense to both parties. The bank would get their money, I would get a little relief. And *I couldn't get them on the phone."*

In the meantime, Kenney was doing everything he could to not let any employees go. He also refused to reduce anybody's pay, even when his Chief Financial Officer implored him to cut salaries by as much as 20 percent. Kenney even made sure that everyone got Christmas bonuses. Two years in a row, he spent most of his own salary filling holes in paychecks, giving bonuses, and providing whatever else the company needed.

A few different times, since he was spending most of his revenue paying off loans and cutting employees' paychecks, some months, Kenney didn't have any money left to cover the bills for the 49 stores he now owned. He was so desperate that he took a $250,000 loan from high-interest lenders, covered the bills, and paid back the loan within a year. It was an aggressive strategy, but to keep the stores open, he had to keep food in the stores.

About a year and a half after taking on that $7 million in debt, by April 2010, Kenney had emptied his $1 million savings account. He'd spent *all* of it paying off the loans, while *still* trying to get the bank to work out a new deal. "It was just fuzzing ridiculous," he says.

■ ■ ■

Kenney, perhaps obviously, did not say "fuzz" there. He said another word, one of those words he made a New Year's Resolution not to use anymore. He's not very good at not using them. He uses them all the time. "I'm too fuzzing good at it!" he says, laughing. It's not something he is proud of, but it *is* part of him, and to leave them out entirely would feel disingenuous. That said, we also understand that printing *those* words may make people uncomfortable in reading or sharing this book, and while we want to be honest about who Kenney is, we also certainly want to respect those who might want to share this book with their kids or others in their lives who may be bothered by such words. So, there will be a *few* times in this book that Kenney says "fuzz," and variations thereof, when in reality, he's using another word.

OK then.

■ ■ ■

Meanwhile, Kenney's personal life also started taking some hits. First, his kid half-brother, Keith, who had been working as the Andy's corporate attorney, left the company to start his own business. Keith just finished law school a few years earlier, and Kenney wanted to help Keith out, so he brought him on and let him learn on the job. But when things started looking bad for Andy's, Keith left.

It always stung Kenney when an employee left him, but for his own brother to leave, and in such a volatile time — it dredged up old, familiar pain and raw fears planted by others, by other *family*, abandoning him when he was young.

3

ABANDONED
Backstory, Part 1

Kenney was born to Tom and Nancy Mosely on March 15, 1963. They lived in Silver Springs, Maryland, near Washington, D.C. They had a daughter, Kelly, three years old when Kenney was born. Tom was a police officer, Nancy a secretary, and theirs was an unhappy marriage. Six months after Kenney was born, Tom left for a waitress named Peach.

That left Nancy with a toddler, an infant, no home, a '34 Chevy wheezing its last, and no job. She moved from their four-bedroom home to a two-room converted garage and took secretary jobs around D.C. Some years, Nancy only made a few thousand dollars. When she and Tom divorced, the court ordered Tom to pay $80 per month in child support, but he used some of his law enforcement contacts to get that reduced to $60 per month, and he almost never paid even that. Tom also almost never saw his kids. Nancy would have let him. He just didn't want to.

Nancy is a tiny woman, 5-foot-2 and *maybe* 100 pounds, a real firecracker, almost vibrating with nervous energy, and not afraid to say what she thinks. She met Dal Moore about a year after Tom left. They shared a favorite pastime: discussing how other people "with poor character" would "look down on them" and "act better than them" and find sneaky, underhanded ways to get ahead — this was the most logical explanation as to why others were able to "find more success in this world." Nancy's favorite stories were about military men for whom she worked, full colonels even, who couldn't spell words that she could as a "lowly secretary."

Nancy and Dal were married when Kenney was three and Kelly was six.

By the time Kenney could talk, a little after his first birthday, Nancy already had him saying *"Yes sir"* and *"No sir"* and *"Yes ma'am"* and *"No ma'am"* and *"please," "thank you,"* and *"may I?"* She taught him to shake hands firmly, to look people in the eye, and to be honest, no matter what. She'd tell him, "The most important asset you'll possess throughout your life is your good character — your good name."

Nancy still managed to cover rent, bills, food, and even Kenney's doctor bills as he suffered through chronic bronchitis. She never earned more than $18,000 a year, and she and Dal had a son of their own — Keith — after which Nancy didn't work for a few years, but she also never once applied for government assistance. She considered it "the ultimate disgrace," believing that it set a bad example for children, teaching them that "inferior behavior" still earned rewards. "I'll dig ditches to support my children," she'd say. "It was my choice to put you on this earth, and it is my responsibility to feed, clothe, house, train, and love you."

She bought their clothes from thrift stores and sometimes she paid off Kenney's medical bills on installment plans. There were no Nike shoes or Starter jackets. "Might not be fancy," she'd say. "But everything'll be clean."

For a couple of years when Kenney was in elementary school, the Moores qualified for the government's free and reduced lunch program, but Nancy refused it. She found the money to feed her kids herself.

Since Dal was in the military, the Moore family lived all over the world, from Japan to California to Alabama to North Carolina. When Kenney was around 10 years old they settled in Havelock, N.C., and by the time he was in middle school, they were living a few towns over in Newport, right near the beach, where he spent his childhood.

As a child, Kenney never doubted that his family loved him. "We knew we were loved," he says. But he also often felt like he was wading through an endless emotional firestorm. "Our family enjoyed a good, robust discussion around the table and food," he says. "And I tell people — they don't believe me once they get to know me, but — I was the quiet one. I was the guy that couldn't get the word in edgewise around the supper table. I was the quiet one. And we all had very strong opinions, and we were never afraid to voice them. That was encouraged growing up."

Nancy also refused to take any abuse from anyone, a trait she passed down to Kenney. When he was around seven years old, a neighborhood bully much larger than Kenney would push him down, throw things at him, mock him, and leave him terrorized. Finally, Nancy told Kenney, "You know the only thing that's going to put a stop to him? You're gonna have to kick his ass."

The next time the bully bothered him, Kenney lowered his head and rammed the kid in the stomach, then tackled him and pounded him with his fists. The kid went home crying. His parents showed up on the Moores' porch, complaining to Nancy about what Kenney had done to their son. "That's right," Nancy said, "and I'm fixin' to do the same thing to you if you don't get off my porch right now."

Kenney and his older sister Kelly would get into fights all the time, and Nancy wouldn't break them up, but rather, she'd get in there and teach them how to hit each other, how to hit the right spots on the ribs that hurt the most.

By age eight, Kenney already felt like the family protector. One afternoon in their Alabama neighborhood, a group of teenagers from a rough neighborhood nearby came down their street and began throwing rocks at people. One hit a pregnant woman across the street from the Moores. She called 911 while Nancy followed the kids back into their neighborhood so that she could tell the cops where to find them.

As she did, she felt like she'd made a terrible mistake: Everywhere she looked, people, adults, grown men, were stepping out of their houses and standing on their porches, staring at her, glaring at her. She felt like she was about to get murdered.

Someone took her hand.

It was Kenney, eight years old, walking tall and tough by her side, chest poked out, fists clenched, ready to fight everyone.

Kenney didn't end up having to fight anybody that day, and they made it back home, but he would always be ready to fight. Kenney started working out with a base boxing team when he was 12 years old, learning from and even sparring with guys three, four, five years older than himself.

When Kenney was a freshman in high school, he learned that an eighth-grader at a local middle school saw Nancy in the bank and said something lewd and obscene to her, so the next day, Kenney went to the middle school, waited in the gym for the kid, and body-slammed him on the hardwood floor.

When Kenney was a sophomore, and Keith was 12, Keith hit three home runs in a Little League game. After the game, as Keith was floating around on cloud nine, a jealous teammate, Scooter, picked a fight with him. A group of kids circled around, urging the two to fight. Keith hit first, punching Scooter in the chin. Scooter punched Keith in the stomach, then they shoved each other a few times — and that was it. Unsatisfied, the other kids started calling Keith terrible names. Kenney appeared out of nowhere and started beating kids up until everybody scattered.

Kenney even protected his family from itself. "Our parents didn't get along great for different portions of time," he says. "They argued a lot. There were some intense fights. And some things thrown. Things thrown out in the yard. That kind of stuff. But I also took the soothing role, too. I would go try to soothe Mom. And hug her and tell her that I loved her when things were going on. But it was normal to us. It was what we knew. There was love. There was just also this somewhat volatile side sometimes that reared its head."

Kenney remembers coming home one day to find Dal in the garage, packing to move out after another blowout with Nancy. (He never really left; he always came back.) Kenney said, "I just want you to know I love you."

Dal said, "I don't want to hear that."

4

TROUBLED ASSETS
The Bank Saga, Part 2

With his $1 million savings account emptied by April 2010, Kenney quit making the payments on the bad franchisees' loans.

That got the bank on the phone.

They finally set a meeting, a real meeting, but the bank didn't send their local banker, with whom Kenney had worked for years. Instead, they sent a stranger, a banker from Florida, and on top of that, they moved Kenney's account into the "troubled assets" group. The banker from Florida was a troubled assets specialist taking over his account.

Kenney was floored. He'd expected the bank to come in *thanking* him for saving them a million dollars already, and for being willing to take on all these loans that didn't belong to him and ultimately saving them many millions of dollars. Instead, they were treating him like a borderline criminal.

The banker cut his monthly payments in half, but gave Kenney a short loan that they'd revisit every other year, with an interest rate well over prime. It was an aggressive deal. And *then* the banker tacked on a $26,000 fee, as a *fine* for *missing* payments *that didn't belong to him,* "to cover attorney costs."

That insulted Kenney. In 22 years with this bank, he'd borrowed several million dollars and paid it all back, never missing a payment, even paying back most of it *early.* Plus, he'd never taken on *this* many stores at one time, but this wasn't the first time that he'd picked up the loan notes of other franchisees who'd let their business go south. "I cared more about doing the right thing than losing a little money," he says. "And I had always, in my mind, done the right thing. And now I'm put into this troubled assets group, with bankers I don't even know, who don't have a clue about my company, who don't have a clue about my business, who don't know who I am as a man, and don't really care."

■ ■ ■

Dealing with the bank, the debt, and the sudden influx of new stores to manage was stressful enough, but Kenney also carried crushing guilt. He knew, deep in that place where we can't hide from our secrets, that these problems were all consequences for when he *had* put making money over doing the right thing. If he'd done the right thing years ago, he would have prevented all of this.

Most of the bad franchisees had come into the company, directly or indirectly, via one man. We'll call him Johnson. Kenney hired him in Andy's early years, and Johnson turned out to be one of the worst human beings Kenney had ever known. But Kenney had ignored all of that, because when it came to selling burgers, the man was also one of the best Kenney had ever worked with. "Money makes good people better and bad people worse," says Neal Dennis. "It reveals people for who they are."

"And you don't even know what they are until they get it," Kenney says. "You see one person, all of a sudden they get some money, and whoa! Mr. Hyde appears."

And there was no bigger Mr. Hyde in the company than Johnson, whose time with Andy's Kenney considers one of his greatest failures not only as a CEO, but as a man.

Johnson worked for Andy's for about a decade starting in the mid-1990s, and every year that went by, Kenney ignored one problem with Johnson after another. Everything about the man was shady. He convinced car salesmen to let him test-drive fancy cars for a few days just because he could and it was fun, never having had the slightest desire to buy. He derided people, not only criticizing their work performance but making personal insults, saying things to cooks like, "You don't cook fast enough because you're too fat."

"And he was a fat guy, which was real ironic," Kenney says. "But we've never condoned anything like that. The only time he'd ever give somebody a raise is after he berated them. A Kenney-ism, one of my things I always teach people, is, _I'm soft on people, but I'm hard on behaviors_. I'm never going to attack you as a person. Now, what you did or what you're doing may need some work. We may need to have a tough discussion. But that doesn't mean you're a bad guy. I'm not gonna attack you as a person. We're soft on people, hard on behaviors. That's one of our mantras. But he used to argue that with me. 'You need to be hard on people, too. You're hard on behaviors, _and_ you're hard on people, too.'"

It got worse. Kenney learned that Johnson, who was married, harassed female employees by offering them money to disrobe or have sex. There were rumors that he even bought some women breast implants.

It makes Kenney sick to his stomach to admit this now, but

Kenney ignored all of these things because, for all his faults, Johnson made the company money. He could take over one of their worst performing Andy's and turn it into one of their best within three months, and all of Johnson's stores were among the company's top performers.

One day Kenney read a book about Jack Welch, the former CEO of General Electric. One passage hit him so hard that he wrote Johnson's name in the margin, underlined it three times, and couldn't stop staring at it. The passage was about Welch's four types of managers. Type Is are those who make your numbers and share your values — they're your superstars. Type IIs are those who don't make the numbers nor do they share your values — they've got to go. Type IIIs are those who don't quite make the numbers, but they share your values, and you can work with them. And then there are the Type IVs — those who make the numbers, but do not share your values at all. "This is your big shot, your tyrant, the one you'd love to be rid of — but oh, those numbers," Welch said. "Type IVs [deliver the goods] without regard to values and, in fact, often diminish them by grinding people down, squeezing them, stifling them."

And, Welch said, you get rid of them.

Kenney knew he had to get rid of Johnson. He cobbled together a group of other owners willing to buy out Johnson's stores, and then he talked Johnson into selling.

But just getting Johnson out of the company didn't mean that Kenney was rid of the man's effects, which lingered like a toxic odor. He'd become a multi-store owner, so Johnson had, of course, hired managers who fanned out to own their own restaurants, managers and owners who shared his values more than Kenney's.

Johnson's offspring didn't do any major damage until the

recession hit, but almost all of the 15 stores whose owners gave up to go bankrupt had a direct or indirect link to Johnson — and to Kenney's failure. One owner was having an affair with a waitress, his wife found out, and they dropped everything and disappeared. Most of the rest were poor owners to begin with, people who believed that owning stores meant hiring managers then sitting back and collecting the money.

And now, here Kenney was, left to deal with the mess. His failure, and Kenney's furor with himself for it, would culminate in Kenney throwing his company to the brink of destruction.

■ ■ ■

The whole situation hurled Kenney back into his prison, which he thought he'd long since escaped, a prison wherein lurked old demons, and the demons went after his scars and reopened old wounds fresh, so that they revived not only in Kenney's heart and mind but also even on his body. He suffered a strange, nightmarish outbreak of big, painful sores all over his legs, sores he'd never had before. He could barely sleep. "Many a night, I'd be up at three o'clock," he says. "Going downstairs, making myself a cup of coffee, sitting, and thinking. Sitting and thinking. Sitting and thinking. A ton of lost sleep. Karen would come down at five and go, '*Goodness sakes, would you go to bed? Get some sleep?*' And there wasn't a whole lot I could accomplish at 3 a.m., but I couldn't sleep either. The wheels never stopped turning. Never stopped."

Kenney was stressed, yes, but he was also angry. "There's two different kinds of angry with him," Karen says. "He gets intense angry if he's in an argument. You know, we all have tiffs. But also, deep down, he's incredibly sensitive, and he gets angry when his heart gets hurt."

They would watch the news in the morning while they all had breakfast, and Kenney would hear another report about some other government regulation getting placed on businesses, or something like that. "And Kenney would just *lose* it," Karen says. "Or, he would turn around to lecture us afterwards, about why that's wrong."

Kenney was angry about what the bank was doing to him, but also because he wanted to do the right thing, and he wanted Everyone In The World to do the right thing, and to be *free* to do the right thing, and when he saw someone getting in their way, it infuriated him.

"That was an intense period," Karen says. "Just years of intense. God, he was so *angry*. We kind of quit having conversations for a little while, because it was more him just lecturing to anybody within earshot."

Karen and Neal and everyone close to him say "it's just passion." But in those days, Kenney's temper went beyond passion to something worse. It got so bad that his kids went to Karen and told her that Dad was scaring them. Finally, Karen had to start doing something about it. "We're not going to live in a house that's chaotic," she says. "We're not going to have chaos. I will not have it."

When Kenney would get too intense, she would confront him. "I'd have to be like, 'Okay, you've gotta take a step back. It's *too intense around here. Everybody's uptight, you're freaking everybody out, you're freaking yourself out.*' And we'd come back down. And when I say down, I just mean, tolerable. And slowly, it would go back up, and again, I'd be like, '*Okay, we can't take this anymore.*' Sometimes it'd be an argument. And sometimes, '*Yeah, yeah, I get it.*' But I would do anything for peace in my house. Even square off with him. You cannot go home and not have peace. Then what do you have? Where can you go? So yeah, if I have to square off with Kenney, I'll square off with Kenney. It's not fun."

Sometimes those fights escalated into furious yelling matches between Kenney and Karen. She would stand in front of him, unmoving. He would storm out and get in his car and drive off. And then she would sit down because her knees had gone so weak.

One time her oldest daughter, Emma, asked her, "You mean your knees go weak?"

"Oh yeah," Karen said with a laugh.

"But you stand there and *stare him back*, just like he's staring at you."

"Do I look as mean as him?"

"Yes."

"Good." Karen laughed. "Because really, I'm about to pee."

She makes sure, if she has to square off with Kenney, that she does it in the morning. "That's when we talk," she says. "We don't talk about anything deep at night. Unless the house is burning down, I bring nothing to him at night. He brings nothing to me at night. He just doesn't get in until about eight anyway. We just watch a TV show all together, or we're all on our laptops, we're all in the same room. So a lot of good stuff happens in the morning. I get my first swallow of coffee, and we talk. But if I feel like we have to fuss, then it's gonna be in the morning, too, which is kind of a rough start to your day.

"If we have to fuss, generally what will happen is, he'll act ugly. And he'll leave. He'll slam the door. He'll carry on. He always leaves, because he cannot seem to calm down with people. He just can't do it. It's like the energy just keeps him riled up. But I know that it's gonna be okay. It's not like we're all left devastated. He's just flipped out. By the time he gets to the office, he's called me, and he's apologized."

Karen found positives in it all, too. "It was probably one of the first times ever I was able to say to the kids, '*You know, this is what your dad's going through*,'" she says. "*"And it's hard. It's really hard. And I know you're not enjoying him as much. And I'm not really either. But we love each other. But this is what we do when we're going through something. And it's pretty serious. It's a pretty serious thing.*'"

Kenney also always made sure to take the time to smooth things over with his kids, too. "He always takes time with each child to explain where he's coming from and what happens to him," Karen says. "He rarely ever makes excuses."

Many fathers seem incapable of telling their children about their failures and their flaws, afraid of showing their children that they are human. And sometimes, yes, a child, especially when younger, needs to think that their dad is invincible. But mostly a child needs to know their dad is strong, and strength is more often seen in how good a grasp a man has on his own weakness.

And this was his righteous fury's dark irony: Kenney getting angry about people hurting people made him explode, which, of course, also only hurt people.

※ ※ ※

One afternoon Kenney and Karen's two youngest children, Isabelle, 13, and Dylan, 11, were playing outside on their trampoline. They started arguing and fighting with each other. Isabelle said something that made Dylan furious. "You know how older sisters know how to use their words," Karen says. "And Dylan's so sensitive. He's got an incredible sense of humor, but he's really intense, like Kenney. Kenney can tease you, and he's good at it, he really is — but you have to be careful when you go back. You really have to time it right.

I've found that I'm not all that good at it with him, because I know his weaknesses, and I can really get in there, and get a good one in, and it's hilarious. But you know, it kind of hurt. He didn't like it. And he'd get pissed off. So I don't do it quite as much as I used to."

That's what Isabelle did to Dylan.

Dylan responded by kicking Isabelle in the face.

Karen grabbed Dylan and put him in the car and drove him to Kenney's office.

Kenney asked Dylan what had happened, and Dylan told him, and Kenney asked him why Dylan got so angry.

"Well, you get so angry," Dylan said, in that innocent and sometimes heartbreaking way that a boy only knows what he's seen in his father.

Kenney told his son, "You do not want to be like me. You do not want to be this."

5

ROCKY
Backstory, Part 2

When Tom Mosely left Kenney and his sister and his mother, he left for good. The last time Kenney saw his dad for nearly two decades, Kenney was two years old. They went to the neighborhood pool together. Like most kids, Kenney started running on the concrete beside the pool, and like most kids, he was told to stop, and like most kids, he disobeyed, and like most kids, Kenney tripped and fell and skinned his knees, cutting them deep. But then, unlike most kids, Kenney didn't scream or bawl — he had the wherewithal to jump into the pool to make the cuts hurt less.

Kenney did not see his father again for sixteen years. When they next met, Mosely told Kenney that story, about the pool, because it was the only story the man had of them together. "Right then," Mosely would say, as though trying to say that Kenney turned out okay, even though he'd been abandoned by his father, because he seemed so tough, "I knew you must have a high tolerance for pain."

It wasn't so much that Kenney had a high tolerance for

pain as much as he had an affinity for finding something to jump into that would distract him from it. Problem was, most of the time, those metaphorical pools weren't quite as safe.

■ ■ ■

Kenney didn't grow up with computers and video games and smartphones to numb him the way he might have today. Instead, he self-medicated with the great outdoors and the most powerful operating system in the world: his brain and his imagination and his wild heart. If Kenney felt like doing something, he went for it, especially if he felt like it would entertain someone else. "I always just made myself the guinea pig," he says. "I was the guy who always said, 'Wouldn't *this* be cool?'"

When Kenney was six, he lived in Iwakuni, Japan. Dal was stationed at the Marine Corps base there. One afternoon, Kenney and Kelly, his older sister, decided to walk to the nearby convenience store and get ice cream. Kenney wore shorts and rubber snap-on boots, and he had blonde hair and a bad haircut, his bangs chopped straight across his forehead. They came upon a railroad track crossing the road, its lights blinking and its bells dinging and its arms coming down. They could see the train coming, but it looked far away. Kenney ran toward the tracks. He didn't want to wait, and he knew he was fast.

What Kenney did not know was that the train was fast, too — a *Shinkansen*, or bullet train, that could go 200 miles per hour.

The train screamed by the instant Kenney made the other side of the tracks, going so fast that its wind picked Kenney up and flung him 20 yards down the road. All Kelly saw was Kenney's boots go flying away. Believing she'd just watched her baby brother die, she screamed and cried and ran for home.

Unbelievably, Kenney was fine. Just a few scratches and bruises. He even got his boots back.

"What were you *thinking?*" Nancy later asked him, furious.

"What?" Kenney said. "I *beat it!* I ran faster than a *bullet train!*"

"But *why!?*"

Kenney didn't know. He said, "I just *felt like it.*"

A few years later, the Moores were living in eastern North Carolina, and one winter, the river near Kenney's house froze over, which almost never happens there. Kenney and his friends wondered if they could walk across it. Kenney the Guinea Pig went first. He made it halfway, then cracks burst beneath his feet and bolted across the river. Kenney froze, then he walked backwards, oh so carefully, until he reached solid ground, sweating despite the cold. "Yeah," he said. "Don't go out there." On cue, they heard an explosive *crack!* A chunk of ice broke off and disappeared, swept under and away by the current.

One summer, after he and his friends had watched a movie about Tom Sawyer and Huckleberry Finn, they thought it would be fun to make their own raft and take it out on the river. Kenney found a big crate, caulked up the bottom, found a long pole, and shoved off into the river. He made it halfway across, then the raft started sinking — and Kenney couldn't swim. He barely made it back to shore.

Kenney learned how to swim a couple of years later after panicking and choking on water during a pool swim test. A lifeguard he only remembers as "Wendy Peffercorn," a.k.a. the bombshell lifeguard all the boys in *The Sandlot* fell in love with, took pity on Kenney and gave him lessons. After finally passing the swim test, in classic Kenney Moore fashion, he didn't ease his way into the deep end; he ran to the diving board and did a flip.

Another time, he and his friends had the bright idea to jump their bikes over an abandoned Volkswagen Beetle. They threw together a launching ramp, and Kenney went first, of course. The launch went off with spectacular ease, and that moment in the air, sailing over the car, felt glorious, felt like being a superhero, felt like Evel Knievel. It wasn't until the height of his jump that Kenney realized they'd forgotten to build a landing ramp. Kenney hammered the ground, his back tire exploded, and Kenney went down hard.

That's pretty much how Kenney went about the rest of his life. He was forever launching without landing ramps, sometimes landing safely, but also often crashing and bleeding.

■ ■ ■

The movie *Rocky* came out in 1976, when Kenney was 13, and as he watched Sylvester Stallone's titular underdog character, he felt like he was watching a version of himself. He felt such a connection to Rocky that at the end of the movie, Kenney jumped up and cheered, right there in the middle of the theater.

Kenney always felt like the underdog, always the odd guy out, always the guy who had to fight for the things that mattered to him — sports, money, love — because nobody in his life ever *gave* him anything. He developed an unrelenting willingness to fight for whatever he wanted. Also, he *had* to win, at anything, and if he didn't, he would explode. He'd flip over board games, and he became such a sore loser that even his parents quit playing with him. He had a temper unlike anyone else, and they never knew what would set it off. Kenney had infinite emotions and no idea how to control them.

The problem goes back to what Kenney said earlier. Dealing with his family's dysfunction, and feeling the need to protect everyone, and having to live with an adult's sense of responsibility and independence as a new teenager — it all created a broiling emotional cocktail that young Kenney didn't know how to handle. He brewed and boiled and festered, a volcano, until Mount Kenney Moore couldn't wait any longer and would erupt, startling, even scaring, everyone around him.

At home, Kenney tried to keep everything bottled up because there was already enough chaos, and he just wanted peace. He acted how his parents wanted, always saying "yes sir" and "yes ma'am" and the like. Problem was, this left his heart in turmoil, and as he became a teenager, his temper started cracking through. Around seventh grade, Kenney was becoming, in his words, "Billy Bad-Ass." He always ran his mouth, and not only to his peers. He loved to challenge his teachers. "I'm sure I probably thought I was hilarious," he recalls. "And they probably failed to see the humor."

Part of his problem was that Kenney was a terrible student. When he would later apply to colleges, he couldn't even get into the state university. School just bored him, and he didn't hide it. Teachers and principals could paddle their students back then, and Kenney was paddled often. They always gave him a choice: three to five swats — the number dependent upon the crime — or stay inside during recess. Kenney always took the paddle.

One of the most important moments of Kenney's young life happened in seventh grade, during Mrs. Whiteman's class. Kenney was sent to the principal, in trouble yet again for running his mouth. Mrs. Whiteman and the principal had another talk with him, and then they told him to choose between recess or getting paddled. Kenney figured he'd get three swats, because he hadn't done anything *that* bad. The principal hit him five times.

Kenney lost his mind. Back in Mrs. Whiteman's classroom, he ripped posters from the walls, he threw books, he flipped desks. Classmates fled their seats and huddled in corners. "I freaked," he says. "And if I did that today, as a middle schooler today — I'd be in some alternative school. And I'm probably not even sitting here talking to you now. Maybe my path goes totally different at that point, that young."

Mrs. Whiteman saved his life. She didn't panic. She didn't call the police. She took him out into the hallway, let him breathe, let him talk. "Thank goodness that she didn't send me off," Kenney says. "Or I would've been pigeonholed the rest of my life as just the angry, mad kid ... She understood that deeper things were bubbling in me."

Mrs. Whiteman didn't know what, exactly, because even Kenney didn't know. "I think I internalized a lot of my anger and things like that," Kenney says now. "And I think I still do sometimes. It's one of the things I work on as a man: To not explode. I internalize so much, and I'm aware of it now, which I wasn't when I was younger. It just happened."

What Mrs. Whiteman saw, though, was that, even as a young kid, Kenney might have been kind of crazy, but he was also deeply sensitive. Underneath his anger and his Billy Bad-Ass-ery, he had a huge heart, but didn't know how to express it.

Whenever Kenney did blow up on somebody, a moment later, he felt horrible for it. Mrs. Whiteman saw that, which is why she didn't treat him like a threat, but rather as someone who needed love and faith. She helped him work through some of his angst on his schedule, not forcing him to change according to what was easiest for everyone else to deal with.

She knew what many in authority forget, driven by fear to cast out the more volatile among us: She knew that Kenney's volatility *could be* dangerous, if he went the wrong way with it, *but* she also sensed that when put to good use, volatility sometimes goes by another word. Passion.

That became Kenney's challenge as he grew up — to turn his pain and anger into passion. Passion can be volatile, explosive, dangerous, but then, the same type of dynamite used to blow up buildings also once cleared the way for the railroads.

The first way Kenney found to channel his passion as a kid: sports.

■ ■ ■

Sports also may well have saved Kenney's life. They were the first thing to give him some sense of control over his life, and so he threw himself into them. From elementary school on, he played everything from basketball to track, but was best at football and baseball. Without sports, Kenney almost certainly would have ended up some kind of drifting, trouble-making burnout.

Sports were by far Kenney's most productive means of escape. Even as a kid, when he felt like playing football or baseball or anything else, Kenney went from door to door in the neighborhood until he'd dragged out enough kids for a game. One summer, Kenney organized a two-on-two Wiffle ball league, complete with statistics and awards. He even organized backyard Olympics, putting on the high jump, long jump, track, boxing, weightlifting — everything. He cobbled together loose change and went to the store and bought pieces of chocolate shaped like coins and wrapped in gold foil to use as medals.

His whole family loved sports. Nancy kept all of the stats and did all of the write-ups for Kenney and Keith's youth league teams, and she often acted as scorekeeper and the public address announcer. They watched games on television together every week — football, basketball, or baseball, college or pro, everything. Nancy was a fine athlete in her own right: she competed in several bowling leagues, averaged in the 160s, and, despite being so small, used a 16-pound ball.

The rest of the family could bowl, too. For several years, the Moores went bowling every Friday night. Keith knew how to put spin on the ball and hook into the pins like pros. Kenney's approach was more basic, slinging the ball down the lane as hard as he could, bowling with an intensity bordering on anger. "I tried to break pins instead of just knock them down," he says.

That's how he did *everything*: Whatever the challenge, he *attacked* it. Most of the time, he either broke it or it broke him, but he never danced around it nor left doubt one way or the other, whether it was a hot ground ball at shortstop or a charging linebacker.

By middle school, sports gave Kenney a schedule, demanding routine and forcing him to make somewhat responsible life decisions. Once Kenney reached West Carteret High School in 1977 and started playing there, he found that the dedication and drive required to succeed at high school sports was the perfect place to deposit all that magma in his chest.

It helped make him one heck of an athlete. He played football and baseball throughout high school, and he played basketball his sophomore year, but never did again because he suffered a sprained ankle that made him miss half of his sophomore baseball season. After baseball season one year, the West Carteret track coach talked him into competing in their conference championship meet, promising Kenney a varsity letter if he earned any points. Kenney was in baseball shape, no kind of shape to be competing in track, but he agreed anyway. He ran the 220-meter dash in 23.8 seconds to place third, and he finished fourth in both the 100-meter dash and long jump.

Of course, Kenney still found trouble. His sophomore year, Kenney and Mike Hunter, the West Carteret High quarterback and one of Kenney's best friends, loved going to a biker bar and betting on games of pool. One night they mixed it up with a gang called the Horror Merchants. Kenney and Mike won their games, but the Horror Merchants refused to pay. Tensions rose. Tempers flared. Kenney used his cue stick like a baseball bat, cracking it on one of the bikers. Kenney and Mike backed their way out of the bar, whipping their cue sticks around like baseball ninjas, then jumped into Mike's brown Pinto, and Mike floored it, and they puttered away.

Marty Giblin, Kenney's backyard neighbor and one of his best childhood friends, says that without sports, Kenney could've easily ended up like another guy they knew, who lived hard and wild and died young. Gilbin says, "Kenney had such a smart, rebellious, intense, addictive personality." Sports gave Kenney real goals, and a way to shape and frame his days. Of course, it helped that he had a natural knack for sports, with the potential to be great.

The only downside was that recognizing how much talent he had for sports forced Kenney to also remember the father who abandoned him. Tom Mosely had been a scholarship football player at the University of Alabama.

6

THE DEVIL RISES
The Bank Saga, Part 3

In May 2011, the bank sent another banker from Washington D.C. to meet with Kenney about working out the loan. "Mr. Washington" informed Kenney that the loan was going from $2 million with two $250,000 lines of credit to $7 million — and a single $50,000 line of credit. And that was just the start.

Over the next couple of years, Mr. Washington repeatedly insulted and demeaned Kenney and his team and their way of doing business. He required them to get his approval to spend more than $25,000 on capital costs, such as fixing or replacing faulty restaurant equipment. That's an absurdly low budget for a restaurant chain the size of Andy's, with more than 100 stores in operation.

Mr. Washington questioned *every — single — tiny — move* that Andy's made. For instance, he was angry when Kenney fired a corporate employee without *notifying him first*. "You could see on my end how I would start to resent this," Kenney says. "Oh, you're running this now, from Washington D.C.?

Is that correct? You don't even know what we do, and you're running this from there? ... So I became a smartass at that point."

He started sending Mr. Washington an email every time a waitress quit. *"Just thought you needed to be aware,"* he'd write. *"She's been with us six months. She made $3.13 an hour. Just thought you needed to be aware."*

And Mr. Washington carried himself with a maddening arrogance, an air of condescension always around him. "As though we should be *honored* that he would *deign* to speak to us," Kenney says. "Like it took this great effort on his part to come speak to us little people. And tell us what we should be doing or not doing ... I was being treated as somebody who didn't know what he was doing. I had a good company, and they acted like my company wasn't any good, and they acted like I was incapable of running my not-so-very-good company, and they had an arrogance — they were the smartest guys in the room, all the time. And I've never professed to be the smartest guy in the room, but don't think I'm the dumbest sitting in here all the time, either. Plus — I live this. This is what I *do.*"

And it just. Kept. Getting. Worse. The bankers continued to demand more and more of Kenney and his CPA firm. Gordon Douglas, Kenney's CPA, says, "The situation was antagonistic from their end, it seemed like, from the very first, when Kenney's not that way as a person. I've known Kenney for over 20 years, and he's been beyond loyal to everybody I know that he's ever dealt with in a business setting, as well as a personal setting. There's no question about it. And I mean, he assumed liability and debts that he didn't have to assume. And then he wasn't treated that way. When you've got somebody treating you in such a completely antagonistic way, when you were doing the right thing, you don't understand it. And then you try to be reasonable, and when you can't get anybody on the other side to be reasonable with you, it's very frustrating."

For one thing, Douglas says, "We were having to jump through hoops to adjust the way the numbers were being reported, which suddenly changed from how they had always been reported."

Adds Butch Talbot, a Dixon Hughes Goodman senior associate who worked with Douglas on Kenney's account, "That also made it more expensive when it didn't need to be. And when Kenney didn't need to be spending more money, they were making him."

One example: They required quarterly financial statements, prepared by a CPA, as opposed to the standard annual reports. Douglas says, "If you're trying to get your money back, you should be reducing expenses, not increasing them."

"And there was never any bend on their part," Kenney says. "At all."

"No," says Douglas. "There was no trying to be helpful, to help you be successful."

The bank also seemed oblivious to how Kenney was running his company and trying to keep it afloat. Kenney owned multiple companies, and he would move money around from one to the other in order to meet payroll, pay bills, etcetera. These transactions appeared on the quarterly reports as "stockholder distributions." When Mr. Washington saw that, he called Kenney and asked, "Just what do you think you're doing?" as though Kenney was trying to hide money.

"Well, bud, I haven't been to the Greek Isles, I promise you that," Kenney said, and he tried to explain. "They *still* didn't understand it," Kenney says. "They *didn't understand*. And they were *a bank*. They also didn't understand some of the things we did to create basis, too. The same issue. They just didn't understand it. It was foreign to them. They thought I was extracting money out in large chunks. Hoarding it, getting ready to flee the country, or something, on them. But finally, Gordon had to call and explain it all to them."

Douglas explains now, "It was, we've got one company throwing off income, and another company that was needing cash, and we wanted to distribute money out of one company, to Kenney, and let him turn around and put it back into the other company. That's just something that made sense from a tax perspective. It wasn't stripping any money out of the overall companies. But — we had to get approval from them, and explain that."

■ ■ ■

Kenney worried that he might have been being a bit paranoid or oversensitive. Maybe because he was under so much stress, he was taking things from the bankers as more personal and insulting than they really were. But as Douglas and Talbot became more involved, they agreed with him. "[The bankers] were used to working with folks who were maybe trying to get out of something," Douglas says. "And that's the attitude they came with, and that's not the attitude [Kenney] had."

"My goal," Kenney says, "was just to pay them every penny that my company owed them."

Of course, it *is* important to remember that banks, in general, were going through crises of their own at the time, albeit crises that they first created themselves. "A bank employee responsible for a loan has to answer to somebody," Douglas says. "But instead of approaching it in a way of communicating that, these bankers approached it in a way of *forcing* something to happen that they couldn't make happen.

I know what was going on — they were getting pressured. They might've wanted to refinance, or been willing to, but they couldn't, not under the pressure that they were receiving. But they didn't come across that way. It was all about the antagonism. It was all about the attitude. I've been in public accounting for 25 years. I've never been in a situation that I felt like was so personal and antagonistic against somebody that was trying to do the right thing."

Kenney says, "I think they wanted me to kiss their ass and say, 'Oh, thank you, thank you, thank you.' And in truth, I kind of wanted *them* to say thank you. And I think it became personal because, when I get angry, I'm not the most eloquent guy in the world."

As if the way the bankers were treating Kenney wasn't maddening enough, Kenney started hearing from franchisees that the bank was also blackballing anybody related to Andy's. He received one email that said:

> "I was applying for a commercial loan to purchase [an Andy's] [...] I was instructed to first apply to [the bank] since that was the bank that our home office used. I met with [a banker]. Earlier today, [the banker] stated that the numbers looked good. He stated that he would get with me in a couple days with an answer. The meeting ended with a positive sounding note [...] After a few days I had not received a return call and I started calling [the banker] back at [the bank]. Several days later I reached him and he stated a loan was not approved. [The banker] said, 'I really don't know what's going on, but apparently the higher-ups have a problem with Andy's.'"

This happened with several franchisees. "And that's illegal," Kenney says. "Because you're supposed to look at each loan on its own merits."

Kenney confronted the bank about it, and of course, they

denied everything.

Chris Lacoe, a franchisee and one of Kenney's close friends, says, "The company had to suffer a lot. There were a lot of owners who suffered. Kenney could've told [the bank] to piss off and screw them, but he ... wanted to be a standup person, and he always took over these loans and tried to get them paid off. But [the bank] didn't give a crap about us. They didn't care about the relationships. They just cared about the money."

And every meeting that Kenney had with the bankers, the worse the situation became, and the more his anger grew. "They got to go home every night," he says. "When they got off at five, six o'clock, they got to go home, eat supper, hang out with their kids, and they still had a job the next day. I got to go home and I got to stay up half the night, making sure that my office employees could feed their kids, and 2,500 other people could survive. I had to go home into that. I never shut it down. And that is a huge difference. So it's very personal to me. So when they come off as arrogant, when they give me the feeling that my company's not good, I take that real personal. And that probably came out in my facial expressions and my words, and everything else. *'No, wait a minute. Everybody in this company, we've worked too damn hard for you to walk in here smugly and basically act like we're not any good.'"*

Kenney would later realize that another reason he took it all so personally was because the way the bank was treating him was also pricking at old wounds and stirring up the demons that made them. The bank was treating him like he was somehow *inferior* to them, the same way people had treated him all his life, and a way that he'd fought and struggled and worked to overcome.

7

KENNEY VS. THE WORLD
Backstory, Part 3

For all the good that sports gave Kenney in his youth, they also crystallized how others viewed him and his family. Even among parents, West Carteret High fell into two cliques: Newport families, like Kenney's, who weren't very well off and who didn't have many parents in the booster clubs, and thus were not well known by faculty and coaches, and then Morehead City families, who were wealthier, and as such, virtually ran the school. This started Kenney's lifelong battle with the rich and arrogant. All his life, childhood on, there were always those who treated him as *lesser than*.

When Kenney was younger, the way his mom dressed embarrassed him. He thought Nancy's clothes were old and worn and out of style, and her pants always seemed several inches short. But when he got older, Kenney realized that she dressed like that because she didn't spend money on clothes for herself so that she could spend what she had on her kids. "And I grew to have a deep appreciation for that," he says. Every new school year, she took them shopping for new clothes. Keith would load up on the newest (read: most expensive) styles, but Kenney felt wrong wearing new clothes when his mom couldn't afford them for herself.

But like any high school kid, there were clothes he *did* want, and other things, like a car. And since there was no way he would ask Mom and Step-Dad for money, Kenney realized that he would have to find a way to get the things he wanted in life. To that end, he came up with a simple and foolproof plan: He would work.

North Carolina was the virtual epicenter of tobacco commerce at the time, so there were endless jobs available for anyone who didn't mind working hard. His sophomore year, Kenney took a job working in the tobacco fields. Kenney woke up at 6:30 every morning, put on grungy clothes, and trudged to the end of his block to wait for a truck to pick him up. He hopped in the back with all the other workers, rode to the fields, and worked from sunup to sundown, picking tobacco, the tobacco gum sticking to the hair on his arms.

The first things Kenney bought with his earnings were a pair of Converse All-Star sneakers and some bright orange OP shorts from Bert's Surf Shop, which he wore almost every day. Kenney also saved up $400 to buy his first car, a 1969 Opel Kadett that looked like a box on wheels. Gross brown with yellow shag carpet, the thing ran like a go-cart. Its clutch cable broke three different times, and it burned oil so fast that Kenney had to keep an oilcan in the back. And none of that mattered, because it was *his*.

Come summertime, Kenney also had football practice twice a day. He'd get up, go to practice, go home, throw on his tobacco clothes, get in the truck, work work work, go *back* home, change *back* into football clothes, go *back* to practice, and then, finally, go home for the night. Between second practice and home, he'd stop at El's Drive-Thru and order three cheeseburgers with the works — mustard, onions, chili, slaw, *everything* — and scarf down all three during the drive home. He loved El's steamed buns, something he'd never had anywhere else. He'd fall asleep at the dinner table, and be in bed by 8:30 every night. The next morning, he'd do it again.

He was proud for working so hard, and he loved earning — not to mention *having* — his own money, but the simple fact was that he and his family were lower class and people at school treated him as a lesser-than. As a result, he played with the proverbial chip on his shoulder, channeling all of his aggression and fire and passion into every play, the only way to get any recognition and playing time.

And as he did in class and everywhere else, Kenney ran his mouth all the time during practices and games. He talked so much that even in his team picture, he's not looking at the camera but at one of his teammates, his mouth wide open.

He didn't care who he ticked off, either. Teammate Vaughan Johnson, a linebacker, went on to play for North Carolina State University and then the New Orleans Saints. A member of the vaunted "Dome Patrol," he was named a Pro Bowler four straight seasons. In high school, Johnson was 6-foot-3 and weighed around 230 pounds. Kenney was 5-9, maybe 170. "I used to always get Vaughan in Oklahoma drills because I was too busy running my mouth when backs and receivers would go to one side," Kenney says. "They would all count, to see where he was in the other line. And I'd end up heads up with him all the time. And he could bust me pretty good."

Not that Kenney ever shied away. The more and the harder that Johnson hit him, the more Kenney asked for. "When you're 5-foot-9, 170 pounds, and you're getting hit 20 times a game by guys that are bigger and pissed off at you — you had to learn toughness," he says.

Working all the time on top of playing football left Kenney passing out at the dinner table, but it also helped him in huge ways. He says, "There was a different kind of strength you got from that — you got some real toughness from that."

Case in point: The Morehead City guys always liked to pick on Kenney and the other Newport kids, the country kids, the tobacco farmer kids, the lesser-thans. When Kenney would show up to practices with his "tobacco arms," all sticky and gummy, one guy in particular always teased him for it. Never one to take abuse, Kenney fired right back. Things escalated one day and they started wrestling right on the hardwood gym floor. The bully had been lifting weights all summer, something Kenney didn't have time for, so he had perfect, bulging muscles and about 20 pounds on Kenney. It didn't matter. Kenney picked the guy up and body-slammed him, and the fight was over.

As it turned out, Kenney could run like a deer, too, running the 60-yard-dash in 6.67 seconds, which made people whistle and go, "That's pretty fast for a white guy." He always fired back, only half-joking, "Why's it gotta be *for a white guy?*"

He played halfback, fullback, or tight end, and some linebacker on defense, and he played as hard as he could as long as he could, outworking the better-thans.

West Carteret's JV team went 9-1 Kenney's sophomore season. Kenney had about 40 receptions and he returned nine punts for touchdowns. The team averaged 40 points a game while allowing six. West Carteret High's varsity football team refused to scrimmage with them. Kenney made the all-conference teams two years in both varsity football and baseball, no small accomplishment for a little guy with a chip on his shoulder at a 3-A high school.

Kenney started hearing from college football recruiters his junior year. Notre Dame sent him a letter, an obvious highlight, and the University of Pennsylvania, an Ivy League school, called and even visited once, seeming excited and asking him to send along his transcripts. "And I never heard from them again," he says now, laughing hard. "That was the end of my Ivy League opportunity."

■ ■ ■

By the end of Kenney's senior football season, no colleges were taking him all that seriously as a football player, and he came to realize, with a bit of a broken heart, that football wasn't his future.

But there was still baseball. He reasoned with himself: "I'm fast, I can hit, I'm a pretty good baseball player. Let's see what could happen with that." A shortstop, Kenney made varsity as a sophomore, and he made all-conference as a junior and senior. His junior year, he went to a Los Angeles Dodgers tryout camp in Rocky Mount, N.C., ran the 60-yard dash in 6.6 seconds, made every play at short, and fired the ball to first with some nice zip, and he hit well. A scout named Jim Garland gave Kenney his card, one of just four that Garland handed out that day.

When Kenney was a senior, Garland went to one of West Carteret's games in Smyrna, N.C. "Where the mosquitos are as big as your feet," Kenney says. Garland arrived early and asked Kenney's coach to hit him some ground balls at short. Garland liked what he saw, and said he was looking forward to the game. Then a bank of lights went out and the game was canceled. Garland had to be in Virginia the next day, so he left, but he told Kenney he'd watch him play with his rec team in the summer.

The scout gave Kenney a surge of hope, showing him a legitimate future in the game. It helped that at the school's sports banquet his senior year, Kenney was named West Carteret's Most Outstanding Male Athlete.

Meanwhile, North Carolina State University was going to give him a baseball scholarship, but told him at the last minute that he didn't have the grades.

As Kenney played baseball over the summer, he dreamed in the way that 18-year-olds dream, dreaming of Garland somehow getting him drafted.

One Friday morning in June, about three or four days before the summer draft, Garland called. "I'll never forget," Kenney says. "I was playing 16-to-18-year-old Babe Ruth baseball. And for some reason, I was pitching. We obviously were really lacking for arms. And I had pitched a game on a Thursday. That Friday, I got a call at home from Jim Garland, and he said, 'Hey, can you get to North Carolina Wesleyan in Rocky Mount tomorrow? We want to work you out before the draft.' So I said, 'Sure!' And I didn't run the 60 quite as fast, and because I'd pitched, my arm was pretty much shot, so I didn't have any zip from short to first."

Kenney went undrafted, and he thought that was the end of his baseball dreams. He set his sights on another way to get out of town and make something out of his life: Hollywood. He and a group of friends made earnest plans to drive across the country, to Los Angeles, and become actors.

But then Garland called Larry Dean, the coach at tiny Mount Olive College, a junior college starting a baseball team, and told Dean he had a shortstop for him. Dean came to one of Kenney's summer league games and made him a scholarship offer on the spot. Kenney's mom was so excited that her son was going to college that she bought him a 1979 Subaru Brat.

Kenney figured Mount Olive College was, well, in the mountains, and looked forward to going someplace far away from home. However, as Kenney discovered, the town of Mount Olive lies on the flat North Carolina coastal plain, smack in the middle of rural eastern North Carolina, in the middle of nowhere. The mountains are a solid four hours away. "That's how naïve I was," Kenney says now. Mount Olive the town is also tiny, covering a grand total of 2.5 square miles, and that's all land, not a single body of water to be found. Maybe 4,000 people live there. It's most famous for being home to the Mt. Olive Pickle Company. It was only a short two-hour drive northwest on US-70, then due west on NC-55, from Newport.

Mount Olive College is a tiny four-year college today, with some 1,200 fulltime students. Back then, it was a two-year school, and even smaller. Kenney had no idea that that's where he would find his whole future, and in ways he didn't even imagine.

Kenney decided that if Garland was going to be watching him, junior college was the way to go. If he played baseball at a four-year school, he couldn't go pro until after his junior year, but at a junior college, he could go pro after his freshman year. That sounded perfect — the sooner he could be done with school, the better. He says, "I signed with all intentions of getting drafted after one year and going into pro ball." That was his way out of Newport, out of his childhood, out of that class war.

8

"LET'S GO."
The Bank Saga, Part 4

Kenney's battle with the bank made him feel like a tobacco-armed Newport kid going up against the Morehead City punks again, only now the bullies wore suits instead of football uniforms. He was still fighting against people who treated him like a lesser-than, people who could rob him of things, only this time, he was fighting to save his bank accounts, and his company, and his life, and the lives of thousands of others who depended on him. Problem was, as an adult, he couldn't solve his problems on a football field, and he couldn't exactly go around body-slamming people, which was a shame, really, because he felt like the bankers could use a good body-slamming.

Worse still, the bank wasn't his only problem.

■ ■ ■

By 2008, Kenney had grown the company as much as he could in North Carolina. They had more than 100 locations, far beyond anything he had ever dreamed of when he'd opened his first Andy's. The only way for the company to keep growing was to expand outside the state, but Kenney didn't know if he wanted to do that.

An investment group from Boston had come down and checked them out and offered him $24 million for Andy's, and Kenney considered it. He says, "This could've been a way for me to cash out and maybe do something else or just take it easy."

Kenney not only ran Andy's, named for his oldest son, but Belle Foods, his food distribution company named for his youngest daughter Isabelle, and Dylan Equipment Company, his restaurant equipment company named for his youngest son, Dylan.

The Great Recession began setting in, and Andy's sales statewide dipped as much as 20 percent. Kenney shut down Belle Foods, deciding he didn't want to be in the food distribution business, especially at such a harsh economic time. "I was a restaurant guy, not a food guy," he says.

And in no time, the Boston investment group's offer dropped from $24 million to $14 million. "That's still a big number," Kenney says, "but it's not a ginormous number for 18 years of your life."

Kenney also felt like he couldn't leave his employees in such a turbulent time. This was also around the same time everything was starting up with the bad franchisees and the bank, so tension had settled in thick around corporate headquarters. Morale sank more every day. People were quiet. There wasn't much laughter. Kenney felt heavy from the stress of finding a way out and from the guilt of knowing he'd brought much of this on himself by keeping Johnson around longer than he should have.

However, even though Kenney was in something of a personal hell, you would've never known it by looking at him. A lot of good things happened with Andy's that year, too, like shooting stars in the eye of a hurricane. They changed the name of the company from Andy's Cheesesteaks and Cheeseburgers to Andy's Burgers, Shakes, and Fries after Kenney got inspired by a movie that included a character who tried to placate his family by asking, "Who wants to go out for some *burgers-shakes-and-friiiies?*"

That echoed in Kenney's head. *Burgers-shakes-n-fries.* He loved how the words sounded, the way they *felt* running together and rolling off his tongue. *Burgers-shakes-n-fries.* "Inspiration can come from anywhere, man," he says, laughing.

He let it marinate for a little while and decided that it sounded better, sounded more '50s, and that it better captured who they were.

They rolled out the rebrand in March 2008. By May, sales in stores that had completed the changeover were up anywhere from 2.5 percent to 28 percent. "In an industry right now that is down 10 percent, just to be up double digits is pretty much unheard of," said Alex Ramos, Andy's marketing director at the time.

They were also working on nailing down a good dessert option other than classic shakes, something that had eluded them for years. They'd tried cookies, pies, cheesecakes, but nothing seemed to stick until they tried frozen custard. Their test runs were hits, and in April 2008, they rolled it out for everyone to try. Kenney named it after his oldest daughter — Emma's Old Fashioned Frozen Custard — and he paid $2.2 million himself to put the proper equipment in every store. (Franchisees paid it back in the form of a small rebate on every box of custard they purchased.) When introduced, sales in some stores went up another 10 percent. The rollout was the most ambitious and aggressive rollout of frozen custard by any American company ever. The result: Andy's became the second largest seller of frozen custard in the country.

That same month, Andy's even received a bit of national recognition for something they'd done back in 2003. Around 2008, people nationwide started becoming far more conscious of trans fat being used in their favorite foods, fried foods in particular. A rising trend was for restaurants to switch from oils latent with trans fat to soybean oil, which contains no trans fat and is far healthier. Andy's had made that switch in 2003, inspiring other, more well-known restaurants to do the same, such as the Ruth's Chris chain of luxury steakhouses.

That was also the month of their first-ever "Big 'A' Challenge." Competitive eaters converged on the Andy's in Greenville, N.C. to race each other in finishing a 50-ounce cheeseburger, fries, and a drink. Wearing a top hat and tuxedo, "Gentleman" Joe Menchetti, who's won more than 100 eating competitions around the country since 2002, won the first Big 'A' Challenge with a time of five minutes, 45 seconds.

They rolled out the contest to all of their restaurants, and if customers could finish the meal in 30 minutes, it was free and they got their picture on the wall. Otherwise it cost $24.99.

That summer, in June, Kenney matched donations given from all of his restaurants to give $50,000 total to the Miracle League. And that September, pop singer Chubby Checker performed "The Twist" live at the Andy's Foundation Golf Tournament gala and helped them raise $125,000.

Yet despite these successes and wonderful distractions, Andy's continued profitability was still uncertain, and there was always something to worry about. The bank was enough of a monster to deal with, but there were many others looming over Andy's, too.

With the Affordable Care Act looming in 2008, Kenney had to overhaul the way that Andy's operated. He owned 49 corporate stores, which meant he had hundreds of employees, and under the ACA, any company with 50 or more fulltime employees is required to provide them health insurance or pay a steep fine.

Kenney decided to sell off almost all of his corporate stores. He felt like, with everything else going on, and thinking long-term, it was the only way to survive the Affordable Care Act. True to his character, Kenney in-house financed the sales of most of those stores, and he didn't require any of the new owners to acquire the debt that came with them — he kept all of the debt on himself. He would sell 41 of his 49 stores within a couple of years, with plans to sell off the rest in due time.

"I had to reinvent my company because of something that came out of Washington D.C.," Kenney says. "And yet, who pays Washington D.C.? People like my company. Washington D.C. creates no products, no services, to generate income. They need more money, they simply say, *'Give me more money.'* If you don't, you go to jail. If I need more money, I gotta get creative. I gotta do more marketing. I gotta train staff. I gotta come out with a great product. I gotta do all that. So I had to reinvent my company. It was tough."

And he knew it was tough for many other businesses in North Carolina. That's why, even though he had a million other things to worry about and work on in 2008, Kenney took time that year to go to Raleigh and meet with state politicians to fight not only for his company, but for companies — for people — everywhere.

Kenney has gone to Raleigh, and Washington, and Capitol Hill several times to sit on panels or to speak with representatives about various issues either his company or his community faced. He went to Washington after Hurricane Floyd put all of eastern North Carolina underwater in 1999, and he went up there again when tornados ravaged the area in the 2000s, petitioning for disaster relief.

And that's why he went to Raleigh in 2008. He didn't go there specifically to fight the ACA, although that was part of what inspired the trip. He went up there to try heading off something he saw as another potential disaster before it struck. This time, it was minimum wage. He hoped to convince lawmakers to reconsider some of their minimum wage legislation, hoping to do some good in his home state first, and, in a greater hope, possibly set a precedent for the rest of the country.

With everything else going on in the country, and with the bank, and in his company, Kenney had reached a breaking point, and he wanted to see if he could accomplish anything in Raleigh, so he got in the car and drove there. The road trip arose out of a sense of noble obligation, but also out of the sort of desperation that made him feel like he had to take *some* sort of control, even if it meant fighting something he had no real power to fight.

■ ■ ■

Kenney believes a lot of what the government does looks good on paper and even *sounds* great when you hear it, but when he looks at how it affects people simply trying to build bigger and better companies, the policies sometimes have an adverse effect. The caricature of the evil CEO taking advantage of his employees and treating them like slaves, devoid of compassion and empathy and humanity, is easy to hate, but the more inconvenient truth is that for every evil CEO, there are many more small business owners with good hearts and big dreams quietly trying to do their best for their employees and their families. And yet the more the government steps in, the more it seems like they hurt rather than help. They shackle business leaders from doing what they do best, which is best for everyone: growing their business.

"There's a role of government," Kenney says, "but it goes so far. Madison said it best in the Federalist Papers: The role of the federal government should be limited and few. Give me rule of law, roads, ports, defense. And then leave me alone. You stop there. But one of their big problems is they don't trust people to do the right thing. So they try to control everything."

Years ago, Kenney explored getting into politics, but he realized there's no way he'd be able to play politician. "I would be the most frustrated man on the planet," he says. "I kind of like being able to say, *'Let's do this,'* and then we go do it. But having others disagree with me and outright lie would probably make me very frustrated. I would probably be like one of those old school Congressmen, where I'm hitting somebody with my cane or something. I'd be on the 24-hour news cycle, *'This guy's gone nuts again.'* So I decided I would probably be best to do what I do, to try to make my impact through our restaurants and get involved with my restaurant association and maybe have a little bit of impact through that."

■ ■ ■

Every time he went to Washington, and sometimes even in Raleigh, Kenney found the environment surrounding politicians and the people who control our country profoundly disturbing. "People *fawn* over these politicians," he says. "Every night there's a cocktail party. Or some lobbying group that wants your ear. I can see how you could get real impressed with yourself real quick up there. And I think that they do. I think that that's why they don't want to leave. They love that. They love that power.

"It's exciting. I mean, you think about it — you're one of a handful, of a few hundred people, who control trillions of dollars and all that. It is an absolutely intoxicating environment. These kids, these young people working in D.C. — it's like they're walking around with a semi-god, when you watch these people walk around and watch how they act. And if you have a little bit of a narcissistic edge to you, it's just gonna feed that. And it's so wrong that all that power and all that money sits right there, in that one little small area. It's backwards from the way it should be."

There are games Kenney knows he could play with politicians, ways of cozying up to them, making them his friend, making campaign donations, "earning" favors. But no — no games for Kenney, just the grind-it-out blue-collar work ethic he's always had, and when it came to Washington, that meant talking, and talking, and talking until enough people hear his proposals and understand them well enough to agree with them.

If there's one thing Kenney had mastered, it's talking.

He had long, productive conversations with many men and women who agreed with what he proposed: Go ahead and raise the minimum wage for people 18 and older, but keep the old rate for anybody under 18. "And I got kind of beat down, in the process, to 18," he says. "I really think the age should be much higher than that [...] It just seems like there are a lot smarter ways to go about minimum wage other than just a flat rate across the board."

Kenney talked everyone's ear off. He so inspired a member of the state's Black Caucus that the man said he'd arrange to have Kenney talk to the whole Caucus. Even state senator Tony Rand, a Democrat and one of the most powerful political figures in North Carolina at the time, agreed with Kenney's proposal so strongly that he called Kenney on Kenney's last night in Raleigh, the night before the committee meeting, and said that Kenney should be pleased, that he felt like they had enough votes to push the thing through.

But it never happened.

Kenney never did get to speak before the Caucus. And then, from what Kenney was told, another representative trying to get minimum wage raised to $11 an hour threw a fit and stormed out when they put Kenney's proposal on the table. They took the proposal off the table so as not to upset this person. "That was that," Kenney says. The frustration was horrible. "You gotta have some *feel*. And I think politicians sorely lack that. They don't have any feel. It's almost like they have a checklist. *I'm now elected, I'm going to get healthcare, I'm going to raise the minimum wage, I —* and regardless of what's going on in the economy, regardless of what's going on in the country, by all means, let's check off the next box."

Feel is how Kenney had built everything he'd built. *Feel* is why, in 2007, he sold the Andy's corporate office building: He looked at the shifting economy, and he looked at the real estate bubble, and he has no better way to explain it than *instinct* or *gut* or *feel*. He just *felt* like he should sell the building and get into cash instead of staying in real estate. "Looking at the horizon, looking at what I read, looking at the economy and where things were kind of going, I just got that feeling," he says. So he did a sale-lease-back and brought the company a nice lump sum of cash. "I didn't do a long statistical analysis on anything," he says. "I didn't crunch a lot of numbers. I said, *You know what, I need to be in cash, I feel, for the next few years moving forward and not be in real estate.*"

About 30 days after he sold the building, the real estate bubble burst, and then the economy crashed, and if he'd been stuck with that building instead of flush with the cash it brought him, he would have been in even more trouble.

"All because of *feel,*" he says. "I just think that that — feel, instinct, again, whatever you call it, that gut feeling, that *intuition* that we all have — gets too ignored these days in favor of data and statistics and overthinking. I think we often know what we need to do without really knowing why."

Kenney's far from the first person to think this — some of history's greatest minds have bemoaned the loss of respect for and appreciation of intuition, which seems to give way more and more to logic and rationality with every generation. Steve Jobs said in his biography, "The people in the Indian countryside don't use their intellect like we do, they use their intuition instead, and the intuition is far more developed than in the rest of the world ... Intuition is a very powerful thing, more powerful than intellect ... Western rational thought is not an innate human characteristic. It is learned and it is the great achievement of Western civilization. In the villages of India, they never learned it. They learned something else, which is in some ways just as valuable ... That's the power of intuition and experiential wisdom."

Albert Einstein himself once said, "The intuitive mind is a sacred gift and the rational mind is a faithful servant. We have created a society that honors the servant and has forgotten the gift."

■ ▥ ▦

Whatever the case, Kenney went to his government in 2008, and he lost. Afterwards, he ranted. He ranted a lot. A selection: "Every year it seems like, we get these regulations piled on regulations piled on regulations," he says. "And business people, we sit back here and we go, 'What the fuzz, man?' I mean, do you want me to open stores or not? Do you want me to grow or not?

Look at the Wright brothers, Kenney says. He loves the Wright brothers. "A couple of bicycle guys from Dayton, Ohio, made an airplane," he says. "Did you know that the government — there was a $200,000 grant back in the 1900s given to a man to come up with the first aeroplane. There's film of it. I think it was in New York, and it was going to take off and fly over the Hudson River. And it fell in the water. That was government. *Bloomp.* Two hundred grand in a watery grave. And here are these two bicycle guys without a pot to piss in, in Kitty Hawk, and they fly."

Andy's wasn't exactly a little bicycle shop, and they were already in the air, but that didn't mean Kenney didn't want them to fly higher. And if he could, he wanted to help business owners and leaders all over the country fly higher, too.

But there was nothing left to do but drive back home, another ambitious and well-meaning businessman having wasted his time with his government, and get back to his life and his fight with the bank.

■ ■ ■

Everyone in the corporate office was concerned about the company's future and the future of their jobs and careers. Mistakes were being made, and passion was lagging. Kenney started to get the sense that everyone was easing off and looking at their jobs as little more than a paycheck. Then one day someone in the office failed to meet a deadline, and Kenney lost it.

He picked up his phone and punched the intercom button and barked to the entire office, "Everyone, go home. I don't care what you do. Just get the fuzz out."

Confused and startled — and, for some of the newer people with the office, a little scared — everyone went to Neal Dennis's office and said, "What do we do?"

"Well," Neal said, calm and matter-of-fact as can be, "you heard him. I reckon we oughta get the fuzz out."

They all left, but they didn't go home.

They all visited various stores to audit them or to just check in. "We felt like we had really let him down," says officer manager Amy Lancaster. "He'd never done that before. He'd never said to get out of the office. And so it was weird. In the middle of the day, only one car, his car, being here. That was hard."

"Every now and then I slam my spatula," Kenney says. "When I used to work in the stores, if I felt like everybody was just kind of dragging along, I would *ting* the spatula really hard on the grill. It was for everybody to go, *Oh, okay, I guess we're dragging today.* It's me saying, *Hey, I'm working here, let's all get after this.*

"I believe that leaders not only have to be able to organize people and get them on the right seat on the bus and make sure they're effective and do all the right things, but occasionally you have to disorganize things. You have to get everybody's attention. You can do that with one-on-one meetings, you can do that in a group setting, you can do it by sending everybody home. Telling everybody to get out of the office.

"It was really a day when I really felt like everybody was just going through the motions, and I'd felt like that was going on for a while. That everybody was kind of looking at this as a job and just punching a clock mentally, and I wanted to remind them that we don't punch clocks mentally in here. That's not what we do.

"We're on a mission. We're on a mission, culture-wise. We're on a mission to help young people become better people, and better parents, and better workers, and better whatever. We're on a mission in here to open up great restaurants.

"And if I feel like you're just pulling a check on me — I didn't like it when minimum wage people did it to me when I ran stores; I'm certainly not gonna like it when salaried folks with benefits are doing it. And that's kind of what happened that day.

"Talk about cutting off your nose to spite your face. They were all gone, and of course, there were numerous times I reached for the phone to hit an extension because I needed something, and I was like, *Oh, guess I gotta go find it now.*"

The next day, Kenney held a meeting and apologized for losing his temper, and then he updated everyone on everything that was going on — the poor sales numbers, how hard things were, how he'd even considered selling the company, all of that. After the meeting, he told them it was his turn to get out of the office. He needed to just get away. He left the conference room, got into his car, and drove off.

"There were a lot of us in that meeting," Amy says. "Everybody was like, *I don't know what to do.* I was like, *Let's pray.*" She laughs. "So we all held hands and just prayed for Kenney, because we knew how much stress he had on him, and a lot of times he shelters us from that."

So where did Kenney go?

Same as his staff the day before, he went to his stores.

He drove all around the state, visiting whatever Andy's he felt like stopping by. "Sometimes you get weighed down with negative," he says. "Sometimes it's just good to go out to a store and watch a girl greet a customer and run and open the door for them, and sit and eat a cheeseburger, and go, *'Wow, that's really good.'* And just get out there, and say, *'You know, we're not bad. We're actually pretty good.'* There are things we can't control sometimes. We're in some smaller communities, and they get hammered. Big cities got hit in the recession, but small communities got *hammered.* So our sales are gonna dip some there. But: Are we still taking care of the guests? Are we still getting the food out in four or five minutes? Is there hustle? Is the atmosphere good? Is there music playing? Are people smiling?

"If I go out there and see that then I know, *'Hey, we're still okay.* It's just that our customers don't have a lot of extra money in their pockets right now, and we're battling other people in the community for those one or two days they go out to eat, and we're battling all of these other things from the government, and the bank, that are out of our control in a lot of ways. And it just makes it tougher, but that just means we gotta be a little bit better, too. We just gotta be better."

But Kenney had no idea how good he was going to have to be.

■ □ ▥

He coped with everything the best way he knew how: By jumping into something else to get away from the pain. As an adult, he'd found more productive ways to do so, turning to those closest to him, and working.

He started a tradition, opening his office late every Friday afternoon for "Drink Think." He opened a bottle of something and members of the executive staff — Neal and April Dennis, Guy Guthrie, Keith, others — came in and had a few drinks, took some deep breaths from the week, and talked about the business and life, venting, brainstorming, dreaming.

Sometime in 2010, in the middle of all the chaos and stress, Kenney and his inner circle had a breakthrough. They started kicking around the idea of franchising Andy's beyond North Carolina. Business was rocky, things with the bank were terrible and stressful, and they were tired of *fighting*, of *surviving* — they wanted to *create* again. They wanted to *build*. The franchisees they already had were pretty settled with what they owned and were stable, looking to just ride out the recession. No one in the company had much desire to open any new stores. And North Carolina had about as many Andy's as the population could handle. But they thought they could sell franchises in neighboring and nearby states such as Virginia, South Carolina, Georgia, and the like. That way, they reasoned, they could grow, but not too fast to handle.

The idea came up almost every week for months until, one night that November, after daydreaming about it for what felt like the hundredth time, Kenney looked at everyone and said, "What are we waiting on?"

"What do you mean?" Neal said.

"Let's go," Kenney said. "Let's change the model. Let's *grow*. Let's fuzzing go."

It was a wild decision, and scary, with everything else going on in their own state and with the bank crushing them. But nobody was surprised when Kenney said that, and if anything, they were excited. They knew Kenney. They knew that this was how he'd built the company in the first place. Same as when he'd outrun a bullet train in Iwakuni as a kid, when Kenney felt like doing something, and he saw where he had to be, he fuzzing went, and his people fuzzing went with him.

Of course, they immediately ran into problems.

■ ■ ■

First: How *does* one go about selling franchises, anyway?

Kenney had zero experience with mass franchise sales, but there were companies that specialized in it, and that November, Kenney hired one company we'll call The Franchisers. It was not a cheap investment. Before The Franchisers decided whether they'd even work with Andy's, Kenney had to fly the CEO and his team from Chicago to Mount Olive, put them up in a hotel, and cover all of their other expenses, which included a $100 restaurant meal, *and* he had to pay them a $2,500 fee. "That should've been my first red flag about them," Kenney says. "But I was so excited about franchising, and I really didn't think we could do it ourselves at the time."

Kenney signed a contract that bound The Franchisers to finding and signing 10 franchisees in the first year. Eight months later, Andy's had spent $70,000 on The Franchisers, and they in turn had sold a grand total of zero franchises and generated exactly three leads, one of which was a man who'd known Kenney and Andy's for 20 years because he had been the first-ever Andy's landlord in Goldsboro. He was pretty sure they could have sold him on a franchise without The Franchisers' help. On top of that, The Franchisers kept bragging about their great work with a few other companies. To Kenney, they seemed far more excited about those companies than they were about Andy's. Kenney was unimpressed, to say the least.

Kenney fired The Franchisers in August and brought the Andy's franchise sales operation in-house. He said he'd still pay them through the end of the year to fulfill the contract, and that if he closed a deal with one of their leads, he would pay them the commission. But he was sick of dealing with them. He wrote in an email, "You have [the other companies] and you obviously are more excited about these concepts than you are ours. You have expressed your enthusiasm for [the other companies] many times. I feel that we are pretty special as well and I would like to share our concept with the world. And there is nobody better to do that than me."

The president called Kenney and railed against him, claiming that he had invested $90,000 into the Andy's company. Kenney called bull, reminding him how much, rather, *he* had spent on *them*. Their discussion escalated. The president, in Virginia Beach on business, said he should kick Kenney's ass. Kenney invited him to try, and said he'd even drive up and meet him for the occasion. The president declined.

Kenney didn't know what to do next. He didn't want to hire another company like The Franchisers, but he wanted to sell franchises. So he kept moving forward, his only real plan being to work hard, and try to work smart, and figure out the details along the way. Not that that was anything new. He'd always been sort of winging it.

9

A REVELATION OF STAGGERING IMPLICATION
Backstory, Part 4

The 10 years between Kenney graduating high school and starting Andy's were no easier than his previous eighteen years. Baseball showed Kenney a way to conquer his class war, but more than that, it also saved his life in a whole new way.

The summer after he graduated, Kenney worked as a lifeguard at Morehead City's Oceana Resort. One day, Kenney saw a man walking down the beach toward his lifeguard stand. Kenney knew before the man introduced himself: "That was him." His father. Tom Mosely. For the first time in sixteen years.

They went to Mosely's hotel room, where they spent an hour drinking beer and having a tense conversation. Mosely told Kenney about taking him to the pool when Kenney was two, and he asked a lot of questions, and they talked about sports and about Kenney's mother and stepdad and his life growing up.

Kenney was polite, but he didn't want to get close to the

man. Mosely was his father, but not his dad. "I have one dad, and his name is Dal Moore," Kenney says. "We had our troubles, but that man raised me as his own." Mosely had abandoned him. Kenney couldn't forget that, or forgive. "I just didn't understand," Kenney says. "If something had ever gone sideways with me and Karen, and we split up somehow — no. Things could go wrong with me and her, but I could have never just forgotten about my kids the way he did. And I didn't give him an out on that. I just didn't understand it. I still don't understand it."

Mosely tried to explain himself. He said that he and Nancy were too young, that they'd grown apart, that Nancy would mock and make fun of things he liked. He said he even met with his priest, who told him that life was too short to stay in a relationship that made him unhappy.

Kenney just nodded and listened and kept thinking, *Yeah, but still — you left us.*

■ ■ ■

When Kenney went home that night, he told his mom about meeting his father, which prompted Nancy to tell him all over again about how Tom had run off with Peach. But this time, she added something new to the story. She told Kenney that she'd *known* about Tom's affair for a year before Kenney was born. Desperate to make Tom grow up and be the husband and man and father he ought to be and quit cheating on her, she seduced Tom with the sole intention of getting pregnant, hoping that giving Tom another child would somehow change him. She had a son. Tom swore at Nancy for it, and he swore even harder that the boy could not possibly be his. That's how Kenney was born.

Kenney had always figured his father didn't want him, but

that — he'd been a *pawn* in a *game* between two unhappy people, and not only that, but a pawn used in a gambit that *failed.* The revelation cast Kenney's childhood in a brutal new light.

He handled the pain same as always, by jumping into something else to block it out. That summer he slept with one girl after another. Kenney sums himself up this way: "I was a [jerk], man." (He actually said something far less family-friendly there, but *jerk* pretty well covers it.)

Kenney kept up his [jerk] ways when he went to college, too, to the degree that he earned himself a nickname: Kenney Moore The Man-Whore. Without baseball to keep him responsible, he would have failed out of Mount Olive his first semester. But he needed baseball to avoid being a lesser-than, so he did *just enough* to stay enrolled.

It's also a minor miracle he didn't get kicked off the team. He frequently butted heads with Coach Dean, a devout Baptist. When Dean reprimanded him for smoking cigarettes, Kenney cussed him out. Dean benched him. He didn't care if Kenney was a bona fide prospect with scouts coming to watch him play. In the first game of one doubleheader during Kenney's freshman year, Kenney hit two home runs off a pitcher who later went on to play several years of pro ball. Between games, he and Dean got into an argument about something — he can't remember the details now — and Kenney spent the second game on the bench.

■ ▪ ▫

When Kenney tells these stories of youthful indiscretions and such, he isn't *bragging*, but he's not ashamed, either. He laughs and shakes his head and his face turns a little red. He knows these aren't exactly stories that most company presidents might tell, especially a CEO who also recently became a Christian, but he shares these stories openly. You might ask, "Why?" Why keep bringing up his failures, his "life before Christ," as most good Christians put it? Why not act like that life never even happened, like many Christians do?

Kenney believes what all good Christians believe about Christ's grace and forgetting of sins, but he also believes in the healing and redemptive power of human beings being honest with one another. After all, why paint pieces of coal pretty colors if you can open them up and maybe find diamonds inside? Plus, if he doesn't acknowledge where he's come from, if he's not honest, he provides nothing for people who might be trying to work through the same sort of place he made it out of, too.

Also, it gives him a deep appreciation for where those dark places led him.

* * *

Kenney was wild, but one girl in particular utterly struck him: Karen Williams. Mount Olive College is one of those schools that are so small that when you meet someone you like, or even find attractive with a passing glance, you don't forget them because you see them all the time. When Kenney was a freshman, Mount Olive was even smaller. Kenney and Karen noticed each other right away.

Kenney looked like a surfer bum, with shaggy dirty blonde hair and short corduroy OP shorts. Karen still remembers those shorts. A history major, she was a gorgeous green-eyed blonde, and fit, a former competitive swimmer, and nearly as tall as Kenney. On paper, it was a classic bad-boy-good-girl situation. They were polar opposites. Karen was Mount Olive born and raised, a good Christian, the daughter of two loving parents, both calm, rational people working in education. Her mother, Frances, was a high school English teacher. Her father, Jimmy, was a principal. They were neither wealthy nor poor, and they managed to run a well-adjusted family.

Kenney, on the other hand, had lived all over the world as a military brat, spent much of his childhood in poverty, didn't think much about God, came from a dysfunctional, chaotic, turbulent family, and he was a mess, a punk teenager, always swearing and smoking and chasing girls, with a wild streak and a temper that no one could predict or tame.

Karen has always had a weakness for strays, always bringing home lost cats and dogs, and the few guys she dated in high school were always somewhat lost, in one way or another. And when her parents first met Kenney, they saw another stray.

Kenney and Karen became friends during his first semester, getting to know each other through some shared classes. She kept Kenney at a distance. They liked each other, but Karen's friends warned her away from him, and she knew his nickname. She even got an up-close view of Kenney In Relationships, watching him date not just one but two of her girl friends, one who lived right in Karen's hall. "Yeah," Karen says, laughing. "They were sort of all the time yelling at each other."

By his second semester, Kenney realized that he *really* liked Karen. There was more to her than the others. She was strong, confident, and intelligent like few girls he knew, and she carried herself accordingly. She didn't waste time on meaningless small talk or gossip. She was authentic through and through, same as him. She was the sort of girl he wanted to *be with,* not just sleep with. He eased off of the partying and the chasing of other young ladies to focus on her.

And Karen, despite all her friends' objections, was drawn to Kenney for the same sort of reasons. She came from a private school background where the emphasis was very much on "what you will make of yourself" and "what you will accomplish," all about reputation and status. Her parents both took a logical, calm-natured, rational approach to life. And Kenney, for better or worse, was the opposite. He never went with the status quo, and his was a personality that Karen craved.

Kenney didn't care about status, except for when people of puffed-up status stood on the necks of those "below" them. He didn't have money, to the point where he wouldn't even eat pizza that his baseball teammates ordered because he couldn't afford to pitch in. They'd tell him not to worry about it, but he didn't want to feel like he owed anybody. And Kenney knew where he'd come from, although he *did* talk about it too much, always joking about his mom getting pregnant with him to keep his dad around and how it didn't even work. Karen finally told him one day, "Dude, you *gotta* stop bringing that up all the time."

Kenney *did* have big dreams and ambitions and passions, but Karen wasn't drawn to him for that. She didn't see him as some rocket headed for the moon that she should hitch herself to. She saw a guy who, beneath all his wildness, wanted to be a good person, and that's what she valued most. Plus, he was a lot of fun to be around.

Kenney was the charismatic type who could sit back at parties and draw people to him, like he had his own gravitational pull. Karen was the social butterfly, going from person to person, table to table, talking, catching up, whatever, and then hitting the dance floor and making a beautiful fool out of herself.

Karen knew she'd fallen for him one day that February. They had a history class together, and he had her giggling and flirting with him so much that after class, her professor pulled her aside and scolded her, saying she was acting like a sophomore *in high school.*

Kenney waited for her outside the classroom, and asked her what the professor wanted. Karen refused to tell him.

Later that week, one of Karen's friends offered to cut Kenney's hair. He said he'd meet her at her house. The girl called Karen to tell her Kenney was on his way over. Karen hustled over to the girl's house to get there before Kenney, and then she made sure to be *just* conspicuous enough when he did arrive. "And then she butchered his hair!" Karen says. "It was *really bad.* But we had a good time."

Karen invited Kenney to a party, and a few days after that, Kenney asked Karen out. Karen was babysitting that night, but she said Kenney could come by to help. Not a dummy, Kenney did. They've been a couple ever since.

Karen had never been with a guy like Kenney. "Whatever he puts his mind to, he pretty much accomplishes," she says. "And so, for a year, he put his mind to me. And that was nice. That was really nice. It was pretty intoxicating."

What they valued most about each other was their authenticity. Kenney didn't play games, didn't show up late or stand her up, didn't make her come pining after him. Karen never had to wonder if he'd walk her to class, or call, or if they were going out on Friday nights. He wanted her, and he made sure she knew. "He didn't toy with me," Karen says. "He was just always available."

Karen was the same way. Whatever she felt about things Kenney said or did, for good or for bad, she let him know, and she didn't hold back. "I have to do authentic," she says, "or I can't do it at all. I can't do *not real*. And some people just aren't equipped for that. But Kenney's 100 percent authentic. All the way. You pretty much know him when you know him, and I really liked that."

And in Karen, Kenney found a girl — no, a woman — who came to know the worst of him, and embraced it with him, and told him when to quit doing some of it — like talking all the time about his parents — and still loved him.

They both say that they knew they wanted to marry each other after dating just three months.

※　※　※

Jim Garland, Kenney's number one scout, always *just missed* some of his best games, such as the game-winning home run he hit in the regional tournament during his sophomore year — and Garland always managed to make it to Kenney's worst games, such as the worst game of Kenney's freshman season, when he struck out twice and made two errors. So, no, Kenney did not spend get drafted to play pro baseball after his freshman year.

That hurt, but Kenney still realized how much baseball saved him. It got him to college and then kept him there, even in wake of family revelations that made him want to flee to the other side of the country.

Baseball also kept him focused after he met Karen. It was, as sports had always been for him, an anchor. Until Karen, Kenney always felt adrift in life, always felt like things were out of control. "I think that's because I didn't really know my dad," he says. "I just never felt like I had that anchor in my life that a good father gives his son, you know? Dal was a terrific stepdad, but I always struggled with Mosely abandoning us, not being in our lives. And between that, and my mom telling me why she'd had me, at that point in my life, I was just a mess."

As he grew up, Kenney still thought he could maybe make it as a ballplayer, but more than anything, he wanted to build something of his own. Then, he reasoned, the better-thans of the world could no longer look down on and step on him. "I wanted to build something and surround myself with people I could consider family, real family," he says. "I wanted to build my own empire."

There was just the small matter of figuring out exactly *what* that empire should be. Hollywood always popped back into his head. But he stuck around Mount Olive so that he could keep playing baseball and so he could stay with Karen. And because of Karen, Kenney realized he had more potential than he thought. He thought she was the smartest woman he'd ever met, and she told him that he was as smart as she was, and he believed her. After Karen graduated from Mount Olive her sophomore year, Kenney's freshman year, Kenney decided that he wanted to graduate, too, which he would've never imagined himself believing was possible a year earlier.

When he told Coach Dean of his plans, however, Dean wasn't exactly encouraging. "Moore," he said. "You only have 26 hours."

"I know," Kenney said. "I want to take 19 and 19."

"But — but — you can't do that."

"Yes, I can,"

"No, really," Dean said. They had a 50-game schedule in the spring, plus practices and conditioning, but on top of that, they also had 20 to 30 exhibition games in the fall. "You can't do that and still expect to play baseball well."

"Tell you what," Kenney said. "You see me dropping on either side, in baseball or in school, then I'll drop a class. But this is what I want to do."

As he got into the schoolyear, Kenney realized that when he was busier he was better at everything. Not only did he handle the 19 hours per semester without dropping a class, but he also *improved* his GPA.

Baseball taught Kenney a lot that year. When the season began, the local newspaper ran an article about how Mount Olive's team was in a rebuilding year and wouldn't be any good. They won the conference championship and ended up as the only team not nationally ranked to play in that year's junior college regional tournament. Kenney realized that they played so well not because of their talent, but because he and his teammates were all good friends. They played harder than the year before when they had future pro ballplayers on their team, because they cared about each other and wanted to do well for each other.

Kenney himself had a good season, too, but he still went undrafted that summer. He had some scholarship offers from some decent Division I programs, but he wanted to be with Karen.

Karen had spent her junior year, Kenney's sophomore year, at UNC-Greensboro with some of her friends. She majored in history, but thought she wanted to get into fashion advertising, and UNC-G was a good place for that. She ended up not liking it, and she wanted to be with Kenney, but that meant a three-and-a-half hour drive from Greensboro to Mount Olive and back every weekend. For her senior year, Karen transferred to Atlantic Christian, a tiny four-year school in Wilson, N.C., just 20 minutes from Mount Olive, so that she could live at home while finishing school.

Kenney asked Coach Dean to see if AC, a Division II school, had any interest. AC's coach, Jack "Doc" Sanford, a 70-something gentleman who'd played for the Washington Senators in his day, watched Kenney play for his summer semipro team in Newport, where Kenney was living for the summer. Sanford liked Kenney enough to offer him a scholarship on the spot.

After that, Kenney went and bought a $300 diamond ring he knew Karen would like, then he drove from Newport to Mount Olive. He picked Karen up in his Brat. "Hey, I have the ring," he said, pulling it out of the box. "Here you go." Beaming and crying, she put it on.

■ ■ ■

Kenney's junior season at Atlantic Christian was a good one. He led the team with a .364 batting average and was named an honorable mention Division II All-American. More importantly, the season was similar in many ways to his sophomore year at Mount Olive: They weren't supposed to be a good team, but they liked each other so much that they played great. Kenney realized again that the talent of the people around you isn't as important as the type of people they are and how well they work together.

And his next season drove that point home. AC was expected to be one of the best teams in its conference, but ended up having a mediocre season. Kenney and his teammates remember that season more for drinking beer while laying new sod on the field in the fall and burying their empties under the new grass. They had a new young coach, Dave Jauss. He's a coach with the Pittsburgh Pirates now, but at the time, he was only 27 years old. The team had more talent, but less camaraderie, less heart. Jauss obviously knew the game, but he was a young guy trying to prove himself, and since he was practically a peer, the guys had a hard time respecting him.

And of course, Kenney and Jauss had their conflicts. They were both fiery, tell-it-how-they-see-it guys, and they often crossed each other. The hardest thing Jauss ever told Kenney was that he didn't think Kenney could make it as a pro. Even today, Jauss recalls why: Kenney maybe *could have* made it, but Jauss doubted it because Kenney had an unusual throwing motion, for one thing — he could throw the heck out of the ball, but he had this whipping side-arm motion that strained his elbow, which Jauss thought couldn't hold up over a pro season.

Some of Kenney's teammates disagreed. Rick Olivere says that Kenney was never the smoothest, most polished player, but he was effective as they come. He made plays, he got hits, he was a leader. He rose to the level of his competition. Another teammate and one of Kenney's best friends, Billy Godwin, who's coached nationally-ranked Division I baseball teams and now scouts for the Yankees, says the same things about Kenney, and all his old teammates agree that had Kenney been given a legitimate shot, they wouldn't have been surprised in the least if Kenney made it to the majors.

Jauss says he saw better things than baseball in Kenney's future. He saw in Kenney a bright young man who was far more intelligent than he let on. "He just wanted to be a jock first," Jauss says.

By the end of his college career, Kenney agreed with Jauss. He also realized when he was older that if he'd worked harder, he would've had a better shot. He always played his guts out in practices and games, but he never lifted weights, never took extra batting practice, never gave baseball the extra work and extra time that he could have.

He had some offers to play overseas, where he could make

a living playing the game and hone his skills enough to maybe make it as a ballplayer back in the States, but by that point, Kenney was ready to move on. Baseball hadn't been the route to a better life that he thought, but it led him to the right exit ramp. He would've never in a million years gone to Mount Olive if not for baseball, thus he would've never met Karen, who helped him believe in himself beyond sports.

So now, he might not have a baseball career, but he had a fiancée, and by then he had ambitions greater than a game. He graduated with a bachelor's in business management and a minor in industrial psychology, ready to get married and start conquering those demons from his old life, the ones that had always tried to stand on top of him. He wanted to take some control in his life. He wanted to build himself an empire.

10

THE LONG, HARD
ROAD TO ANDY'S

Part 1: Welcome to the Real World

Kenney and Karen joke now that they almost didn't make it down the aisle. They felt too young, Kenney didn't even have a job yet, all that. But make it down the aisle they did, getting married the summer after Kenney graduated, on August 10, 1985, in a humble and simple ceremony at the First United Methodist Church in Mount Olive, about 100 friends and family in attendance. "We just wanted to go ahead and be married," Karen says.

They got an apartment in Raleigh, where Karen had been working for North Carolina's Office of Archives and History for a year. She'd tried fashion merchandising and realized she hated retail work, so she put her history major to good use.

Their first married argument came when Kenney was cleaning up the kitchen after dinner and ate the last piece of meatloaf, which Karen had planned to eat for lunch at work the next day. Getting used to living with each other was something of a shock. Karen lived at her parents' for most of their relationship, and she had her own apartment when she started working in Raleigh. Kenney lived in a house with a bunch of baseball players his senior year, but that is, of course, somewhat different from living with a wife.

More than that, however, and far more stressful, was living with each other's personalities.

Kenney was trying to find something he could give his all and turn into his empire, and he believed he could do anything, and he wasn't afraid to explore a million different possibilities, wide-open as ever. Of course, being 22 years old, Kenney's ambition proceeded in fits and starts.

Karen might have craved that sort of carefree, do-whatever personality in a man in college, but she *is* her parents' daughter, and as such is extremely logical. "Not quite Asperger's logical," she says, "but I'm up there." Her big creative leap back then was working in Box H in the archives rather than Box A for a day. She needs the rationale behind every decision, and she loves a set routine.

Karen would wake up and the first thing she'd hear was Kenney's new big idea for the day and the way it would change their lives and the world, before she'd even had her first cup of coffee. And she'd hear more when she came home from work. And she'd shoot holes in all of Kenney's ideas. She wasn't being mean or rude, at least not on purpose. She was just thinking out loud, same as Kenney, and her logical mind kept seeing all the ways his ideas could fail. They could argue for days.

"I come home, and Kenney's like, *'I can do this, I can do that',*" Karen says. "I'm like, *'Oh my God, get a job, draw a paycheck.'* You know? I came from two schoolteachers. And they went to work. They were creative in their own jobs, they were successful. So I'm not saying we just clocked in and worked until we got to clock out. We all went into jobs we cared about. But I'd never come in contact with somebody like Kenney, who was just — all the time, he just had a different idea."

It took Karen a long time, several years in fact, to learn how best to talk with Kenney about his ideas, which was almost every day: Instead of going at him right away, she learned it was best to listen, and digest, and process, and *then* talk. These days, she and Kenney talk for an hour every morning, Karen easing into the day with a cup of coffee and Kenney, who can wake up and be ready to go in an instant, spelling out his next big vision. "I had to learn," she says. "He would come in and say something and I would just shoot him down, and be like, *'Yeah, well, you can't do that because so and so.'* So, after probably a lot of arguments and a lot of hurt feelings, I finally started to understand — *just listen. It never hurts someone to just listen."*

Every once in awhile, the Hollywood idea reared its head again, especially after Kenney had a few drinks. He never did go to L.A., but he did star in some local productions over the years.

In the meantime, however, Kenney *did* break down and take a job to pull a paycheck. He loaded trucks for a moving company. He took a minimum wage job in the computer department at Manpower, this back in the mid-1980s when computers were the size of an office and they needed strong guys like Kenney to haul stuff around. "Now, people who know me think it's hilarious that I used to work for a computer department," he says, laughing. After six months of that, Kenney went to a headhunter, who found him a $15,000-a-year job with American Tobacco Company. Kenney drove all over the region, setting up store displays and stocking products.

That was his first "real" job — the company offered profit-sharing and benefits and everything else adults tell kids to get. He also appreciated how it brought his life full circle, in a way, from his first job in the tobacco fields to now selling the cigarettes that tobacco made. He had a company car filled with cartons that he could buy at discount prices, and he and Karen and all their friends were all big smokers back then, so when they were hanging out on weekends and ran out of cigarettes, Kenney grabbed a new pack out of the car.

There wasn't much to complain about, but there were two problems: One, the job did nothing to further the building of his empire, and two, he hated his boss.

The man taught Kenney much about how *not* to be a boss. He threw cigarette packs at people when they made mistakes and he insulted his employees, equating their humanity with their job performance. "He was just negative," Kenney says. Kenney knew he was fine at his job, but every time the boss evaluated him, Kenney never got higher than a C. He worked for the man for two years, and he can't remember a single compliment the man gave him. Not that he needed compliments, but working for a man who didn't seem to value what he provided made Kenney want to quit.

After riding around with his boss for three days for an evaluation, Kenney sat through another round of criticism until he finally looked at the man and let loose all of his pent-up frustration with a simple, biting question: "Do you *ever* see *anything* good?"

The man sat back and blinked.

■   ■   ■

Kenney left American Tobacco in the summer of 1987 to sell life insurance and mutual funds, which he felt like was a true opportunity, with the potential to be something he could grow and make his own. That's how he often makes his decisions — where Karen is logical and calculating, Kenney goes off instinct and figures it out along the way. When he attended an orientation meeting, Kenney saw example after example of people who became successful and wealthy with the insurance company, and he was sold, with no doubt he could be one of them one day.

He worked for the company for a year and a half. He learned how to speak in public, how to get up in front of groups of people and sell, and how to get cynics and skeptics excited about what he had to sell them.

But not all skeptics: At the same time, his new career and his ambitions were threatening his marriage.

Part 2: His Wife, the Hero

Karen never liked the insurance company. From the first meeting she went to with Kenney, something felt off. There was a cult vibe about it. The meeting wasn't about selling life insurance — it was about "changing your life." She felt like the company was "basically brainwashing people." And her bad feeling about the company only grew worse as Kenney became more involved. "They just kind of surrounded you," she says. "They took over everything." She and Kenney never had any free time alone together. They never had time to do things with friends. The company had them doing some-thing every night and every weekend. Plus, the company also expected their employees' spouses to be supportive. Employ-ees whose spouses weren't engaged in every company activity ended up derided and pushed out.

As if all of that wasn't bad enough, in a fit of naïve ambition, Kenney up and moved to Morehead City — right near his hometown of Newport, remember — because the company didn't have a branch there, which he saw as an opportunity. He lived with his parents for a little while, and then he rented a room at an acquaintance's house — and he left Karen behind, alone in Raleigh.

She would drive to Morehead on weekends, but this was before a bypass was built from there to Raleigh, so the trip took a solid three hours, sometimes four. This was long before the Internet, and long-distance phone calls cost a small fortune back then, so when they weren't together, they were very much apart.

Capping things off, the job wasn't going well. His salary depended on commissions and on his salespeople under him making sales. It didn't help that the American economy was slipping into a recession sparked by a stock market collapse in October 1987. But the biggest obstacle to making any money was the way that the commissions were structured. If Kenney sold a policy, he received 80 percent of the premium, but if the client dropped their policy within 60 days, then Kenney had to return the money. That happened over and over again, to the point where they were living off of Karen's income alone. "It was just one of the darkest times ever," she says.

Karen had a good salary and she was building a great career. She was promoted three times in three years at the North Carolina Office of Archives and History. But with Kenney in Morehead City, Karen spent all of her time working and explaining to her friends why Kenney was away. "It got to the point where I quit answering the phone," Karen says. "Ninety-five percent of my time was spent explaining that it was all going to be okay."

They knew she loved him, and they *thought* he loved her — but he *had* moved three hours away, and he seemed a little crazy, chasing after his dream with *this* weird cult of a company. Some of her friends even went to one of Kenney's insurance company meetings and came out of it saying, "Oh. My. *God.*"

"I didn't like what we were doing at all," Karen says. "And I hated that, too, but after awhile, what are you gonna do? Sit around and bash him with everybody? I mean, I'm not gonna do that. So I'm just gonna have to say, 'It's gonna be okay.'"

■ ■ ■

After about five months of living the way they were, Karen says, "I had to make a decision: What kind of married couple did we want to be? And I didn't like what I saw at all." It came down to choosing either her marriage or her career. Did she want to keep working where she was, keep building her own life, stay near friends, and ensure her parents' peace of mind? Or did she want to give up all of that to be with Kenney?

She chose Kenney. "I chose to quit my job and move to Morehead and support him any way I could," she says. She bursts out laughing, telling the story all these years later, and says, "And saying those words sounds like, really selfless, and, *'Oh, wow, she's amazing!'* But, no. I was conflicted. It was *hard.* It wasn't, like, *'Oh, totally, I'm gonna stand by him and I'm gonna support him'* — no. I was like" — She fakes crying sounds — *"'I don't know what the hell I'm doing!'* I had to tell my parents! I had to quit my job! And I *hated* it. It was awful. I think my dad was gonna have a stroke. It was so sad."

■ ■ ■

Kenney and Karen rented an old house in an old, run-down

neighborhood near the river in Morehead. The house was drafty, which neither of them had experienced before, and it didn't have heat, and there were snakes in the basement.

"Oh my God, we were so poor," Karen says.

"We ate a lot of fried egg sandwiches and yogurt," Kenney says. "We became master egg chefs."

Karen's grandmother had given her a big set of 50-cent pieces, and they took one at a time to go buy two biscuits from a corner store for dinner. They kept hats and scarves and winter coats by the door to *put on* when they came home. They found an extra $50 of credit on one of their cards, so they used it to buy a space heater that they dragged with them from room to room. And they decided it was prudent to heat up only certain parts of the house once instead of twice, such as the bathroom when they, you know, needed to shower. "So, you know," Karen says, laughing, "it wasn't *all* awful."

* * *

Karen found a job at Mary Anne's Pots and Pans, a little store on the waterfront where boats come into Morehead City. Mary Anne, a sweet older lady, asked Karen, "Do you cook?"

"Yes!" Karen lied. Now she says, "Which, *no!* I knew *nothing* about cooking. I mean, I could cook things, but *really cooking* — no! And she caught onto that pretty quick." Karen laughs. "But she was awesome. We became fast friends."

Mary Anne was going through a divorce, and she and Karen bonded over the struggles of marriage. Moving to Morehead hadn't magically repaired Kenney and Karen's marriage. If anything, they fought *more,* because now they were around each other all the time. Mary Anne was an excellent sounding board, because she would get so angry that Karen couldn't stay angry herself. "I remember one time Kenney and I were having an argument in the car," Karen says, "and he was yelling so freakin' loud."

Mary Anne came out of the store and stood on the sidewalk, clearly watching them out of the corner of her eye. "I think maybe she can hear you," Karen said.

"She can't fuzzing hear me!" Kenney roared.

Karen got out of the car and went inside.

"That was him yelling at you, wasn't it?" Mary Anne said.

"Yeah," Karen said. "Maybe."

Mary Anne went off, screaming at the top of her lungs, saying things like, "Carteret County men think they can treat women *any way* they want to!"

"She went berserk," Karen says. "It was really off the hinges. Like, *Oh my god. She's losing it.* And she left. Mad. I thought, *Oh my gosh, she's going to go kill Kenney.*"

People working in the store above theirs walked down and stuck their head in. "Is everything okay?"

"Mary Anne's just losing it today," Karen said.

"Men?"

"Yeah."

"So I guess it was kinda like that," Karen says. "She would kinda take all the anger. I mean, how could you even be angry after that?"

■ ■ ■

Karen helped Kenney with his job however she could. She tried talking to people for him, but "I was not comfortable with that at all," she says. "You know, the cult-like part."

But she *was* comfortable with the more practical side of his business. While Kenney was out hustling to make sales and network, she organized meetings and events. "I could do all that," she says. "I could set things up." She laughs. "I could get coffee!"

She also found free spaces for him to use, because he couldn't afford to rent out a room or office. "We were so broke," Kenney says. "And man, she was such a jewel."

So were Karen's parents. They "just happened" to visit Morehead City quite a lot, and they would always "pop by" to see how Karen and Kenney were doing, and they just so happened to swing by the grocery store first. They accepted that Karen loved Kenney, and they talked with Kenney enough to understand Kenney's heart, and they came to love him, too. They tried to give them some money a couple of times, but Kenney wouldn't have it. He couldn't accept anything from someone else unless he felt he had earned it.

■ ■ ■

After working with Mary Anne for a few months, Karen saw an ad in the paper for a social worker position with Carteret County Social Services, and showed it to Kenney. "It says here you don't need a social work degree — you just need a college degree!"

Kenney said, "Do you want to be a social worker?"

Karen replied, "I want a social worker's paycheck."

She talked her way into the job and took a position in crisis intake, meaning she was the first person people saw when their lives were falling apart.

Meanwhile, Kenney kept working all the time, trying to make sales, generate leads, and build a network of salespeople beneath him. But it just was not going well.

For all their frustrations, Kenney with work and Karen with Kenney, they remained a team, and that's what saved them. "Once I moved down there, that part, it was still hard, but the way it was hard changed," Karen says. "At least we were in it together."

They fought like they hated each other sometimes, but never like enemies, always like teammates frustrated with each other's performance. "Not only did I stay when things were hard because I love Kenney, but because he loves me," Karen says. "We love each other and we show it, now and in the past, in hundreds of ways. We are each other's family. His dreams are my dreams. Mine are his. Asking why I stayed in my marriage is like asking why you eat or breathe. I guess I don't take a lot of things lightly. I certainly did not take getting married lightly. Kenney always made me feel like I brought something to the table in this marriage. I felt valued. We each have lost our way before, through neglect, boredom, or depression, but we always want to be together regardless of circumstances. I don't even know where I stop and Kenney begins anymore. I hear or see things that he would be interested in or like, and I can hardly wait to share it with him. He is the same way with me."

■ ■ ■

Something else that would prove invaluable was when Karen realized where much of Kenney's anger and intensity came from: He thought she might leave him. As she got to know his family Kenney's scars came to make more sense as Karen recognized ways that Kenney had been emotionally abandoned. Just one example: Kenney's older sister and younger half-brother had various issues over the course of their lives that required various types of rescuing, but Kenney was always independent, never needing his parents to rescue him, and he even ended up the rescuer sometimes, but this also left him feeling like a forgotten stepchild.

And so Karen saw how, over the course of his life, a fear

had grown and grown in Kenney that everyone in his life would, at some point, abandon him. He says, "Karen really didn't know me for a long time because I always had this fear of people leaving me, so the best way I handled that was to go on offense. Which was totally wrong."

Karen says, "I found out that once he understood that I was never going anywhere, that, you know, I got married to him *to be married to him,* not to have drama with him, and not to leave him, that helped tremendously. That's just not my nature. I'm going to figure out what's going to make it work. If he's not into it, then obviously, it's not going to work, but once he realized that about me, he was able to open up a lot more, too, with no fear of me packing the bags."

That fear of abandonment is also why, remember, Kenney wanted to build an empire. He not only wanted to create a business of his own, but also a family. The fear would flare up again and again, the driving force behind everything he would become, for better and for worse. When it was good, it inspired him so greatly that it felt like God himself reached down and flipped a switch in his soul. But when it was bad, it was the demon spark to his worst eruptions, and a demon that he could never quite kill, that he would always have to fight.

■　■　■

A few months after moving to Morehead City, Karen came down with the flu. She had a headache for two weeks. She was always at the doctor. And then the doctor discovered that single surprise that can all at once be the most terrifying and the most amazing thing in the world: Karen was pregnant.

Part 3: Rob's Cheesesteaks and Cheeseburgers

One day in March when the weather was starting to get warm, Kenney went to the beach to try to relax. Between learning he'd be having a child and his struggles at work, Kenney knew something had to change, but he had no idea what to do. And then the answer walked right up to him, wearing nice clothes and a shiny gold watch and even shinier gold chains. It was Kenney's old high school football coach. We'll call him Roberts. They man-hugged and Kenney said, "Man, you're doing okay, aren't you?"

Roberts said he was. Roberts was on his way back to his car, and he told Kenney to walk with him. When Kenney saw the car, his mouth fell open. Roberts was driving a brand-new Jaguar, Kenney's dream car.

"I'm in the restaurant business," Roberts said. "And I'm looking for sharp young guys like you, Kenney. You need to come see me sometime. Let's talk about getting you into the restaurant business."

Kenney didn't take the offer seriously, at least not the part about getting into the restaurant business. He was a tobacco field kid, a frustrated ballplayer who became a salesman, able to talk anyone into almost anything. He'd never worked in *restaurants*. He'd never even *thought* about it. But he thought that maybe Roberts could use a million-dollar life insurance policy, so he called him, and he drove to Roberts's home in Greenville, N.C., a small college town about an hour and a half north of Morehead.

Kenney never opened his briefcase. He and Roberts spent their whole meeting talking about the restaurant chain Roberts had started in eastern North Carolina. We'll call it "Rob's Cheesesteaks and Cheeseburgers." He went on and on about the food business and how great it was. And then he offered Kenney a job, right then and there in his living room, and not as a cook or waiter, but as a manager, on salary. As in, a real job, with a real, consistent paycheck.

When Kenney got home and told Karen, she shrieked. "We'll be able to really eat! We'll have *heat!*"

* * *

But getting a new, good job didn't solve all of their problems. For one thing, Kenney was gone all the time again. He went through management training in New Bern, about an hour from Morehead City, and then Roberts wanted Kenney to manage a store in New Bern, and of course, Kenney went all out. He *felt* this was an opportunity to become a key player in an exploding business. Roberts was doing well, even franchising, which meant even *more* opportunity, so Kenney threw himself into his work. Kenney and Karen didn't live apart, but between restaurant hours and Kenney's hour commute, they barely saw each other. Karen, now pregnant, once again felt alone. It felt familiar.

"He was still a little frustrated," Karen says. "And I guess I was a little frustrated. But that's just part of our makeup. That's just who we are. We're a little intense."

And then Karen's health insurance company decided to make life even more interesting.

* * *

Being the logical person she is, after leaving her job with the archives in Raleigh, Karen kept her health insurance through COBRA, a federally-legislated program that requires continued group health insurance coverage to be made available when workers change jobs. She'd paid her bill every month without fail, keeping it when she worked at Mary Anne's Pots and Pans and then when she went to Carteret County Social Services, even though the county offered its own plan.

Everything was fine until she found out she was pregnant, and then she learned that her COBRA plan didn't cover her pregnancy. She tried to switch to the county plan, but it wouldn't cover her pregnancy, either, since she'd become pregnant before applying. Karen spent hours upon hours on the phone and meeting with people, trying to work something out, and to no avail. Eventually, Kenney and Karen had no choice but to work out a payment plan with the hospital and her OB/GYN.

It was a horrible ordeal. Telling a doctor you don't have health insurance is demeaning enough. Telling your OB/GYN that you haven't taken the precaution even for your child was humiliating.

■ ■ ■

Kenney worked at Rob's in New Bern for five months.

To his surprise, he found that he liked the food business, maybe even loved it, cooking in particular. It reminded him of theater — he'd done a little acting in local productions after college, and cooking reminded him of being on stage and the center of attention. He loved that he could make people happy in an instant. The food business also tapped Kenney's competitive side. When things were busy, he had to be fast. He made it his goal to get food out in three to four minutes, remarkable for a short-order cook. And then there was the management side. That was easier, as he'd been managing others his whole life, from organizing neighborhood football games and Olympic competition, to college, where he was team captain. Every good business has to have good managers, and good managers have to be good leaders, pure and simple. And Kenney loved leading and learning how to lead better.

Plus, he was making and serving food like he loved as a kid — burgers like the ones from El's Drive-Thru, the ones that he'd eat three of after his evening football practices.

He did so well that Roberts promoted him to district manager. Roberts was setting up franchise groups around the region, and Kenney started by managing two Rob's owned by two CPAs in Greenville. He would handle new stores as the CPAs opened them.

* * *

Kenney and Karen couldn't quite afford a house in Greenville, but they didn't want to get an apartment. They didn't want neighbors waking the baby, and they didn't want the baby's crying to wake the neighbors. They found another old house in the small town of Ayden, twenty minutes outside of Greenville.

Karen scored a great new job with a law firm called Ward and Smith, building their law library. The job not only came with health insurance, but it covered her pregnancy, even the doctor payments they had already made. She and Kenney got back almost everything they'd spent on her doctor's bills. And that was something of a godsend, because when Andrew was born, in November 1989, Karen ended up having him delivered via C-section.

Andrew was born healthy, and things finally began looking up. *At last,* Kenney's passion had landed him a stable job with a future. Kenney saw himself owning a Rob's restaurant some day. Maybe even more than one.

After about six months in their Ayden house, Kenney and

Karen bought Karen's late grandparents' old house in Pink Hill, a one-light town about 45 minutes from Greenville on Highway 11, between Greenville and Wilmington.

In Pink Hill, they were finally stable, and that felt like Paradise. The house was a white two-story Colonial that Karen's great-grandfather built in 1905, and there, she felt *at home* — safe, grounded, secure, for the first time in a long time. In that house, Karen found herself at peace with Kenney and his intensity and all his wild ideas. She kept working at Ward and Smith part-time, and on days when Andrew slept well and Karen got bored, she went to the back of the house and picked through old boxes of her grandmother's keepsakes. Life felt good. Anytime Kenney dreamed up something new, Karen could say, "Okay! Do it!"

■ ■ ■

Kenney gave Rob's his all. He was a district manager, but he didn't just supervise; he kept flipping burgers with the cooks and he waited tables. He *worked*. One time, when he thought someone was breaking into one of his Rob's stores after hours, he spent three nights camped outside the store, hiding in the bushes, trying to catch the thief.

He became friends with Dan Jones, whom Rob hired to run one of Kenney's stores. Kenney knew it was absurd that, with a mere eight months in the business, he was going to be Dan's boss — the man had *14 years* of restaurant experience. The first time he met with Dan, Kenney went to his restaurant and said, "Look, I'm your district manager. That's my title. But every time I walk in here, I want you to look at me as another set of eyes and hands. I'm just in here because we both have the same common goal: We both want this store to get better. So I'm gonna work with you. You can clock somebody else out, save yourself some labor cost, and I'll just get on the grill or do whatever you need, and we'll work side-by-side."

That set the tone for how Kenney dealt with everyone. He had no desire to be a "snoopervisor," reporting everything wrong. "I wanted to get into the fray," Kenney says.

The result was a less adversarial relationship with his store managers and more of a teamwork-based one. And in Dan's case, that relationship became a great friendship.

Dan wasn't the Type A, fiery volcano of a guy that Kenney was. He was much more Type B, withdrawn, quiet, reasonable. They were a good fit because they both wanted the same goal: build a better company.

The longer they worked for Rob's, the more frustrated they became with how Roberts ran the business. They had their own ideas, too. Kenney and Dan spent hours and hours on Kenney's back porch, Kenney smoking cigarettes and both of them drinking beer and solving all of the company's problems and dreaming up what they'd do if *they* ran things.

Their frustration built as Rob's expanded. By early 1991, after Kenney had been with Rob's for about two years, Roberts had opened 32 stores. It was too much too fast. The company was too spread out. Roberts began losing control of his operation. Stores were changing the menu at will. Franchisees began turning on Roberts. Relationships broke down. Roberts didn't seem to be doing much to improve things, either — and, as Kenney and Dan learned later, some of Roberts' decisions were making things *worse*.

One: When you negotiate a lease, landlords sometimes offer tenant improvement money. That is, they'll say, *yeah, we want your concept, we want this Rob's here, so we'll give you $50,000 in tenant improvement to come in here and build out your space.* Well, Roberts would keep the money, then sell the restaurant rights to the franchisee for something like $200,000, and wish them luck, having started them drowning in debt. Making matter worse, landlords wanted to recoup their investments, so they hiked rent on the bewildered franchisees.

Two: Roberts owned an equipment company and a construction company, both of which he required his franchisees to use, and he charged them inflated prices for his goods and services.

Three: Roberts's franchisee fee was, in Kenney and Dan's opinion, way too high, requiring 10 percent of all sales from the franchisees each month. Standard franchising fees were closer to 7 or 8 percent.

All in all, his business model seemed greedy, designed more to make Roberts rich than to build a good and profitable company.

Meanwhile, Roberts kept living large, spending all the money he made off of franchisees on himself. He even bought a second Jaguar.

Kenney looked into buying Rob's restaurants that he could run his way. Maybe he could work his way up to help Roberts run the company. But he and Dan also started seriously considering starting their own chain of restaurants. Three of the four stores that Kenney oversaw, including Dan's, were in the company's top five. They knew what they were doing.

But then everything fell apart.

■ ■ ■

Kenney and Dan didn't know this until later, but the equipment that Roberts was selling to his franchisees, he had *leased* from vendors. It was lucrative, but also insanely illegal. This should go without saying, but *you can't sell some-*

thing you don't own. Roberts got away with it as long as franchisees made their royalty payments, but if they fell behind, then Roberts, who blew through all his other cash, was in a bind with the company he'd leased the equipment from. The equipment companies sued Roberts, so then Roberts sued the franchisees, and then the franchisees sued Roberts in return. "There were just lawsuits flying all over the place," Kenney says. That cost everyone.

Toward the end of January 1991, between Roberts's treachery and a lagging United States economy, Rob's fell apart. Roberts declared bankruptcy. The two CPAs who owned Kenney's four Rob's restaurants stripped them all of Rob's branding, leaving Kenney to find some way to draw customers into restaurants with no name, serviced by employees wearing jeans and t-shirts as uniforms. But Kenney being Kenney, he kept busting his tail. He was 28 years old with a wife who'd stuck by him, and he had an infant to provide for. They were safe and comfortable, and they could afford food, and heat, and diapers. Kenney would do whatever it took to maintain that lifestyle. He had no idea he would have to do things he never thought he'd ever do.

■ ■ ■

One cold Sunday afternoon that February, around 6 p.m., the phone rang at the Moores' house. One of the CPAs wanted Kenney to drive to Greenville for a meeting. Right away.

Kenney got in his company car, a blue Volkswagen Jetta, and made the hour drive. The meeting was brief and abrupt. The CPAs were "making a change" and wanted to sever all ties from Rob's and start fresh. They'd already hired a new district manager. They asked Kenney to hand over the keys to his stores and his company car. They had a rental car that they said Kenney could use for a week.

Kenney felt blindsided. He knew things weren't going well, but he had no idea he'd be *fired. I have three of the top five stores in the* company, he thought. *I thought I meant something to these guys. I've worked my ass off for them. How could they do this to me? To my wife, to my kid? This is a horrible way to treat a human being.*

"Keep your fuzzing rental car," Kenney said. "Shove it up your ass."

He invited the CPAs outside to discuss the matter further. They declined.

Kenney stormed out. He found a payphone outside and called Karen and told her what happened, and that he needed her to come pick him up. Yes, even though it meant waking up Andrew and putting him in the car, and — just hurry up, please, could you?

■ ■ ■

While he waited, Kenney went to a bar with an assistant manager's boyfriend. Over beers, the guy told him, "This is going to be the best thing that's ever happened to you. You're going to do your own thing, and you're going to be great at it."

Kenney appreciated that, but he felt on fire. Once again, people important in his life had abandoned him, just cut him loose.

■ ■ ■

When Karen arrived in their black two-door Nissan Pulsar, Kenney climbed in and told Karen more about the meeting, and then he rambled on, wondering what they would do next. Karen said, "It's going to be okay. You'll find something better. And as for them — they messed up by getting rid of you. And they'll realize that."

She was calm and supportive and that meant a lot to Kenney, but he could hear it in her voice, too: She was scared. Of course she was. They had a mortgage, and a baby, and all Kenney could think was, "What are we going to do?"

Karen reached back and took his hand, and Kenney reached out with the other and Andrew took hold of his finger, and they all held on, together.

11

BIRTH OF ANDY'S
Or, the Stupid Idea That Started All of This

Kenney was tired of losing work and money and peace of mind because of matters out of his control. If he was going to fail again, he wanted to fail at *his* thing.

Kenney knew that several Rob's had closed down near Pink Hill, and he knew that *that* meant whoever owned those stores had nothing more than an empty restaurant and a bunch of restaurant equipment.

He had an idea. He would buy an old Rob's and resurrect it into a restaurant of his own.

It was a perfect, insane, maybe kind of stupid idea. Rob's began breaking down because Roberts was swindling seemingly everyone he could, but in eastern North Carolina back in the early 90s, even the most upstanding of businessmen were struggling. After a brief boom in the late 1980s, the American economy went into another recession in 1990, and although parts of the country had recovered, small rural towns like Greenville, and especially the tiny towns like Pink Hill, were still hurting. "Recessions hurt everyone in the country," Kenney says, "but what a lot of people don't realize is that during recessions, little towns like these get *killed*."

But Kenney just *felt* he could make it work, same as he'd *felt* he could outrun that Iwakuni train as a kid, so he took off running.

Less than a week after the CPAs fired him, Kenney started calling around to the groups who owned the old Rob's stores, asking if he could buy the equipment and re-open under a new brand. John Howard was part of a group in Greenville that had a closed Rob's in another nearby eastern North Carolina town, Goldsboro, about 40 minutes from Pink Hill, and Howard and his group liked Kenney — they'd even tried to hire him away from the CPAs before.

Kenney said that if Howard would in-house finance the Goldsboro store's equipment — that is, provide him with his own loan instead of making Kenney go to a bank — then Kenney would pay him $32,500 for it. "You know that if you go to a used equipment dealer with it, you'll get 10 or 15," Kenney told him. "But I'll give you 32.5 with an interest rate. You'll just have to start the payments next month, obviously."

Howard said that he wanted Kenney to secure the store's lease first, but then he'd be happy to do it, and he said, "I believe in you, Kenney."

Howard was one of the first people other than Karen to ever tell Kenney that.

       ■ ■ ■

The landlord unequivocally denied Kenney, saying, "No. You don't have *any* financial backing. You have *no money*."

That could not have been more true. Kenney and Karen's money was running out. They were so broke that Karen floated the unthinkable — maybe Kenney could go down to the unemployment office? Just once? So they could eat?

"I didn't know what, right away, I was going to do when I got fired," Kenney says now. "I didn't know if I was going to go work for another restaurant chain, or what. But I knew I wasn't gonna take that check. I was gonna find something. If it meant working the cash register at the local convenience store, then so be it. That's what I would've done. But I was going to earn my way through this world and not look for a handout."

"But," Karen told him, "you've paid into it. It's *for people who lose their jobs. It's for people with children to feed. It's for people like us.*"

Kenney says now, "Even though I paid into the system, and I had every right to collect it, and all of that — to me, it made me feel like I was less than the man my wife had married. I know that sounds kind of hardcore, but I wasn't put on this earth to get *paid* for doing *nothing.*"

Karen told him, "Look, we have *no money.* I've *done* the finances. It's been stretched as far as it can be stretched. We're going to have to ask *somebody* for help."

Never in his life had Kenney ever imagined he would walk into an unemployment office and ask for free money, for money he would owe nobody, for money he would never have to pay back. He heard his mom's voice resonating in his head, saying her family was her responsibility, not someone else's. He felt shame in his heart.

"But *you have paid into it,*" Karen reminded him, over and over. "You *deserve* some of that money. *It's yours.*"

He knew she was right. His wife's voice drowned out all the others in his mind long enough to help him swallow his pride and silence his shame.

He had to sit in a room with a few other guys and watch an educational video about searching for jobs, or something like that. He can't remember the details now, except for what he was thinking: He couldn't believe the conversations he was hearing. Several people were there to renew their welfare, and they were complaining, saying, "Man, can you believe they make us do this to re-up?"

Kenney could only look at them, able-bodied men and women complaining about having to *watch a video* for *free money*, and say to himself, "Come *on.*"

He was thinking nonstop, *This is embarrassing. This is humiliating. I do not belong in here.*

■ ■ ■

Kenney's first unemployment check came the next week. He would never take another. "But it also fed us for the next couple of weeks," Karen says.

After that, Kenney refused to let the Goldsboro Mall landlord ignore him. He would've gone to his house, but he lived hours away, in Shelby, so Kenney did the next best thing. He found the man's home phone number and called first thing on Sunday morning, when he knew he'd be home.

The man answered, sounding groggy. Kenney told him who he was and what he wanted. "Well," said the landlord. "You're persistent. I'm going to give you a chance. But your rent is $3,000 a month."

The store was maybe 1,400 square feet, holding 32 total seats: four tables, 16 bar stools. And in 1991, $3,000 was worth about $5,500 today. "Just *outrageous,*" Kenney says now. "But I didn't have a choice, basically. Not if I really wanted to do this."

Another problem: he had nothing to use for collateral to sign the lease. He needed someone to co-sign with him.

He went to his mom and step-dad, Nancy and Dal Moore.

They said no.

He went to his real father, Tom Mosely. He also said no.

He went to friends, other family members, more — no, no, no.

Desperate, he finally went to his father-in-law, Jimmy Williams, who believed in him. Williams likes to joke that he co-signed because he was afraid that if he *didn't,* then Kenney and Karen would end up moving in with them. But Williams knew Kenney's passion, and his work ethic, and his heart, and the truth is, when he talks about Kenney asking him for help today, it makes Williams swell with such pride and joy that he cries.

■ ■ ■

The day after Kenney signed the lease papers, he called John Howard with the good news. Howard's wife answered, sounding broken. Howard had a heart attack the night before and passed away. The first man to tell Kenney he believed in him, "the man who really helped me get started," Kenney says, "never really got to see me get started."

Kenney went to the funeral, grieving Howard's death and the death of his empire, of his dream.

And then two people from Howard's investment group called him: Rod Williams, a doctor from Roanoke Rapids, and his wife Betsy. Howard's faith in Kenney had been contagious. Like Howard, they'd loved Kenney when he was a district manager for Rob's, and they were thrilled about what he wanted to do. They saw to it that Howard's deal with Kenney worked out, and they even loaned Kenney an extra $3,000 to pay his first month's rent.

Then it was time to get into the store and get to work.

Kenney took his and Karen's last $500 and bought a used

light blue Chevy Citation so that he could get from Pink Hill to Goldsboro.

One morning in early March, Kenney drove to Goldsboro, walked into the mall, walked up to the gate over his store's entrance. Here it was, the first physical step into the future that was his empire. Kenney unlocked the gate and slung it up.

A million roaches ran across the floor.

It quickly became apparent that when the previous managers shut things down, they *shut things down,* without even bothering to clean. There was old grease and grime coating the fryers and the grill, and there was food in the pantry that had been rotting for seven months. When Kenney pulled a freezer away from a wall to clean behind it, the white wall looked brown from all the cockroaches living back there.

Kenney spent a full week scrubbing the restaurant from top to bottom. Maybe the worst part was cleaning out the grease traps. To this day, Kenney says he's never smelled anything as horrible as a grease trap that's been sitting dirty for seven months. "It's just *toxic,*" he says. Kenney worked on his hands and knees, attacking the dirt and grime caked around everything. Karen came to help him, Andrew in tow. Their bodies hurt everywhere. Their knuckles split and bled.

After three or four days, the manager of the K&W Cafeteria across from them walked over one night. "What are you cleaning with?" he asked.

Kenney said, "Soap."

The manager laughed and said, "Man, I'll be right back." He returned carrying a jug of oven cleaner. "Here," he said. "Use this. That'll get it right off for you."

The way oven cleaner stripped away grime was nothing short of magical. "What!?" Kenney exclaimed to Karen, exhilarated and feeling stupid and embarrassed. "Look at that! It comes off pretty easily!"

■ ■ ■

Come time to open the place, Kenney was still short on money. Rod and Betsy Williams came through for him again. They loaned him another $3,000 out of their own pockets so he could make his first food order and get some change in the drawer. "That was awfully kind of them," Kenney says now. "Of course, I promptly paid them back within 90 days, as soon as I could. But they didn't have to do that. They'd already gone out on a limb with me on the equipment, so they didn't have to do that."

Kenney also had to name his restaurant, and he didn't want to name it after himself. However, he also couldn't take his heart out of it, and every time he looked at his son, Andrew, he knew why he was doing this. He didn't want Andrew to grow up struggling the way he had. Kenney's childhood had left him with many deep wounds, some of which had only just scarred over. He named his restaurant Andy's Cheesesteaks and Cheeseburgers.

He kept the '50's concept, because he loved it and because he knew many others did, too. One of his favorite places to eat in Mount Olive had been a 1950s-themed burger joint called Smitty's. And he kept the same general name — "Cheesesteaks and Cheeseburgers" — even though, in his mind, the cheeseburger would be his signature creation. He cooked his burgers like nobody else, in a way he'd only had a burger one other place, at that beloved El's Drive-Thru of his youth. He kept "cheesesteaks" first in the name because most malls develop exclusive contracts with burger joints that prohibit the opening of more than one burger-centric restaurant.

Putting "Cheesesteaks" in the name meant his restaurant wasn't burger-centric, getting him around the ban.

Theme-wise, Kenney's concept was, in his word, "confused." He decorated the walls with sports team pennants he bought from the mall's sporting goods store. He hired the cheapest graphic design shop in Greenville, Mojo's, to create a logo. The place was run by a few college-age kids, and Kenney was pretty sure he smelled marijuana when he first walked in. He told them he wanted a baby with big cheeks wearing a baseball cap and a diaper and holding a bat and maybe eating a cheeseburger, or something like that.

Later, when Andy could talk, he would point at the logo and say what he saw. "Pig! Pig! Fat pig!"

Meanwhile, Karen, who would help with the bookkeeping, made a desk out of some old cabinets and set it up in their bedroom, where she worked between naps and nursing. That was Andy's Corporate Headquarters.

■ ■ ■

Kenney opened Andy's at 4 p.m. on Saturday, March 9, 1991, with a staff of four — another cook, a waiter, and two waitresses.

They did $400 in sales.

That wouldn't exactly put a dent in his debts.

The question flared in Kenney's brain again: *What are we going to DO?*

But he was very much still the kid who'd outrun the bullet train. He knew sales of $400 a day wouldn't build an empire, but that didn't mean he wasn't going to slow down. He worked open to close, and hours before and after, especially after losing his first two waitresses in the first two weeks. One of them went to the beach and never came back. The other stole from him.

That *did* lead to an important lesson, though. A college girl, Kristin, came in the first week Andy's was open, asking for a job. Kenney had a full staff at the time and didn't think he needed her, and besides, he thought she sounded kind of ditzy. He told her he'd give her whatever extra hours became available.

Kristin taught him what a great waitress was. When the first girl left for the beach, Kristin stepped right into her shift, and she worked hours upon hours, working hard the whole time, always smiling and making the customers feel good. "She practically saved the store," Kenney says. "She was a stud." And that's how Kenney learned to never consider a staff "full," and to never write someone off because of how they look or talk.

12

THE VOICE IN KENNEY'S HEAD
Growth of Andy's, Part 1

In early 1991, the economy was still down, and most companies were minimizing risk and trying to tread water, but Kenney saw that as an opportunity. He looked at other struggling Rob's stores and, one by one, he bought them out.

Only a few months after opening the Andy's store in Goldsboro, he bought a Rob's in Washington, a tiny North Carolina town on the Pamlico River, for $50,000, once again convincing the owner to in-house finance it for him.

Soon after that, Kenney called his old friend, Dan Jones, who had moved to Alabama, and convinced him to come back to North Carolina and work with him. He said that he was taking on the world, and that he was building the second coming of McDonald's, and that things were going *great*.

It was all pretty much a lie. Kenney's Washington store was deep in the red, and on good weeks, the Goldsboro store, where he was working open to close every day, was *maybe* breaking even.

Dan packed up his old Camaro, which was held together by little more than bumper stickers, and came back to work with

Kenney. His calm Type B personality was a perfect counter-part to Kenney's Type A drive. They bounced ideas off of each another, and Dan wasn't afraid to challenge Kenney. He was like Karen in that way, and Kenney needed that. "He kept me tempered in the early days," Kenney says. "The ice to my fire, if you will. But at the end of the day, when I said, 'Here's what we're going to do,' he was an amazing executor. He would get it done, and he would get it done in a big way. He was very, very valuable to me. And he was a beast. He worked open to close just like I did. And yeah, things weren't going great in the company, but I knew that with his work ethic and his passion, we could do it together."

■ ■ ■

A few months after buying the Washington store and bringing Dan on, in the late fall of 1991, Kenney had a bit of revenge. Two stores owned by the CPAs who'd fired him were going under, one in Kinston (between Greenville and Pink Hill), and the Greenville store Kenney managed, the one where they had fired him. Kenney went to them and worked out a steal of a deal: $26,000 each, in-house financed, *at no interest.*

That was a bit of a chest-thump moment. He was the boss now. Those who had abandoned him, who had deemed him worthless, now needed him. Their stores were now his, the next pieces of his empire.

He liked the sound of that. *His. His* empire. Right within reach.

Kenney went after it every minute of every day. Five restaurants wouldn't be enough. He set a new goal: Open 20 restaurants around North Carolina, *be* somebody beyond his hometown. "And," says Karen, "when he wasn't working, he was thinking about it, and when he wasn't thinking about it, he was talking about it. He talked about it all the time."

If you made the mistake of asking him, "How's it going?" you were in for half an hour of How It Was Going. "Oh, heaven *forbid* you asked that question back then," Kenney says now, laughing. "It didn't matter. I remember going to a Guns N' Roses concert, and Keith and I were with a couple of other guys, and they made the mistake of saying, 'How's business?' So they got it. They knew how business was. And Keith was laughing at me because he was like, 'He never shuts up about this!'"

Karen remembers one night when they had a little family gathering at their house in Pink Hill. Kenney was smoking on the porch — Kenney smoked a *lot*, so much that whenever he was home, pretty much, he was on that back porch — and Karen was in the dining room setting the table. She heard Kenney's sister walk in from the porch and say to Karen's brother, "Okay, I've done my time. Your turn." Kenney was still talking.

Over the years, some people have faded out of Kenney's life because they couldn't handle a certain aspect of his personality. Putting it simply, the man comes on *strong*. Karen says, "What Kenney does is, Kenney works things out as he's talking about them. Sometimes he'll say something outrageous. And I used to believe everything he said. And I would go, 'Oh my god! How can you *feel* that way?' But I came to know, when it comes out outrageous, he's just testing the waters. And I'll be like, 'That's pretty extreme.' He's like, 'Is it?' I'm like, 'Yeah. It is. You don't want to go down that way.' He'll be like, 'No, but this is what I want to do!' And he'll give you this *impassioned* speech about why. And I'll be right back at him about why it doesn't hold water. And this may go on for two or three days. And then finally, either I'll say, 'Yeah, I see your point,' or he'll say, 'That *was* kind of over the top.' And that's how he does it. That's how he figures things out. He just beats it around. Beats it to death. And you just have to, you know, decide if you can sign up for that or not."

Over the years, Kenney and Karen worked out a pretty good schedule for the discussion of his outrageous ideas. "I would be nursing and cleaning up, and he would be following me around and talking," she says. "And that was kind of where we got this routine we've got in the mornings now. Where, I get my coffee and *(Karen snaps her fingers)* he's awake. God love him. He wakes up and he's awake. I am not. I start, first thing I get up, I get two cups of coffee in me, then I gotta start emptying the dishwasher, or something. But that's an hour! I can sit still and listen and stare for an hour. And be engaged, I guess, is what I'm saying. I just sit and I listen, and I nod, and I'm there. And he gives me his opinion on whatever. And I can do it for about an hour straight now. I can sit still for an hour."

■ ■ ■

Back in those early days, the vision Kenney was sharing — or beating people over the head with — and what he was telling people about Andy's was all the same as what he told Dan Jones to convince him to come back to eastern North Carolina. "We were getting better. Our sales were growing double digits. We have a great concept. I have four restaurants, and everything is great. I'm getting some really good people around me. Everything is *great.*"

But the truth is, everything wasn't really all that great.

■ ■ ■

"Everyone likes to say these days that if you're passionate

about what you do and you're working hard, you're going to be successful," Kenney says. "Well, that's a crock, man. There's got to be more to it than that."

He agrees that it's important to have passion for what you do, and work as hard as you can at it, and believe that it will pay off, but that's also too simplistic. The American Dream doesn't come that easy, and sometimes working hard isn't enough. Like everything else in life, there is nuance to this concept of the passionate chasing of one's dream. If passion is all you have, as Kenney was learning, you won't get much in return.

■   ■   ■

For the next year, Kenney worked his tail off, working with fire and passion, chasing the ever-loving heck out of his American Dream, and after that year, all he had to show for it was debt. The Goldsboro restaurant was barely breaking even. The other three Andy's stores were deep in the red. He was $35,000 behind on his food bills. And he was obsessed with finding some way to make sure that Andy's — to make sure that *his empire* — made it.

He kept costs as low as possible by working open to close, and cooking, and taking orders, and doing anything else that needed to be done. He worked as many hours as he could. He trained employees to answer the phone not only to take to-go orders and answer customer questions, but also to play secretary. He negotiated leases and explored investment possibilities on the phone behind the counter between order tickets.

But for all that, Andy's continued to struggle. The K&W Cafeteria across from Andy's had lines on Sunday so long they almost blocked the Andy's entrance. Meanwhile, Andy's was empty.

"When I was in front of everybody, it was great," Kenney says. "Especially my staff. I wanted them as positive and motivated as they could be. When I was riding home in the car alone, that's when the realities — the bills and the payroll coming up this Friday, and us not being able to quite turn that corner financially, and all that — that's when all that reality would hit me."

Then one night, driving home after his millionth open-to-close shift in Goldsboro, Kenney had an epiphany.

■ ■ ■

He was puttering along in his cheap old Chevy Citation, trying to figure out why the business was struggling so much. *I've been working so hard. I've been missing family reunions. I know that Karen, great and strong though she may be, has to be wondering when this Andy's thing is going to really get going. I haven't been able to watch my infant son grow up.*

And then he had a thought that felt like something more, almost like a voice in his head, sent from somewhere else. *"It's not about you."*

"What do you mean?" Kenney said. "What do you mean, *it's not about me?*"

It's not about you.

Kenney wondered if he should get some professional help. He decided he was okay — he hadn't *heard* any of it out loud.

But the words stayed in his mind.

He went home and showered and went to bed, still smelling of onions and grease. "As anyone who works in this industry knows, you can never get that smell all the way out," he says.

But he couldn't sleep. He watched television. Then he turned that off and stared at the ceiling. *It's not about you.*

It's not about you. For the next two weeks, that's all he heard, those four words, a relentless echo.

Kenney decided that wherever the thought came from, it was right. So far, he'd been focused on himself. On building *his* empire. But businesses don't grow if they are all about their owner — that's the mistake that Roberts had made. A good business, even a chain of restaurants, has to exist for a bigger, better reason than one person's ambition. Good businesses, Kenney thought, are about the people the business serves, right? And why did restaurants exist in the first place?

To feed people.

So Kenney started there. He had always believed the customer was always right, but he had still viewed the customer as serving *him*, as this amorphous entity he had to please to build his empire. Same thing with his employees. They were important for what they did for him, nothing more. But that mindset wasn't working.

Kenney turned it on its head. He took *his empire* out of the equation and replaced it with *their experience.* In other words, on the top of the Andy's totem pole, he replaced *Kenney Moore* with *The Customers.* He looked for every tiny way he could make *their* experience as good as possible. This led him to changes in how he viewed other aspects of *his empire* as well. The restaurant staff, the cooks, the waiters and waitresses, and the cashiers were all direct links from the business to the customers. The happier they were, the better the customers' experience would be, right? So Kenney also worked to make their experience great, too, putting The Staff second highest on the totem pole.

Kenney followed that logic further, deciding that if creating the best experience for the customer meant creating the best experience for the staff, then he needed to also create the best experience for the managers, Andy's direct link to the staff. Make the managers happy, make the staff happy, make the customers happy.

And on and on that went, until the totem pole looked something like this:

> Customers
> Staff
> Managers
> District Managers
> Store Owners
> Corporate Staff
> A million other things

> Kenney

From the bottom up, each served those above them. As Kenney read the popular 1998 book *The Servant* by James Hunter, he discovered that this was a business concept labeled *servant leadership,* first conceptualized in a 1970 essay by Robert K. Greenleaf.

Kenney also realized that same as he wanted to build an empire for himself, others wanted to build empires of their own. To further serve people, he had another idea: Focus less on building *his empire* and more on helping others build theirs by enabling them to buy into his franchise and therefore launch their own small business. He decided to focus on giving everyone that opportunity. He wanted to help people do what he always wanted to do for himself.

"I realized," Kenney says now, "it's okay to extend yourself for people. The model for businesses in the early 1900s, and all the way probably through the 1970s and 80s, the model was based on the military model of general, lieutenants, and on down. It would be CEO, vice presidents, all the way down to the store level people, the grunts, and the guest underneath them. Well, I flipped that over and said, *No. We're at the bottom. The guest is at the top. And we're gonna have relationships. And it's okay. It's okay to care about each other.*

"Because what I've found is that people will do a lot if you have great influence with them. It's not a demand thing. It's not 'Do it or your fired.' I think that model of business, that military model, that structured model, is so dated it's scary. People who worked for me, if I looked at them and said, 'God, man, you have let me down on this one,' or 'You've upset me on this one, or you've disappointed me,' that would crush them worse than me ever yelling at them. And that's authority. That's influence."

His mantra became *Extend yourself.* For whoever might need it, extend yourself. Help people how you would want to be helped.

When he was working the grill, Kenney had a clear view of the mall, and when someone met his eyes, he flashed them his easy smile and said "Hi! Hope you're having a great day!" When someone came in, he or his staff made sure to greet them at the entrance and walk them to a table. When that K&W's Sunday afternoon lines wrapped around in front of his store, Kenney and his staff offered drinks and snacks to the people in line.

Karen says she heard all kinds of questions from her family and friends about the way Kenney went about his business. "Oh, all the time! *'Why's he doing it this way? Why's he doing it that way? Why's he doing this? Why's he doing that? Why does he cook instead of walk around the restaurant and be a manager?'* Because that's what managers at other places did. They just walked around and asked customers, 'How was your food?'"

Kenney didn't write up specific sets of guidelines about how to make the customers' experience better or anything like that. He simply went from store to store, setting an example, helping everyone in his company buy into this concept of giving of themselves for the customers — and, for that matter, for each other, too. "I just realized," he says, "it's okay to love people." And that's what he told his staff: Love people.

Within six months, Andy's was turning a profit.

■ ■ ■

Along the way, Kenney, never slowing down, merged Andy's with another company, The Little Mint. They'd been big back in the 1960s and '70s, with up to 37 restaurants in and around North Carolina, and they'd gone public along the way. By 1992, however, they'd been beaten down by the recession, left with just one store.

Their owner saw Kenney's success and liked his concept. In exchange for a piece of Andy's, Kenney took over what was left of The Little Mint, including their corporate office in Winterville — a tiny town right beside Greenville — and their eastern North Carolina store. This worked perfectly for Kenney. He'd been thinking about taking Andy's public and testing his concept on a larger scale, and merging with Little Mint made that easy. So he went for it.

Kenney's experiment with going public wouldn't last long. Within a few years, Kenney negotiated a reverse-split, buying back people's stock in the company and taking it private again. That was prompted by a board meeting where he had to go in, as the CEO of the company, and discuss, with several old men, why he wanted to give raises to some of his employees, and then he had sit outside while they voted on it. That was totally opposite of what he was trying to build. "I realized pretty quickly that I wasn't much of a board meeting type of guy," Kenney says, laughing. "And that's putting it lightly."

Plus, he didn't want his company to exist to serve a Board of Directors any more than he wanted it to serve a CEO.

■　■　■

When Kenney moved to The Little Mint's corporate office, he got two new secretaries who could take the burden of bookkeeping from Karen. She still likes to joke that it took two women to replace her.

More importantly, the Little Mint merger gave Karen peace of mind about what Kenney was doing. "I felt like, you know, this is real," Karen says. "It wasn't a restaurant or two. It was a real business."

13

SALESMAN DOWN
The Bank Saga, Part 5

Kenney did away with The Franchisers in 2010 for the same simple reasons he'd done away with The Little Mint board back in 1992. They didn't share his vision, and he believed he could do the job better on his own. To replace The Franchisers, Kenney hired his former banker, who we'll call Arthur, to be Andy's Chief Financial Officer and primary franchise salesman. Arthur was a fellow Atlantic Christian alum and, it seemed, a good guy with a good heart.

It's worth noting that, for all the tension and drama, The Franchisers weren't a total waste. Andy's did end up signing one of The Franchisers' leads, and when they did, Kenney cut The Franchisers a commission check. Plus, The Franchisers taught him a great sales method: Discovery Day, a detailed walk-through of the Andy's operation given to prospective franchisees. Discovery Days typically started at the Andy's in Raleigh's Crabtree Valley Mall, where they sampled the entire menu and saw how the restaurant was run. Then they went an hour southeast to Mount Olive, where they had a grand tour of the Andy's corporate office and warehouse, and where

Kenney met with everyone in the conference room and spilled his heart on why they should buy in.

■ ■ ■

Arthur started working for Andy's that August right after Kenney fired The Franchisers. He brought in Terrell Rhye, a wealthy franchisee from western North Carolina. When Kenney went to meet with Rhye, he cut his hair, shaved, put on a suit, the whole nine yards. When Rhye walked into the meeting, he wore an ill-fitting, untucked polo shirt, sweatpants, and sandals, and he had a big beard and a long ponytail. Kenney picked up a vibe from the guy, a vibe he liked, so he shook his hand and said, "I can't believe I cut my fuzzing hair for you."

Rhye burst out laughing.

Kenney learned that when Rhye was a younger businessman, he'd been flat broke and homeless and in all kinds of trouble, and he'd begged his dad for $200. He turned that into more than $200 million. He and Kenney now call themselves brothers.

■ ■ ■

As it turned out, state-by-state restaurant franchise law was an absolute labyrinth.

Regulations varied by state. All Kenney had to do to franchise in Texas was fill out an online form and pay a small fee. In Maryland, on the other hand, the requirements were so complicated they gave him headaches and would have cost some thirty grand.

"I'm sitting over here going, 'What the fuzz, man?'" Kenney says. "Why can't I open a restaurant in this state, or that one? It's a hindrance. You hear, 'We need more jobs!' Some states — Texas — 'Oh, go online, fill out an application, send us a check. Come on down!' Maryland? It takes a small act of Congress. Why is it so difficult? And Adam (Beaudoin, Kenney's attorney) is over there going, 'Kenney, it just is.'" Kenney laughs. At himself. He laughs at himself a lot. "He kind of reigns me in. And once again, I may have a tizzy or shake my head. But the end of the day, you need smart people to make that happen, and that's what he's been."

■ ■ ■

Arthur turned out to have a serious drinking problem. Terrell Rhye was the only franchisee he closed. Arthur would disappear a few days at a time. After the first episode, Kenney pulled him into his office and they had it out. Arthur broke down crying, swearing that he'd turn things around, that he'd never let Kenney down again.

That lasted until October, when they went to Tampa for their first-ever franchise show, a giant expo of countless franchising concepts for people to explore. It was a big deal, and they only barely had an idea what they were doing. All Kenney knew for certain was that he was excited.

He took Arthur and Neal and April with him. "We had more people in our booth than anybody else there," Kenney says. "We didn't know what it was all about. We were just gonna wow people. We were proud of what we did. So anybody that walked by, we were greeting them. *'Hey, how ya doin'?'* And they're like, *leave me alone, I'm here to look at a carpet cleaning franchise, not a burger franchise.* But we were speaking to everybody."

Well, they all were except Arthur. Come morning on the second day, Kenney couldn't find him. Arthur, who should've been more pumped about it than anybody else, the man in charge of selling his franchises and recharging the company, and pretty much *the* main man they needed in the booth at this franchise show, had disappeared.

It was horrible, but it was also funny, in a way. It forced Kenney to improvise on the fly, which is pretty much how he'd done everything, including franchising within North Carolina, ever since Andy's became a viable business back in 1992.

14

READY, FIRE, AIM!
The Growth of Andy's, Part 2

Once Andy's was making money in 1992 and the economy was recovering, Kenney started franchising, but only to people within the Andy's organization, so that he could fulfill his vision of enabling his employees to own their own business. That voice in his head wouldn't let him forget: *It's not about you.* It had migrated to his chest, to his heart, tugging at him every day. "I *needed* to get these guys owning their own business," he says. "I *needed* to create opportunity for people."

First up: Dan Jones, Kenney's invaluable righthand man.

The process was simple. Kenney asked Dan if he wanted to buy some stores. Dan said he did. They worked out the details, agreed on a royalty fee, shook hands. After that, Dan deposited his store's money into his own account instead of Andy's. That was that.

Kenney's second franchisee was Keith, his kid half-brother. Keith started working with Andy's in early 1992, just as Kenney started thinking about franchising. In the fall of 1991, Kenney went to Chapel Hill to visit Keith, who was getting his law degree at the University of North Carolina. They went to a football game together, where Kenney talked Keith's ear off about how he could work up to owning his own business, not within years, but months. Kenney says, "Back then, by the time we'd be done talking, I'd either have you ready to flip burgers or I'd have you running away from me."

Keith was ready to flip burgers.

Keith forewent a law career to start working at the Andy's in Goldsboro at minimum wage. "But I didn't view it as a risk," Keith says. "I mean, Kenney's a persuasive guy. He sold me on the opportunity. It's food like we loved when we grew up, and he was like, 'Look, you can be in business for yourself and own your own business.' And he was right."

After Keith waited tables and cooked for three months, Kenney called him and said he needed a manager at his New Bern store. It was another former Rob's, and it was struggling. The store manager overreached and bought billboards and radio ad spots that he couldn't afford. In short, he was awful, so Dan Jones fired him.

Keith went to New Bern. After he worked there for a few months, in June 1992, Kenney offered him an old Rob's in the Wilson mall for a ridiculously low price: five grand to Kenney for the store, another five to the mall for the equipment. Like Kenney's first Andy's, this one was filthy, and Keith had to clean it all himself. But he was in business for himself for a mere $10,000. "Kenney didn't make anything off of it except for a royalty fee moving forward," Keith says.

■   ■   ■

That was an intentional strategy on Kenney's part. He wasn't showing Dan and Keith favoritism. As he sold more franchises, he treated every franchisee the same way, finding ways for them to buy into Andy's for as little money as possible.

This strategy was a direct result of watching Roberts rip off his franchisees and send them into their stores with enormous debt. Kenney took an approach as opposite as could be, in line with his *extend yourself* philosophy. Making his franchisees as happy and motivated as possible created that trickle up effect to the managers and staff and, ultimately, their customers. His goal was to get franchisees going without being strangled by debt, allowing them to meet the royalty fees without stress and make money for themselves. Nobody could complain about that.

Kenney didn't even realize at the time that this was a legitimate business strategy. It felt like some sort of mystical concept he'd stumbled across.

■   ■   ■

After his first few franchisees got rolling, Kenney saw his vision becoming real. "There were people out there going, *He's not just dangling a carrot in front of my face,*" Kenney says, thinking of his experience with the insurance company. "They realized, *Hey, I can own my own business here.* And once we started doing that, the whole attitude of the company changed. There were people who would come to work as a 20-year-old fry cook or whatever, just thinking it's a part-time job, and all of a sudden they realize, *I can own one of these one day!* It wasn't about your education or what side of the tracks you grew up on. It wasn't about who you knew. It wasn't about being a good soldier. It was about, *Hey, come in here, produce, run a great store, and you'll get a shot.*"

Kenney understands that this is unorthodox, and probably kind of crazy. "You don't make minimum wage people owners of their own business," he says. "They're minimum wage people because they're minimum wage people. But that's not how we looked at it."

Kenney thought, *Our food is awesome. Our cheeseburger is great. We have a wonderful product. We have a wonderful culture that surrounds us.* He just *knew* that he could do something special. Sure, some minimum wage people are minimum wage people for a reason. He knew that. But many, if not most, just need an opportunity — they just need to be shown a way to get there.

■ ■ ■

Serve people and love people and believe in them. Those were the most important factors in the growth of Andy's in the early to mid 1990s. As the years went by, however, Kenney learned it was equally important to surround himself on the corporate level with people who shared his philosophy.

He had Karen. She might not be handling Andy's books anymore, but her influence trumps all, of course.

Then there was Dan Jones.

But he would need more than close friends and family to grow the business the way he envisioned.

The first new guy was Neal Dennis.

Dan Jones hired Neal to run his Kinston store in May 1992. Neal and Dan had worked at a Domino's together years earlier, after which they opened and ran a restaurant called Mr. Gatty's. Neal burned out on the food business, telling Dan it was too much. "It's all-consuming," Neal says now. "It's not a career, it's a lifestyle. It's all in, all the time. It's almost twenty-four-seven. I mean, sometimes, I was on the phone at nine, ten, eleven at night. It just takes over your life."

When Neal left Mr. Gatty's, he told Dan, "I'm never going to do this again. I'm done with food. It's just too much."

THE HWY 55 CORPORATE OFFICE has been in Mount Olive since 2003.

REAL '57 CHEVY sits in the lobby of the Hwy 55 corporate office, having been converted
o a desk. Kenney leans against it here in 2011, and behind him hangs the original Andy's
n from his first store in the Berkeley Mall in Goldsboro.

THE MOORE FAMILY circa 1970, in California. That's Kenney's mom, Nancy, and his stepfather, Dal, with Kelly on the bottom right and baby half-brother Keith in the middle. Nobody's sure why Kenney's looking at the ground, or why Nancy is putting devil horns on his head.

KENNEY AS A LITTLE KID sometime around 1965, with his older sister, Kelly.

BASEBALL is the only reason Kenney originally went to college. He's pictured here (top left) with his baseball coach Rodney Kemp, top right, and some baseball teammates as a senior in high school.

NOTICE NUMBER 5, the only player not looking at the camera — because he's running his mouth at a teammate. That's Kenney; this is his senior football team picture.

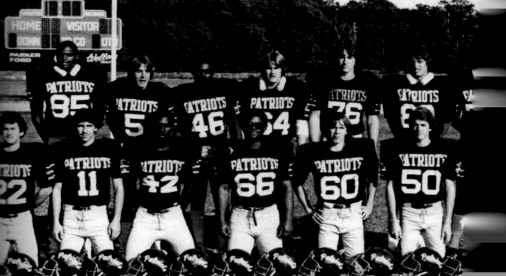

KENNEY AND KAREN cutting the cake at their wedding.

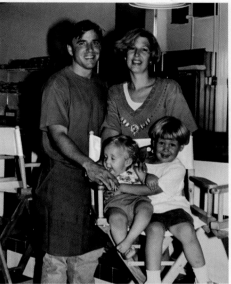

KENNEY, KAREN, DAUGHTER EMMA (bottom left, biting Kenney) and **SON ANDY**, sitting inside the now-famous 1993 Mount Olive, N.C. location, their first Andy's outside of a mall.

IRST-EVER ANDY'S was located in)oro, N.C.'s Berkeley Mall. The first time then 2, saw the pictures on the wall, he them fat pigs. They're supposed to be rs.

"WE'S FREEWHEELIN'!" was scrawled across the conference room wall in the Kinston corporate office in the early '90s — it was the unofficial company motto.

KENNEY AND HIS CREW cutting the ribbon on a new store in the '90s: (from left to right) Guy Guthrie, April Dennis, Kenney Moore, Neal Dennis, and Dan Jones.

Kenney dressed up to "perform" the song **"PLAY THAT FUNKY MUSIC WHITE BOY"** at a company rally.

THE FAMOUS JESSE, pictured here with Kenney at an Andy's Foundation event, inspired Kenney to quit smoking.

BREAKING GROUND ON THE NEW CORPORATE OFFICE in the early 2000s was a huge moment. Here's Kenney (second from left) with, from left, his mother-in-law Francis Williams, son Andy, daughter Emma, wife Karen (carrying son Dylan), daughter Isabelle, and father-in-law Jimmy Williams. The Williamses were essential in helping Kenney start the company.

E INFAMOUS "ANDY MAN" mascot is always a hit with kids.

Kenney (second from left), out to eat with some members of his **CORPORATE OFFICE FOR BOSS'S DAY** in 2014.

CHUBBY CHECKER, the former pop star behind the song "The Twist," has partnered with Andy's/Hwy 55 on multiple promotions in the past.

THE FAMILY — Karen, Isabelle, Emma, Dylan, Kenney, and Andy — at their favorite vacation spot, Disney World in Orlando.

Kenney, behind the podium, **INTRODUCING THE NEW HWY 55 REBRAND** and their new master franchisees at his February 2012 press conference. Seated to his left are master franchisees (from right to left) J.R. Cottle, Chris Lacoe, Terrell Rhye, and Brett Rhye.

ABU DHABI master franchisee Khamis Al Rumaithy opened the first Abu Dhabi restaurant in March 2014.

Standing on the stage at the Durham Performing Arts Center, Kenney speaks to more than 2,000 people at the August 2014 Hwy 55 rally. His message, as always, was simple: **LOVE YOUR NEIGHBOR.**

THE CORNERSTONE FOR HWY 55'S SUCCESS has always been two things: serving others, and working hard. Kenney, pictured above in the fall of 2014, doesn't just preach such things to his employees — he lives them, and is known for occasionally dropping into a Hwy 55 restaurant, putting on a t-shirt and hat, and working on the grill, cooking burgers and cheesesteaks alongside teenagers working for minimum wage. Hwy 55 is now working on developing more than 1,000 new stores across the United States and in multiple countries around the world, and was named Best Food and Dining Franchise in the U in 2014 by *Franchise Business Review*.

For the next several years Neal drifted from job to job and played drums for a heavy metal band. He and his wife, April, moved to Kinston, and one day, Neal went to a minor league baseball game for the Kinston Indians, the single-A affiliate of the Cleveland Indians, where he bumped into Dan.

They exchanged pleasantries, and then Dan said, "Hey, I want to talk to you about something, but first I want you to go ahead and laugh at me."

"Why?" Neal said.

"Just go ahead and laugh."

"Okay," Neal said, laughing.

Dan said, "I want you to come get back into the food business."

Neal laughed again. Hard. "Man, I told you, Dan — I'm *never* going back in the food business."

"Just come talk to us," Dan said.

Neal followed Dan to his seats, where he met Kenney.

Over the course of an hour-long conversation, Neal realized there was something different about Kenney and his business than anyone or any business where Neal had worked before. "I don't know what it was," he says now, "but I just knew that guy was different from anybody else I'd ever worked with. I'd worked for Mom-and-Pop companies. I'd worked for Trans America, which at the time was the biggest finance company in the world. I'd worked just tons of jobs. And I just had a feeling this was different. And I don't know why. It was just different. And it has turned out to be very, very different from anything I've ever done."

Neal went home and told April he thought he wanted to do it. "Worst comes to worst," he said, "at least we'll have somewhere to eat."

After about 90 days, he burned out again. "I was right back

where I was at in the food industry the first time," he says. "I was like, 'Oh my god, this is taking over my life again, I don't want to do this — I just don't want to go down this road again'."

He quit.

About 90 days later, Dan called him up and said, "Look, we've got a situation in the Washington store." Either their manager was going to quit or get fired. "Could you just come help us until we put somebody in there?"

Neal said okay, but not for long. That was 25 years ago. And now, of course, Neal is the company's Chief Operating Officer.

▪ ▪ ▪

At first, Neal's job was to be Kenney's go-to fixer, going wherever a store was having trouble. Then, in early 1993, Neal and Kenney started talking about Neal buying the Kinston restaurant and becoming Kenney's third franchisee.

Neal went home and told April one night. April, who worked in the corporate offices of Bojangles, a Cajun fast food chain, asked Neal to see the franchising documents *she* was familiar with at Bojangles. "Yeah," Neal said, "we don't have anything like that."

"Wait, so how's this going to work?" she said. "This can't be legal."

A few days later, Neal came home and told April, "He turned it over to me — I own the Kinston restaurant now."

"Well," April said, "where's the contract?"

"There's no contract," Neal said. "We shook hands."

"This *can't* be legal."

"All I know is," Neal said, "today, I put the money in his bank account. Tomorrow, I'll put the money in my bank account. We shook hands. That's all I need."

Neal opened two more stores in the next three years, *and* he convinced April to leave Bojangles and work for Andy's. Not long after that, Kenney ended up convincing both of them to come work for him in the Andy's corporate office.

"I was very self-centered when I met Kenney," Neal says. "I was 28, 29. I'd been in all different kinds of business, but I did not have a career path. I was still just trying to figure out what I wanted to do when I grew up. He's really taught me that business is about who you are as a person — it's about integrity first. If that's right, then everything else will take care of itself. It doesn't mean you won't have problems and struggles, but if you take the focus off yourself, and put it on other people, then everything else falls into place."

For instance, when Kenney asked Neal to come work in the corporate office in 2008, Neal wasn't sure if he wanted to. "So I had to make a decision at that point," Neal says. "Again, do I do what's best for me, or do I do what's best for other people in the company? So I said, *I'm going to help Kenney build the company.*"

Kenney would inspire that sort of loyalty in plenty more people like Neal. Because the more Neal worked with Kenney and got to know him, the more his understanding of what made Kenney a little different became clear.

In November 1993, Neal was opening an Andy's in a small eastern North Carolina town called Grifton, about 20 minutes outside of Greenville. They were all set to open on a Monday, but when he and Kenney were giving the store a final once-over the Friday before, he found sewage was backing up into the restaurant.

Neal called the plumber.

"Dude, I'm at the beach."

"At the beach?"

"At the beach. But I can probably tell you what it is."

The restaurant was an old building that they had remodeled, and with new waste moving through old sewage lines, something called a distribution box buried in the parking lot had clogged.

"Okay," Neal said. "So what do we do?"

"Clean out the distribution box," said the plumber.

"How do we do that?" Neal said.

"Well, you'll have to dig it out and then empty it."

"How deep is it buried?"

"Probably four or five feet at least."

Kenney told Neal, "Meet me here tomorrow. We'll figure it out."

The next morning — a Saturday morning — Kenney met Neal in that parking lot, having brought his own shovels. He got out of his car and said, "All right, let's get to work."

They spent the day digging through four feet of gravel and ended up, as Neal puts it, "Knee-deep in piss water." But they got to the distribution box, and they cleaned it out, and they opened the store that Monday, as planned.

Neal was amazed. "This is the CEO," he says. "He could've just said, 'Here's the shovels, man. Let me know how it goes.' But he's in the parking lot *with me*. Digging up *a sewage line*. But I just learned, that's who he is. He gets it done. And he's not afraid to do any of that."

■ ■ ■

By the summer of 1993, Kenney's life and business were both going well. Andrew was healthy, and although business didn't feel *totally* stable yet, Kenney had a real vision, and he saw it working, and compared to 1992, the business had come along

way. And that's why Dan Jones told Kenney that what he proposed toward the end of the summer of '93 seemed insane.

Until then, all 10 Andy's stores were in malls. Malls were
what they knew, and they were working. Andy's same-store
sales were growing by 20 and 30 percent most places, and as
much as 40 and 50 percent in some.

But Kenney wanted to try something different.

Smitty's, the popular burger joint in Mount Olive that
Kenney loved in college, had closed, and Kenney knew that
with Smitty's gone, the town would be hungry for a good
cheeseburger. Kenney figured they should open an Andy's
where Smitty's had closed — in a strip mall.

"Dan thought I'd flipped a cog," Kenney says. "If he said it
once, he said it five times. *'Are you sure?'*"

And no, Kenney wasn't *sure* that it would work, but he
was sure he *felt* like trying it. "You've gotta have some *feel*,"
Kenney says.

Dan tried and tried to talk him out of it, as against the
idea as a person could be. They were already successful in
malls, Dan said — why leave that comfort zone? Why face the
unknown when you can keep growing with what's already
working? Dan wanted a statistical analysis, a logical explanation, a full-blown report on why it would be okay to risk
trying something other than malls.

This was one of those times when, after beating the idea
to death for a few days, Kenney didn't change his mind. He
wanted to open an Andy's in Mount Olive, and Mount Olive
didn't have a mall, and darn it, he just *felt* like the strip mall
would work. "You could call it *feel*, you could call it *instinct*,
intuition, *gut*, you could call it whatever you want," Kenney
says. "There are times you have to make decisions in business
that have absolutely nothing to do with what's going on in the

world at that time. In business, you gotta have *feel*, just like in athletics. What separated Michael Jordan from other six-foot-six guys that jumped as high as he could? It was Michael Jordan's feel for the moment, feel for what's happening in the game at the time. That's the differentiator between him and other people. Well, in business, it's the same thing."

Looking at that vacant Smitty's, Kenney saw a chance to make things work *better*. Plus, Kenney liked having success in malls, but *hated* dealing with malls. He had no control of when they could open and close, and a mall manager was always snooping around and scolding them for making *just a bit* too much smoke. Mall rent was at least 20 percent higher for the same space just about anywhere else, and once they passed a certain sales threshold, the mall charged them *more*.

In a strip mall, they wouldn't have to deal with any of that. The rent would be cheaper, and they'd have more autonomy, and if there's one thing Kenney Moore always wants, it's more autonomy. Besides, Kenney reasoned, if they pay 20 percent less rent, and they still do the same sales, or even a little less, *and* they have that autonomy — why *not* take that risk?

■ ■ ■

Kenney sold the Mount Olive store to his father-in-law, Jimmy Williams. And when he pulled into the shopping center parking lot to open the store for the first day in August 1993, Kenney felt a wave of relief — there was a big crowd in the parking lot and a long line of people on the sidewalk. He didn't realize there was an event in the strip center, but whatever brought all these people here, that should lead to a *great* first day of business.

And then, walking from his car toward the store, he realized that the line led right to his restaurant's doors. The crowd was there for Andy's.

Right then, Kenney knew he'd made it.

That Andy's was packed from the moment it opened, keeping Kenney so busy he didn't even have time to eat. He lost 30 pounds in 30 days, surviving "on Gatorade and cigarettes."

That's not to say there weren't a few problems. In that time, he had the first of far too many encounters with the one and only Johnson, the man who would lead to Kenney's whole problem with the bank.

* * *

Jimmy Williams knew Johnson's mother-in-law through work. Johnson had worked in the Air Force and then at McDonald's before Jimmy hired him to manage the Andy's in Mount Olive. Johnson came and went as he pleased. He barked orders and criticized staff, and together, Johnson and Jimmy often questioned Kenney's decisions. Within a week of opening, Johnson was complaining about being tired. Kenney, meanwhile, cooked, worked open to close every day, mopped, cleaned, did everything.

About 30 days into this, Johnson and Jimmy came into the restaurant as it was closing to have a business meeting, leaving Kenney, the company CEO, doing all of the work while they talked.

Kenney had enough.

He called over to Johnson, who was sitting across from Jimmy in a booth. Johnson looked up at him with a smug, annoyed frown. "What?"

"You see this mop in my hands?" Kenney said, holding the mop up.

"Yeah?"

"You'll never see me holding it again." Kenney threw the mop at Johnson.

Johnson, a tall, fat man with a solid hundred pounds on Kenney, stood like he was ready to fight. "What's your problem?"

Kenney stalked around the counter and over to Johnson, pointing a finger in his face. "I've been doing all your work, you lazy fuzzing fatass."

"Whoa, hey, whoa," said Jimmy, standing and holding up his hands.

"You stop," Kenney said, glaring at him. "You're not talking to one of your fuzzing students here. You bought *my* concept, you bought into what *I* am doing. Stop questioning every decision I make."

Kenney left and went home. Jimmy showed up at the house in Pink Hill later that night and they talked. "If this is the way this is gonna be," Jimmy told him, "you can take your company and shove it where the sun don't shine. I am *not* gonna be part of a company that is going to destroy my daughter's family."

Kenney said he was sorry. He wasn't mad at Jimmy, and he shouldn't have lashed out at him. They forgave each other, and they haven't had a fight like that since.

But for years, Kenney *would* regret something from that night: "I should've kicked Johnson's ass right then and there," he says. "Maybe he would've quit, and all these problems with the bank would never have happened."

■ ■ ■

Kenney relived that first morning in Mount Olive countless times over the years, remembering how he'd seen the crowd and wondered why they were there and then realized *they were there for Andy's.* "It just boomed, man," he says. "That risk was one of the pivotal points in our company's history. It literally changed the direction of my company."

They moved out of malls and into strip centers and even free-standing buildings, such as the Grifton store with the infamous distributor box that Kenney and Neal had to dig up. When Kenney's lease expired on his first store in the Goldsboro Mall, he moved it to a strip center in town, and sales went up 28 percent.

That morning in Mount Olive was also the first time he'd ever seen a crowd like that lined up for Andy's. Until then, he knew that he'd been playing a classic game of fake-it-till-you-make it, a lot of smoke and mirrors and marketing to make Andy's look bigger and better and more successful than it was. That opening day in Mount Olive, though, showed Kenney that this crazy, bottoms-up business vision was working. That day, Kenney knew that Andy's was real, that he was making it, that he didn't have to fake it anymore.

◼ ◼ ◼

The Mount Olive Andy's also put Kenney in contact with Guy Guthrie, the first person Kenney would sell a franchise to "outside the family."

Guthrie was a 26-year-old from Kenansville, yet another *small eastern North Carolina town,* with maybe 700 residents. He was a young entrepreneur and did his banking in Mount Olive, coming to town at least once a week. He had always gone to Smitty's, so after it closed down, he tried Andy's. He had a shrimp burger and loved it, and he loved the Andy's concept, and he couldn't stop thinking that Kenansville could use something like that.

Guthrie called the Andy's corporate office in Winterville to talk to Kenney about meeting to discuss buying a franchise. Kenney never called him back, so Guthrie called again. And then again, and again, and again, and when Kenney still didn't respond, Guthrie kept on calling, until *finally* Kenney called him back.

Guthrie told Kenney that he'd already found a building they could use, and that it was vacant, and that Kenney just needed to come meet with him, and he'd get it.

Kenney didn't feel like going *outside the family,* but he wanted to at least meet Guthrie. His relentlessness reminded him of himself. So went to Kenansville, about 20 minutes from Pink Hill, about an hour from Winterville.

Guthrie arranged for them to meet at the building he'd found, and he set the meeting for 4 p.m., with a plan. They talked for about an hour. Kenney liked Guthrie fine enough, but the town seemed dead.

Until five o'clock.

Kenansville, though officially home to only 700 people, was the Duplin County seat, home to the county courthouse, hospital, and every other sort of official facility. At five o'clock, a parade of cars began streaming by, people heading home from work. "And I was astounded," Kenney says now.

Guthrie — fair skin, short blonde hair, blue eyes — is far more even-tempered than Kenney, but they are much alike in one way: When Guthrie decided to do something, he got it done. His meeting with Kenney was in January 1994. His Andy's opened just 42 days later, on March 5, 1994. It's been open ever since. And nearly two decades later, it would be the unexpected site of one of the most important moments in Andy's history — but we'll get to that later.

■ ■ ■

Same as Neal and Keith, Guthrie signed on without any sort of contract, but Kenney was working on getting something a *little* more official, something more legal than "Here you go" and a handshake. He consulted with some attorneys about drawing up a franchising contract. They said it would cost about $25,000. Andy's was making money, but $25,000 was a big hit to take, so Kenney passed. Instead, he went to a local convenience store and talked them into giving him a copy of their Subway franchising contract. He sat down and spent hours and hours rewriting one for Andy's, writing by hand on a legal pad, copying Subway's language and inserting *The Little Mint* and *Andy's* accordingly. Then he hired an attorney to look it over for him. After a bit of polishing and a lot of typing, Kenney had himself a franchise contract for just a few thousand dollars. He knew it wasn't the strongest in the world, but it was good enough.

Over the years, he polished it up, but that was another important lesson: Perfection is fine to pursue, but it can be a waste of time, especially in the beginning. Good enough needed to be good enough.

And it was. By early 1997, Andy's had opened 17 stores.

■ ■ ■

Kenney was going to work one morning when his then-five-year-old daughter Emma said, "I wanna go to work with you today, Daddy."

"Emma, no, you'd be bored," Kenney said.

"No, I wanna go to work with you today."

Kenney told her no again.

A few minutes later, he looked outside, and Emma was sitting in his car. Unable to resist, Kenney took Emma for a walk around Kinston's quaint downtown area and they bought grape sodas. Their little date changed the future of the company.

As they were walking down the sidewalk, Emma looked up and pointed and said, "Daddy! That's a *pretty* building!"

It was an old bank building with big columns in the front and a FOR SALE sign in the window. And Kenney *did* like it. He took down the realtor's number, and when he got back to his office, he called and asked how much the building was. Turned out it was around $85,000. Kenney went for a tour. The building was cheap for what it was: three stories, plus a basement and a huge vault. The building had its issues, too. The elevator sounded as if it might quit working any second, grinding its way up and down. But Kenney loved the place. He bought it and sold the Winterville office and relocated Andy's corporate headquarters to Kinston.

It was a rash decision, but it played out fine, and that's just how Kenney ran the company in those days. Their mantra was *"We's Freewheelin'!"* — a line from an old scene in *The Little Rascals* when two of the kids are zooming down a hill in their go-cart.

"Where are the brakes!?" one yells.

"Ain't got no brakes!" the other shouts. *"We's freewheelin'!"*

Kenney had *WE'S FREEWHEELIN'* painted on the conference room wall.

"I just loved it," Kenney says. "Because that was us, man. *'Ready! Fire! Aim!'"*

15

SALESMAN DOWN AND OUT
The Bank Saga, Part 6

After Arthur disappeared at the 2010 franchise show in Tampa, Kenney decided he would just deal with him back in Mount Olive. Meanwhile, Kenney took over, saying, "Fuzz it. I can still sell if I want to."

Firehouse Subs had the booth next to Andy's. The second day there, Kenney got to talking with their representative. "They had this little Irishman," he says. "Little round guy, red goatee. And he and I started talking, and we found a kinship."

The man told Kenney that he was something called a master franchisee. He explained that he owned the rights to 20 stores in and around the Tampa and St. Petersburg area. For the right to open up those 20 stores, he paid Firehouse Subs $100,000, or, $5,000 per location. Moving forward, he could own and operate all 20, or he could own and operate however many he chose and franchise the rest himself, splitting the franchise fees and royalty fees.

The more Kenney thought about that, the more he loved it. "Because what happens — now we have that master," he says. "We have a guy who is financially obligated to open those stores. He's already made an investment in the area, and he has a real incentive to open up 20 great stores, because that's how he gets paid. And it helps spread the risk." Before they made it back home, Kenney had decided. "We're gonna do it that way," he said. "Now we just have to find the right people."

■ ■ ■

Back in Mount Olive, Kenney met with Arthur, who again cried and pledged repentance. Kenney gave him yet another chance. He wanted to believe in Arthur. He wanted to believe in people, period, and he believed that people could change, and he wanted to do what he could to help. Maybe if Arthur saw that someone could forgive his sins, could embrace his past failures and believe in his future, then Arthur could turn things around and beat alcoholism.

That was in October. Two months later, Arthur disappeared again. Kenney had to fire him at that point.

In February, Arthur's mother called Kenney and told him that Arthur had spent January in rehab, and now he was clean and sober.

Kenney met with Arthur once again, and once again, Arthur cried and repented. Kenney hired him back, thinking of the redemption story, envisioning how great it would be if Arthur turned his life around.

Three weeks later, Arthur disappeared yet again. Kenney let him go for good.

And so, in the middle of launching a major effort to sell franchises, Kenney was left without a franchise salesman.

Karen said there was someone Kenney *could* call who might want to take Arthur's place, and who should be great at the job: Guy Guthrie.

Guthrie had left Andy's a few years earlier, but people

leaving him had always been something Kenney handled worse than most people, so the fact that Kenney hadn't burnt their bridge when Guthrie left was a huge deal.

16

IN WHICH RELATIONSHIPS ARE HARD AND PEOPLE GET HURT
Growth of Andy's, Part 3

After buying Kinston's old bank building in 1997, wild although it was, *Freewheelin'!* was working. Almost every Andy's was performing well, and it's not like they were opening in booming metropolises. Most Andy's were in small rural communities. Not that Andy's didn't do well in big cities, too — they did — but Kenney wasn't afraid to take a chance on small towns. He'd read that Sam Walton did the same thing when he was launching Wal-Mart. Plus, small towns were always *so excited* about Andy's.

Over time, Andy's developed a dedicated following. They even had their own superfans, such as one woman everyone knew as "Miss Phyllis." She went to every Andy's and detailed her experiences in a travel journal, and she's collected every menu Andy's has ever put out, every cup design they've ever used, and pictures from almost every restaurant.

Kenney met one of his major goals in 1997 by opening his twentieth Andy's, a second one in Greenville. And of course, that didn't mean things were getting any easier. No one likes failure and many fear it. But as Kenney soon learned, success can be even more terrifying. As Andy's grew, new challenges arose, some of them even more difficult than his early ones.

Kenney realized that in order to keep going in a way that served others, he needed to build real relationships. Relationships were as valuable to him, if not more valuable, than the company itself. Through his work with Andy's, Kenney cultivated a lot of love for other people, more than he ever thought he'd have for fellow human beings. He loved being a friend, and making others feel loved and valued.

He was building that family he wanted.

After their monthly manager's meetings, Kenney and the managers and Dan and Neal and April would sit around until all hours of the night, some two dozen or more of them, talking and dreaming about the future of the company, about life itself. "I'm sure my wife thought I was having an affair," Kenney says now, laughing. "And every other spouse of every other person in the company. The meeting would end around eight or nine, and then we'd sit around until two or three in the morning."

His empathy set an example for everyone around him. He was building great relationships for himself, yes, but also among his employees. Many of the people from those late-night meetings are still with his company today. Says Jaclyn Smith, his assistant of 20-plus years, "He just makes you feel comfortable. Whenever I started working in the office, it was just like I'd known him forever."

But not all of Kenney's relationships were so simple.

■ ■ ■

As a newly successful CEO, Kenney had to re-learn how to navigate relationships with women. Women suddenly found him far more attractive than before. Kenney has an outgoing, friendly, affectionate way about him, and back then, he was a natural flirt. Many times Karen warned him, "You give off *signals.*" He admits that he enjoyed attention from women, and he always has. However, as he became successful, women became more responsive, and when a woman took things the wrong way and made an advance on him, he ran away. "I'd get scared!" he says, laughing. "Like, *no, I'm sorry, no, I love my wife, go away!*"

Some women misinterpreted Kenney's friendship as something more, something romantic even, and when they came to realize that it was not, they felt rejected. One in particular lashed out, and really exacerbated the situation, to the degree that she even made aggressive phone calls to Karen, causing her and Kenney no small amount of grief.

Kenney learned to make it abundantly clear where he stood with the females in his life. He remains the friendly guy today that he's always been, but he's extra cautious. He makes sure his friendships stay within certain boundaries, even as he tries being helpful and kind as a CEO and friend. Now, to make sure no one gets the wrong idea, he avoids one-on-one meetings with women. If he does have to meet with a woman, he'll bring along another woman. At a company event a few years ago, Kenney was approached by an attractive waitress who'd posed for *Playboy* before, which was no secret. They'd never met, but when she arrived, she asked someone, "Which one is Kenney Moore?" They pointed his way. She adjusted her cleavage and bustled over to his side and introduced herself. He said, "Nice to meet you," then walked away and found someone else to talk to.

Jaclyn Smith, his assistant, started with Andy's as a waitress at the Goldsboro restaurant when she was a 20-year-old student at Wayne Community College. One day, Kenney came into the restaurant to check things out, and Jaclyn overheard him say something about looking for a new assistant.

"I'm going to school for business," she said, dead serious. "I'll do it."

Kenney laughed hard, doubling over and slapping the counter. But he wasn't laughing *at her* — laughter is also often how Kenney expresses approval. He loved the fact that she spoke up for herself, and so frankly at that. And when he realized that she was qualified, not to mention married — which would make life easier on everyone — he seriously considered it. He called her store manager to ask about her. The manager told him that as far as he knew, Jaclyn — an attractive, dark-haired, blue-eyed girl — was happily married and quite the wholesome young lady.

Kenney went home and updated Karen. "She's *married!*" he said.

"Well, that's good," Karen said, knowing that a woman married is not a woman faithful or kind.

"Not only that," Kenney said, "but I asked around. And she's *happily* married."

"Really?" Karen said, laughing. "You asked?"

"Yes!"

"Okay!"

Kenney hired Jaclyn, the weekend came and went, and then Kenney came home from work Monday night to report, "Jaclyn left her husband this weekend."

"Well of *course* she did," Karen said.

But Jaclyn still works for Kenney to this day, some 20 years later, and she's proven herself to be one of his most invaluable employees, helpful and resourceful and smart, not to mention one of his toughest, too. She's also been in a good relationship for a long time, and she has a child, and she and Kenney have never had any drama.

Kenney looks out for everyone else, too. In the corporate office, he has zero tolerance for inappropriate workplace advances. He understands that co-workers might date, though he'd prefer they didn't — but if someone tries hitting on someone who's married, it's not long before they get shown the door.

■ ■ ■

As the '90s gave way to the 2000s, Kenney had built a loyal, even loving, team that he considered family. But making sure women didn't get wrong romantic ideas about him wasn't the only problem Kenney had with relationships. His fear of abandonment remained visceral as ever, and it made him paranoid and volatile, sparking the worst of his eruptions. And not just with Karen. His demons would set him on anyone.

One symptom of Kenney's fear was that once someone became important to him, he expected them to never leave. The problem is that in business, of course, people inevitably *do* leave. And when his employees left, a fury arose in Kenney that sometimes cost him not just an employee, but a friend.

Carrie, an office manager, was married and had a baby. She didn't need her job. Her husband could support the family, so Carrie decided to become a stay at home mom and gave two weeks' notice.

A little over a week before her last day, Kenney enacted "strictly business week" — no goofing around, no family meals around the conference table, and Kenney didn't speak to anybody. People came in, got work done, went home. "Just reminding them of what it's like to work in the real world,"

Kenney says, laughing. "Just so they remember how good they've got it here."

At the end of the week, Kenney made the rounds, chatting people up, working out the tension, letting everyone know everything was back to normal. And then he got to Carrie's desk. Nobody remembers what she said, except that it was some sarcastic remark about how Kenney didn't need to be so strict in the first place.

He *lost* it. He yelled, cussed, swatted an acrylic tray on her desk, accidentally sending it flying into a drink that spilled on her. "Get the fuzz out," he said. She was done, she didn't need to finish her two weeks, and he'd be *happy* to see her go.

And as she left, he felt horrible.

Karen told him that night, "This has got to stop. You can't keep doing this. Someone's going to have you arrested. And it's *Carrie!* Nice Carrie. You love Carrie!"

"I do, I do," he said. "I don't know why I got so mad."

She hadn't even said anything that *bad.* He would realize later that it was all because he was really angry that she was leaving the company in the first place. Even though he knew that her leaving work was perfectly reasonable, in Kenney's mind, that meant her leaving *him.* And only years later, while working on this book and talking through it, would he realize that his anger at people leaving him had anything to do with his abandonment issues.

Even still, back then, Kenney quickly went to Carrie and apologized and begged forgiveness, and she forgave him. Today, Carrie, Kenney and their spouses are all friendly.

Another employee who became close to Kenney was Brian. He and Kenney even played poker once a month. But when Brian wanted to leave for a different opportunity, Kenney took it personally again, as though Brian had some problem with him. The two argued until Kenney literally chased Brian out of the office.

And then Kenney felt horrible again. He went to Brian and groveled and apologized, so much that Brian had to tell him to stop. "It was just important to me that they know that I didn't know who that guy was that went off the rails on them," Kenney says now. "That's not who I am, and I wanted to find a way to stop letting that guy, whoever or whatever he was, come out of me."

But there was one terrible blowout in 2004 that has yet to be rectified — and, to Kenney's regret, maybe never will be.

Kenney's righthand man Dan Jones was married to a woman we'll call Jessica. Kenney hired her years earlier. She fell on hard times as she worked through a messy divorce, Kenney gave her some financial help, she eventually started dating Dan, etcetera. Along the way, Kenney came to realize that Jessica was, in his words, "Not a good person at all." He says, "I remember when they opened a store. They were rolling. Dan was working a lot. And she jumped me after a manager's meeting. *'We're never home to see our baby,'* this and that. I said, *'I'll take the store. Do you not want it?'* And of course, she didn't want *that*. But you see, the whole thing is kind of twisted. She never understood our culture. She never understood what we were. Part of our culture is, we work hard."

It seemed she dragged Dan away from Kenney. At first, Dan went to Kenney and told him that he wouldn't be able to make the weekly executives' meetings because he was too busy running all of his stores. There were probably five or six. Kenney could acquiesce to that. But then, about six months later, Kenney started hearing from those stores' managers, saying they hadn't seen Dan in weeks or months. Conversations with Dan became tense, stilted, downright *strange,* and Kenney could sense that Dan was looking to ease his way out of Andy's. After all the years they'd put into the company together, Kenney couldn't believe it, and he felt that old familiar anger rising.

And then, in 2007, Jessica went to Kenney's sister-in-law and started talking about Kenney and the woman who'd lashed out at him and Karen after misconstruing Kenney's friendship as something more. Jessica went on and on about it, blowing it out of proportion, saying that a *truly* good guy would *never* have allowed such a thing, never *ever.*

Kenney called Dan and Jessica into his office. Their conversation rapidly became uncivil as Kenney tried to put Jessica in her place and Dan stood up against Kenney in defense of his wife. After a few minutes of that, Kenney snapped. *"Get the fuzz out."*

They were done. He didn't want them in the company.

Dan sold him his stores, and when Dan signed the papers, Kenney got up from the conference table, looked at him, and said, "When she leaves you, don't you fuzzing come back to me. Because she will." And then he walked out.

Kenney couldn't believe he treated Dan that way. Dan didn't deserve that, especially with all they'd been through together. Today, as with all his past explosions, Kenney's ashamed for acting like that. "I didn't need to say all that," he says. But to this day, their friendship hasn't recovered. They've crossed paths once or twice, shaken hands, but they barely speak. Dan wouldn't even agree to an interview for this book.

Kenney beat himself up about all of it for a long time, and talking about it now gets him choked up. His only solace is that good came out of it.

First, he needed to replace Dan, which prompted him to

bring Neal Dennis into the corporate office fulltime. Neal had been splitting time between corporate and running the Andy's restaurants he owned with his wife, April. This is also why Kenney bought Neal's and April's stores, so that they could focus on corporate work instead of having to run their stores at the same time.

Second: It registered in Kenney on a new and visceral level how wrong it was for him to treat anybody that way. He needed to get himself under control.

He changed by changing his perspective. He forced himself to stop taking things so personally, which was hard, because to him, everything was personal. He forced himself to see that when people left, it wasn't about him — they were just doing what was best for them. He realized that taking everything personally all the time was a self-centered, even selfish perspective on relationships.

Not long after Dan left, a few others did as well. One had been with the company for 17 years, but only gave Kenney one week's notice. When Kenney asked him why just one week, the man said, "Well, I assumed you'd tell me to go ahead and leave right now." Kenney said he could take two weeks if the extra pay would help his family. "So that's when I knew I was making it," Kenney says. "Because it hurt. That old separation thing again. You know. We were like brothers. But I held it together."

Another one who left around that time was Guy Guthrie, who wanted to start his own company. Kenney called Guthrie into the conference room on his last day, where Guthrie was shocked. "I thought he was going to yell at me," Guthrie says. But instead, Kenney had a cake, and he'd called everyone else in there, too. Kenney had everyone share Guy Guthrie stories, and they all celebrated the time Guthrie had spent with the company.

"I was proud of myself when Guy Guthrie left," Kenney says, with a heavy chuckle. "You know, not telling him to fuzz off, not throwing him out of my office. Hardheads like me take a long time to learn, but because I did it the right way, when this position came open for a franchise sales person, because I had separated from him properly, I could call him."

Guthrie took the job, coming on as Andy's Vice President of Franchise Sales. He's still there, and he plans to be for a long time. "And he's wonderful at what he does," Kenney says. "I couldn't have a better person doing what he does. It was one of the best hires I've done in a long time."

Guthrie saw so much potential. "We've been around 22 years, almost 23 years," Guthrie says, "but we're still the new guys, because we were kind of hidden in North Carolina for 21 years. But the good thing about our company is, we've got all that experience, but we're the new concept to the rest of the country. And that's why I came back. This isn't a company I feel like I have to sell people on. Once people get it, they get it. I just have to help get the word out."

17

LAST DAYS OF ANDY'S
The Bank Saga, Part 7

After solving the franchise sales problem by hiring Guthrie in 2010, Kenney ran into another major problem. In December 2010, Kenney called his law firm, Ward and Smith, to work on their franchise documents, which Kenney knew needed retooling if they were going out of state. This introduced Kenney to a lawyer who would become invaluable: Adam Beaudoin, a tall, big, hardy sort with a clear, strong voice and a mind to match. Beaudoin liked Kenney right away. "He's somebody who's a risk-taker," Beaudoin says. "I'm risk-averse. That's what I do. I manage risk. I help people manage issues. So it's exciting to be around somebody who's got energy, and who wants to do something positive, not, *'I want to take somebody out, I want to sue them,'* any of this. It's, *'Hey, I want to grow this thing.'*"

Beaudoin started working up new franchise documents, which would cost Kenney $100,000 by the time they were finished. "Now, once again, this is kind of a hindrance sometimes to business," Kenney says. "How many people out there can afford to have the proper documents prepared for them?

They can have a wonderful concept, but can't grow their business because they can't afford $100,000 in attorney's fees. Just to cover the legal side, which you gotta make sure you cover in order to grow your business."

More upsetting, however, was that they were going to have to change their name. They had the North Carolina trademark for "Andy's," but they didn't have the federal trademark, and Ward and Smith's homework showed them that someone in Missouri had the federal trademark, specifically for Andy's Frozen Custard. They knew that there was no way for Kenney to get a federal trademark on a name so similar.

In other words, if they wanted to grow, Andy's had to overhaul its very identity.

Kenney railed. "This is *B.S.* I'm not even doing the same *thing* as that guy."

"There was a lot of thrashing around about the name," says Beaudoin. "And we were kind of curmudgeons."

"I got so frustrated at one point," says Kenney, "that I said, 'Can I put a symbol up there saying, *The restaurant formerly known as Andy's?* Like Prince did at one point?' Adam was the only one at the table who chuckled. The rest of the lawyers failed to see the humor."

Once Kenney realized there was no way around it, he and his staff started tossing around new ideas. At one point Kenney thought they were going to change their name to Chubby Checker's Burgers, Shakes, and Fries. Kenney had a few meetings with Chubby about it, but they decided against it because Chubby had given his name to other products before — hot dogs and beef jerky and the like — and more than that, Beaudoin knew that Checker's Drive-Thru, the national drive-in restaurant chain also known as Rally's in some states, would challenge that.

Beaudoin suggested maybe choosing something related to their history, like the name of a street in one of their first towns. Kenney said *Hwy 70*, after a state highway that ran through Goldsboro and Mount Olive. Then Neal said, "What about *Hwy 55?*"

Hwy 55 is a state highway that ran right into Mount Olive, and it evoked the '50s theme that they were going for, and it *sounded* good. *"Hwy 55 Burgers, Shakes, and Fries,"* Kenney said. "That's brilliant! You could even probably get Eminem to make that rhyme!"

But before they moved forward with that, in May 2011, they thought they had a chance to keep "Andy's." Back in December, on a whim, Neal had gone to LegalZoom.com and applied for the Andy's federal trademark. The government notified them on May 11 that they had been approved on May 4.

This didn't mean they had it for certain. After getting approval, they had to wait until mid-October for anyone to challenge them. They decided to wait on changing the name until then, just to see what happened.

Andy's Frozen Custard's challenge came through at the last possible minute on October 19.

Kenney looked the company up. They had about 20 stores, most of them in Missouri and Illinois with a few scattered around Arkansas, Oklahoma, and Texas. A couple named John and Carol Kuntz started the company in 1986 and, like Kenney, they named it after their son Andy, who now ran the company. Kenney thought they could relate, so he emailed Andy himself.

"I said, *'Hey, look, you know, I started very similarly to you',"* Kenney says. *"'It was named after my son. We do frozen custard, you do frozen custard. We're in the Southeast, it'll take a long time to get to the Midwest.'* In my mind I was thinking,

If he responds to me positively on this, we may purchase his custard recipe so he can make money on that, and we may actually add a small fee on top of the custard boxes in order to secure the name Andy's as well. Which could have amounted to a very large amount of money for him. And I didn't put all that in my initial email, but I had all that in the back of my head for when we got to negotiating. The only thing I asked in my initial email was, *'Hey, let's just talk, me and you. CEO to CEO, and keep the attorneys out of it for now.'"*

Two weeks later, in mid-November 2011, somebody else in the Andy's Custard office replied, "We are taking it up with counsel."

That was maddening. They had blatantly refused to do the two things Kenney asked. *Why would you do business that way?* Kenney thought. He emailed back, *We'll change the name. Good luck to you.*

"Now, in the wintertime, I bet they don't kill it," Kenney says. "I bet it would be really nice to have that little sideline income flowing in on a monthly basis. Just for letting us share the name. But we never got there, because the two things I asked for in the original email, he basically shot down."

Kenney was ticked at himself, too, for wasting time waiting on that guy, and he was depressed that it wouldn't work out.

He considered keeping the Andy's name in North Carolina and using Hwy 55 elsewhere — a la Hardee's/Carl's Jr. and Checker's/Rally's — but that meant two sets of cups, two sets of menus, two sets of signs, two sets of everything, and that meant losing buying power, which meant costing his franchisees more money, which all meant charging the customer more. It had to be *Hwy 55* across the board.

Kenney went home and held a family meeting with Karen and his kids. He told them the situation. He was especially worried about Andy. He could still call their signature item the *Andy's Burger*, and he didn't have to change the name of the Andy's Charitable Foundation. But, "I want to pull the trigger on this Hwy 55 name," he said. "I just want to make sure you feel good about it. We really do have our hands tied."

Andy, then 21, said, *"Psh,* whatever, Dad. Make it happen."

■ ■ ■

Beaudoin finished the franchise documents and filed for the Hwy 55 trademark. It took six more months for everything to get approved. "A company ready to roll, ready to grow, ready to do things," Kenney says, "and I gotta wait on government. Even though these attorneys were smart enough to know that when we picked that logo, we knew we were gonna be good with it, or we wouldn't have submitted it. We weren't trying to pull anything over their eyes. We felt 99 percent sure we were going to be good with this."

It wasn't all a matter of sit-around-and-wait. Part of the process was proving that he was going to use Hwy 55 for his company, and that he wasn't just buying a federal trademark on something he thought someone else might use one day, the way cyber-squatters buy up website addresses that they think big companies might want to buy from them some day. To that end, Kenney had to create everything he would use, from menus to cups to even buying a brand-new sign to put over a store, all without a guarantee that he'd be allowed to actually use it.

"Think about that process for a second," Kenney says. "This is lunacy. Here I am, trying to open up stores outside of North Carolina. We're chomping at the bit. We're trying to create jobs. We're trying to add tax revenue. I mean, all the things you think would make government go, 'Yay, let's go!

Let's do it!' And now we've got to start sending them samples of things we didn't even know we were going to use. We have to create all that, which takes time, and then get back to them, so they can see all that. Why is the piece of paper saying *this is what the logos are going to look like* not enough? Why do I have to send you a cup? I have to prove that I'm using it, but they're telling me I might not even have it. To me, that is the definition of stupid. To an attorney it makes perfect sense. Poor Adam. He had to hear me rant and rave about it."

Hwy 55 passed the federal filing test in February 2012. They still needed final approval from a trademark examiner, and that would not come through until May, but Kenney was done waiting.

On February 24, 2012, he held a big event and press conference to announce the new name, complete with cups and banners and T-shirts. A few dozen chairs were filled with reporters and members of the community. Standing behind a brown podium, Kenney wore his standard uniform of jeans, a black v-neck t-shirt, and, for the sake of appearing formal, a gray sport coat. Eight people sat at tables on either side of him. The banner behind him read HWY 55 BURGERS, SHAKES & FRIES, and beside it, though not an official part of the new logo, a sign that said *"Formerly known as Andy's."*

"It's very unlike us to have press conferences," he said. "It's not something that we've done, as a matter of fact, the past 21 years. We don't like to toot our own horns. It's not who we are. But we think these announcements are pretty special."

He gave a brief overview of why they were changing the name, and then he introduced the people sitting beside him. They were his first master franchisees. Since October, Hwy 55 already had commitments to 275 stores: 100 in Florida, 50 in Virginia, 75 in western North Carolina, and 50 in South

Carolina. Now that the trademark drama was behind them and their new brand was all set, those master franchisees were finally able to sign on, committing to opening within the next few years.

Among the eight were Terrell Rhye, with his big beard and long hair, wearing a simple red long-sleeved shirt, and two other men worth highlighting here because they had undergone a transformation as drastic as Kenney's: Chris Lacoe, clean-shaven with short brown hair, wearing a dark sport coat and sky blue dress shirt and tie, and J.R. Cottle, with a goatee and shaved head, wearing a khaki suit and open white dress shirt.

For Lacoe and Cottle to be sitting there that day as *master franchisees* made them the ultimate manifestation of Kenney's vision of helping minimum wage workers become successful. When they first joined Andy's years ago, Lacoe and Cottle were spectacular knuckleheads, almost incapable of even cooking a proper burger.

"What I say to people is this," Kenney says. "One of the beauties of what I've done the past 20 years is I've made over 50 minimum-wage people owners of their own business. And probably the most negative thing I've done over the past 20 years is I've made over 50 minimum-wage people owners of their own business." And then he laughs, hard. "If I got the wrong one, well, it's a mess, but if I got the right one, it's a wonderful thing. It all comes down to character. Always. It's not talent, or ambition, or passion. It's always character."

18

BELIEVING IN PEOPLE
ACTUALLY PAYS OFF
Growth of Andy's, Part 4

Kenney met Lacoe first, in 1994, when Kenney was 30 and Lacoe was 19. They played pickup basketball every Friday night at an old elementary school near Pink Hill, in an ancient gym with an old wooden floor and a court so small that the three-point line ran out of bounds.

After playing, all the guys went to a pizza joint and ate and drank. Kenney held court, telling everyone all about Andy's and how great it was going, and how they were going to do big things. Lacoe spent half his sophomore year working up the courage to ask Kenney for a job. Kenney laughed and said sure, then brushed him off. But Lacoe persisted.

Lacoe was even less enthusiastic about school than Kenney had been, if you can imagine it. "I loved college," he says. "I just hated going to class." Lacoe spent one year at Mount Olive College, then one semester at UNC-Wilmington before getting kicked out and having to go back to Mount Olive. He finished his sophomore year at Mount Olive with a grade point average of, by his recollection, "point-zero-something."

His take on school was downright Kenney Moore-esque. He was "majoring" in business, but, he says, "I had a hard time listening to a professor who was trying to tell me how to make it in the business world, and be financially independent, and all this kind of stuff, when they're there making you know, sixty or seventy thousand dollars a year working that job. And it just didn't make sense to me to pay somebody to teach me how to do the same exact things that they're teaching everybody else. It just didn't make sense."

Lacoe knew millionaires set for life, and he'd listened to *them* talk about work, and it didn't always line up with what his professors said. But Kenney — he talked like the millionaires.

Lacoe didn't want to go back to school in the fall. He wanted to *work*. He also knew that wouldn't go over well with his parents, so he wanted a job lined up before he told them. When Lacoe persisted, Kenney saw he was sincere and asked where he wanted to work. Lacoe said Clinton, a little town about 30 minutes from Mount Olive. He wanted to get away from home.

Kenney set up an interview, and Lacoe got the job, starting out as a cook working for minimum wage, $4.25 an hour. Lacoe started in January 1995, thinking it would be a temporary job. He'd grown up in the country, cropping tobacco and working hog farms and tending to horses and turkeys. Andy's was his first "real world" job, and he didn't expect to like it. But then he fell in love with the restaurant business. He loved that Kenney said he could work his way up and one day own an Andy's himself. "That's what I wanted," Lacoe says. "To me, the only way I would succeed was if I owned my own restaurant. There was no other option, no just being manager or assistant manager. I had to be an owner. That's the only way my brain worked. I had to have something that was mine."

Which was, of course, Kenney's whole mission: give people a business that they can own.

After Lacoe worked there for about nine months, and his parents saw how much he loved it and how much future potential there was for him, they came around and even gave him their blessing. "For awhile, I heard it from them and from everyone — *'Oh, you left college to go flip burgers?'*" Lacoe says. "Now, we've always had a joke about that. There wasn't anything wrong with being a burger flipper."

▪ ▪ ▪

After about a year, Lacoe was promoted, though more out of convenience than qualification. His manager quit to open his own Andy's, and Jimmy Williams, Kenney's father-in-law and the store's owner, needed a quick replacement. Lacoe says, "I got the job, but not because I was the best person for the job. I just happened to be the best person in that store qualified for the job."

Neal Dennis says he was "useless" and Kenney says, "I could've fired him 20 different times."

Lacoe himself says, "If anybody today would've done the crap I did back then, they would not last. They would've been gone within two or three months."

He wore board shorts and flip-flops and backwards hats to work. He cleaned as little as possible. He grew his hair out long and shaggy, then he had it braided into cornrows — *then* he cut it and bleached it platinum blonde with purple tips and *went to a corporate managers' meeting.* Kenney liked characters, but he had his limits. When Kenney saw Lacoe's hair, all he did was give him "the eyes" — an intense look, his eyes wide and a little red, radiating disapproval — and then drop his head and shake it and walk away. "I knew what that meant," Lacoe says. "He was pissed. I knew I'd messed up. I knew I shouldn't have done that. It looked immature, it didn't look like the manager of a restaurant, it wasn't grown-up."

One morning, Jimmy Williams was in the parking lot waiting for him. He told Lacoe that Sunday was going to be his last day. He was fired. Lacoe went into the store, so upset he was crying, and he called Neal Dennis, then one of Andy's vice presidents, blubbering, "Mr. Williams fired me!"

"When?" Neal said.

"Right now!"

"Hold on — *right now?*"

"Yeah, *right now!*"

Neal paused. Then he said, "Well, I didn't know it was gonna happen that soon. Let me talk to Kenney."

Kenney wanted to stick with Lacoe because he believed Lacoe would grow up one day and become a responsible adult, and then he'd do a great job. This was based on what Kenney knew of Lacoe's parents, but also, Kenney just liked believing in people.

Neal called Lacoe back and said, "Kenney said, look, do the right thing between now and Sunday, and don't leave that store hanging. Do what you need to do. Then show up Monday morning at the office, and you've got a job working with us. Kenney will sit down with you then."

And that's what Lacoe did.

Kenney told Lacoe that he would have a store for him to buy in about 10 months if Lacoe wanted it. It would be in Richlands, near Jacksonville, home to Marine Corps Base Camp Lejeune. Lacoe knew the area from high school basketball. "I can't *stand* Jacksonville," he says. "But you don't tell

Kenney 'no.' He offered you a store, you took it. You sucked it up and you dealt with it."

Lacoe knew it was the opportunity of a lifetime. He was 23. Owning his own store at that age would give him everything he'd wanted since quitting college four years earlier.

Until then, Kenney said, Lacoe was to work in the corporate office as a traveling area operator, visiting Andy's restaurants and reporting back to the corporate office, and stepping in to help cook and do inventory or whatever the stores might need him to do.

Lacoe ran it by his parents, and they said of course they'd help him get the loan he'd need to buy the store. They were thrilled, even.

So, for now, all Lacoe needed to do was do a good job, and in 10 months, Richlands was his. "If you *want it*," Kenney reiterated.

To prove he *wanted it*, Lacoe had to do his job well, way better than he'd done in Clinton. And of course, that was easier said than done.

■ ■ ■

Andy's exploded in 1997, growing from 15 to 25 stores by the middle of 1998. Part of Lacoe's job was to help open all the new stores and keep tabs on them. "Kenney worked the crap out of us," Lacoe says. "And I had a minimum of an hour drive every day. He couldn't pay for hotel rooms, anything like that. You had to be at work at 10 in the morning, and you weren't leaving until 11 or 12 at night, and you had an hour drive home at least. We'd work, man, like, 80, 90 hour weeks for two weeks. And there was no sitting in a chair. Kenney was like, *if I'm standing here cooking, you can be standing here cooking.*"

Lacoe learned a lot in that time. "I thought I was bad," he says, "but there were some *really bad* owners and managers back then. There were some people who really did not give a crap about their job, or about what Kenney's philosophy on the business was. It was more about them than it was about the greater good of what we were trying to accomplish here."

Kenney preached that they weren't just trying to sell burgers, shakes, and fries. They weren't even trying to build an empire. "You're trying to hire and train young kids to go from being handed everything they need in life to teach them how to grow up and be mature," Lacoe says. "You're trying to teach them to make educated decisions, and how to be responsible, and hopefully how to get an opportunity to own their own business. That's the philosophy that Kenney taught to us — that it's my personal goal that everyone who works for me, whether or not they want to do this for a career or not, they're going to have a moral compass.

"We can't compete with McDonald's and Burger King and Hardee's as far as price points. You can go there to get a dollar menu; we're not a dollar menu store. And we can't compete with them on speed because we're a cook-to-order restaurant. We're not a bar; we don't have alcohol. We don't have TVs. We don't have girls with their boobs hanging out. We want to do all the things that make people absolutely love to come eat with us. We want to treat them special, and we want to make their food great every time."

One of the biggest lessons Lacoe had to learn almost cost him everything.

Lacoe lived with the other four Andy's traveling managers in a house in Greenville, and they spent almost every night out at bars and clubs. They were all single, and splitting rent four ways left them feeling rich, and they invested heavily in good times. "We would drink until we basically passed out," Lacoe says. Then they'd head to local late-night restaurants. "Every. Single. Night."

One of them, who they called "Cracker Head" because his last name was too hard to pronounce but sounded vaguely like, well, "Cracker Head," loved to fight. One time he picked a fight with a dozen Marines. "If you could imagine it happening, it happened," Lacoe says. "Just put it that way. We were idiots."

Staying out so late so often also meant often getting to work late. "Whenever you drink that much, and you're going to bed at four and five in the morning, you know, it's hard to get up for a meeting at nine o'clock in the morning sometimes," Lacoe says. "Kenney was very nice, didn't get too off the handle the first couple times."

But then they were late two times too many, leading to what is now forever etched in company lore as "The Overreacting Story."

One Monday morning in February 1998, Chris and the traveling managers had a meeting scheduled with Kenney. They'd been late too much, so they tried to be responsible. They went to Mount Olive, which was 20 minutes from the Kinston office as opposed to 40 from Greenville, and stayed at Lacoe's parents' house. They didn't drink. The meeting was at 9 a.m., so Lacoe set an alarm for 7:59 a.m. Or so he thought.

The alarm went off at 8:59.

There was much panic and cussing, and then Lacoe called the corporate office and told Neal, "We're going to be late again."

"Don't worry about it," Neal said. "Don't worry about coming in."

"We can be there in 30 minutes," Lacoe said.

"No, don't worry about ever showing up again."

"Hold on — what?"

"Kenney said don't worry about it. You're done."

They all piled into the car and drove to the office. By the time they arrived, Kenney and Neal and were at a new Kinston store, getting ready to open it later that week, which the traveling managers were supposed to help with. Lacoe went by the store and saw Neal in the parking lot smoking a cigarette, so he pulled in to talk to him.

"Kenney said you're all suspended without pay for two weeks," Neal said.

Lacoe was relieved they weren't fired, but still, two weeks without pay? "I couldn't afford anything without two weeks of paychecks," Lacoe says. "I'd blown everything on going out partying every night."

He tried to explain everything to Neal, to at least get the rest of the guys off the hook. "Look, this is not their fault," he said. He tried to tell Neal about them staying in Mount Olive, and the alarm clock thing, and — "What do I need to do now?"

Neal took a puff on his cigarette. "Man, right now?" he said. "You need to get the fuzz off my lot."

"What?"

"I don't want Kenney to ride by here and see me talking to you."

Lacoe left, but he called Jaclyn over and over again during that week until Kenney set a meeting for that Friday.

The traveling managers arrived early. They sat around the table in the conference room, *We's Freewheelin'!* scrawled across the wall. A few minutes later, Neal joined them. Lacoe sat slouched in his chair, head down, a hat tugged low over his eyes, trying to find the courage to face Kenney. He ran through a conversation he'd thought out and rehearsed, one of profuse apologies and promises to do better and vows not to stray.

Kenney walked in. "Well," he barked, not even sitting down. "You guys wanted a meeting. The hell you want to talk about?"

"And Kenney always does this, man," Lacoe says now. "He knew we wanted to meet. He knew what we wanted to talk about. He just likes to throw you off your game. My first words were — and in hindsight, I probably should've picked a better way of saying this — but I said, '*You know, well, Kenney, I just think you're overreacting.*' That was not what I was *trying* to say, that was not the whole sentence, but that's all that got out of my mouth."

Kenney lifted his end of the conference table and then slammed it down. Jaclyn heard it, and she worked two floors down. Sounded like one of the floors was collapsing. Which, given the building's condition, wouldn't have shocked her.

"You want overreacting?" Kenney yelled. "I'll fuzzing *show you* overreacting!"

"Then he starts cussing," Lacoe says. "Every other word you could think of — '*The fuzz you mean? Fuzzing thinking I fuzzing overreacted? My, fuzz*' — he just goes off. I can't remember verbatim. There were some 'motherfuzzers.' And everything else you could think of."

Lacoe looked at Neal, who'd scooted his chair all the way back against the wall. "Like, *what the fuzz?*" Lacoe remembers. "*What do I say? What do I do?* And Kenney goes, '*Are you fuzzing ROLLING your EYES at ME?* I'm like, '*No sir! I'm not rolling my eyes! I'm just looking at Neal for help!*' And he said, '*I oughta knock that fuzzing hat off your head!*'"

Kenney tells the story almost the exact same way, and so does Neal. "You want the good, the bad, and the ugly?" Neal says. "Well, this was the ugly. I'm a grown man, and I was scared that day."

Kenney having an angry outburst wasn't uncommon, but this one was an all-timer. "Thank God, he calmed down after a few minutes," Lacoe says. "He let us know that he was not very happy with us, and not very excited about the way we'd been doing stuff, and if we still wanted to be with this company, we needed to straighten our act up, and all that. And he ended up only suspending us for one week. We went back to work on Monday. And let me tell you, it was not a nice work schedule after that. It was straight 14, 16-hour days for probably the next 12 or 13 workdays. They were some long days, and there was nothing nice about it."

Lacoe straightened up over the next four months. He quit going out every night. He started dating a girl. He cut down on his drinking. He stayed in the Kinston office after meetings talking until three in the morning. "And then I'd have to drive 30 minutes home and get up and go to work the next day," Lacoe says. "It was all about building that relationship, talking about business, how to grow your business, how to grow your people, how to treat them, interact with them. Everything you could think of, we discussed. We had putting contests upstairs. It was the dumbest thing in the world — we would putt down the hall, off the desk to the right, into the cup, and bounce back to — it was the dumbest thing. Did everything you can imagine. And that built the relationships that are still there today."

And in June 1998, Lacoe opened his store in Richlands.

"I felt like from what I wanted out of my employees and what I wanted out of my business and in turn what I wanted out of my life, I had to think differently and act differently," Lacoe says. "You know, things like, I don't cuss in front people who work for me, or I at least try not to. I would always try to find a way to serve them and serve the customers best — like Kenney says, extend myself. I would try to hold employees accountable this way, by doing the things I thought they should do. And there's other owners out there that don't really follow the same philosophy. They have stores and they're owners and they've got employees and they're, for the most part, doing fine. But I realized that this was the best philosophy. I realized that you had to think different, and act different. You had to *be* different.

"You had to be like part of that one percent that thought and acted this way if you wanted to actually be part of that one percent. And that was Kenney. He was not the norm. He was a little bit different. And it took some getting used to. But he stuck with me. He didn't get rid of me when he easily could've gotten rid of me. He was hard on me when he didn't have to be. He has other things to do. He didn't have to deal with me. And I'm not the only one that he did that with."

Kenney stayed on Lacoe's case for a while, but over the years, Lacoe earned his respect and showed that he'd grown up. How? He carried himself like a professional. He didn't get wasted every weekend. He was a productive member of society. "I worked," Lacoe says. "That's all I did."

■ ■ ■

Lacoe has fulfilled Kenney's vision not only by becoming an ideal master franchisee, but also by fostering more and more of his own good franchisees and employees, largely by treating people the way Kenney had treated him, except perhaps with fewer Hulk-smashed conference room tables.

It all began with J.R. Cottle, his future co-master franchisee. Cottle was 15 when Lacoe hired him as a cook, and Lacoe hated him. "He was a total aggravation," Lacoe says. Cottle worked his way up to manager over the years, but, like Lacoe at first, he didn't take his responsibilities seriously. He would open the restaurant at 3 a.m. after a night of partying with friends and cook food for young ladies from the local gentlemen's club. Cottle was eventually subjected to an intervention of sorts by the corporate staff, who told him to stop wasting his future a dollar at a time.

Lacoe was strict with Cottle, same as with all of his employees. "That was the way I felt like I had to run my store," Lacoe says. "And now I feel like my standards are even higher than Kenney's are sometimes. Especially on facial hair."

Until a few years ago, Kenney didn't allow anybody in the company to grow any facial hair. Then he decided he wanted a goatee, and he didn't feel it was fair for him as CEO to demand his employees be clean-shaven if he wasn't. That's always bothered him about Walt Disney, who wore a mustache but required his employees be clean-shaven. Thus Kenney let his people grow goatees if they wanted.

However, Kenney allows franchisees to keep stricter rules if they want to, and Lacoe does. He says, "I'm like, 'Heck no, dude. That's what built this company. I'm not going to relax on facial hair.' And I never set foot in the business doing any kind of business with facial hair. If I go into work, or into a meeting, I shave."

Lacoe has come to resemble Kenney in many ways. Like his boss, he's not content to sit back and rest on his success and live out his days like that, and like Kenney, he's trying to make other people successful, too. "I've done enough and accomplished enough," he says. Keep in mind, this man is only 38. "I've not completely made it, but I've done very well for myself. And I hold all my people to that same standard. Like,

'Look, you are going to have to work hard, and then I will sell you one of these restaurants. I want to sell it to you probably for the exact same price I paid for it, or cheaper. Because I need to make sure that you're going to succeed.' Yeah, it's worth more than that, and it'd be nice to make more money off of it, but Kenney always said, that first restaurant we sell to people, usually you sell it to them for a cheap price. You want them to make it. You want them to succeed. You don't want to put them in financial hardship right off the bat. He sold me a restaurant one time for $50,000 and he ended up buying it back from me for $87,000 like two years later. Another one, I didn't pay anything for. I walked in and the cash was in the drawer. So I tried in turn to do that same thing for some people who worked for me, reward them for hard work. This is a hard business to do.

"Most people go to college, get a degree, get out, get a job, work 40 years, then retire. That's pretty much what you're taught to do. Well, how many people do you see nowadays that are Wal-Mart greeters or they got a job at McDonald's or they go get another job because they can't live off retirement? So I try to teach the people who work for me, *'Look, you need to fit a 40-year workplan into 10 years. Do it while you're young. Do it while you're not married, do it while you don't have kids, do it while your body is able to do it, work your ass off. Don't waste your time and effort on your friends and partying and all that. Get the work out of the way. Then you can enjoy the rest of your life.'"*

Lacoe now lives at the beach, near Wilmington, and he lives well.

"The kids who work for me now, they have a chance to make six figures owning one store and make that their first year," he says. "I've got a 26-year-old that works for me that's already making pretty good numbers because she runs all her stuff. By the time she's 30, this girl's gonna be set. She already owns one house, she already owns 10 acres of land she paid for free and clear. She drives a BMW. She's got it made. But she works her ass off. And whenever I sell her this first store, I'm selling it to her for almost $100,000 cheaper than it cost me to get into it. And her first year she's going to make $150,000 at 26, 27 years old. Not many people get that opportunity. You don't get that opportunity going into college and getting a job — very few are going to make that kind of money by that age."

In fact, in 2014, *The Atlantic* published a study showing that making $130,000 at age 27 puts one in the top one percent of income for that age in the country.

■ ■ ■

Cottle and Lacoe are both married and fathers now, and they are now co-master franchisees of South Carolina. "There was always something there," Kenney says. "It just took growing up. They were just young. They worked hard. They believed in what we were doing. They sat through our stuff — they stayed up until two, three o'clock in the morning talking about business. They just had to get that party jones out of them. We've all been there. I saw a study somewhere that said that men's brains are not fully operational until 28 years old. Women are much earlier than that."

Kenney is referring to the prefrontal cortex, one of the last regions of the brain to mature, which is responsible for planning, prioritizing, and controlling impulses. And he's right. A 2013 *Wall Street Journal* article said that scientists have discovered that in adult males, the prefrontal cortex may not fully develop until somewhere between ages 25 and

28. "A lot of times, you just had to wait some of these guys out," Kenney says. "I was 19, 20, 21 once myself. And I had a good time."

"But [Cottle and Lacoe] were engaged," Neal says. "That's the difference. Some people, you can just look in their eyes, and they don't have it. But the right ones, you can see it, too."

What Lacoe accomplished, and then what he pushed Cottle to accomplish, was what other franchisees did over the years, too, thus fulfilling Kenney's vision, the embodiment of what he heard that one night in the car. *It's not about you.*

19

IN WHICH KENNEY MUST
STOP TAKING A SALARY
The Bank Saga, Part 8

Anybody who watched the Hwy 55 press conference in February 2012, with Kenney introducing Rhye and Lacoe and Cottle and his other five first master franchisees and going on about all the amazing things in the works, would have seen Kenney as a man on top of the world.

But same as when Kenney started and faked his first year in business through deep debt, and then faked it some more until they were profitable, now he was faking it all over again. He always was good at making things seem much better than they were. Around the office, and in his monthly managers' meetings, Kenney appeared strong and confident, projecting an image of success.

He was giving more and more interviews — print, radio, television, it didn't matter — to push his concept out into the world and to bolster Hwy 55's rebranding and expansion. No outlet was too big or too small. He was in scores of magazines. One day, he went on a national television show's business segment and told millions of people how he had fulfilled the

American Dream. A few days later, he appeared on a talk show local to North Carolina.

And in every interview, he was upbeat and positive and driven, as confident as one might expect from a man selling hundreds of his restaurants to franchisees around the country. He seemed like a man in control of his world and at peace with those with whom he shared it. He told Bill Friday, the local show's host, "The last two and a half years have made us a better company." And he told *Today's Restaurant Magazine*, "We've been building a runway for 20 years. Now we're getting ready to take off."

He was excellent at hiding the fact that he was in a fight to the death with his bank, and a fight that he might be losing.

■ ■ ■

By May 2012, Kenney had made *some* progress paying off the debts, and Hwy 55 was closing on its trademark, so Kenney emailed Mr. Washington to update him about that and everything else with his master franchising. Mr. Washington replied that it was all "very encouraging," but then he wrote, "There were a couple of other topics I meant to brining [*sic*] up."

Kenney did a double take. *I meant to* brining *up?*

Among other things, Mr. Washington asked if Kenney wanted his $50,000 line of credit renewed when it expired in June. Kenney wrote back asking if he could get the credit line increased to $100,000 so that he could stop going to the high-interest lender. Kenney also told Mr. Washington that he'd pay off about $300,000 more worth of debt over the next few months, which should free up more monthly cash flow that he could then use to start making larger payment on the other notes. Plus, they had their first out-of-state store opening in a couple of weeks — one of Lacoe and Cottle's, down in Myrtle Beach, S.C. — and they were going to open stores in Virginia not long after that, and they'd open stores in Florida by the end of the year, and there were even some overseas investors looking at taking Hwy 55 international.

Mr. Washington gave Kenney nothing he asked for.

Kenney did all he promised, and those stores opened, and things were looking better by the month, and it didn't matter to the bank. In September 2012, that last $50,000 line of credit disappeared. The bank also didn't renew the terms for Kenney's current loans, nor did they even do an extension. In short, they failed at their job.

The strange thing is, this left Kenney under no legal obligation to keep making those massive monthly payments. "It's on the bank to put me on an extension, or either redo the note or call it," he says. "They have three options. They did nothing. It's almost like they forgot."

And yet Kenney kept making the payments. "If my company owes money to somebody, I feel obligated," he says. "I have always felt obligated."

Part of him also hoped that making payments he didn't have to make would bolster the bankers' faith in him.

But then he got another email from Mr. Washington, saying he wanted to discuss a few more things and "introduce you to another individual in the asset resolution group," a banker from western North Carolina. In other words, Mr. Washington was bringing on even *more* babysitters.

"Are you *kidding me?*" Kenney said. He knew that things were still tough, "But we're doing the right things," he says. "We're heading the right direction. And that was another thing I couldn't seem to get these guys to understand. I don't think they ever cared to get to know my business. And we were starting to grow. We were starting to sell states. We were opening more stores. And those new stores were doing tremendous business in new markets, markets that had no idea what Hwy 55 was. We had changed our model. There was a lot of good going on to where, if you were engaged with me and you were truly a banking *partner,* you would actually put value to all that."

Butch Talbot, a senior associate who worked on Kenney's account at Dixon Hughes Goodman, says, "And bankers used to do that. The bankers could come in, and they said, *'I see what you do here, this is a pretty good idea.'* And that was it. They understood what you did, they understood why you needed money, they made you a loan."

Kenney says, "We went from one extreme to the other. You went from banks backing loans for people who never made their first mortgage payment before the mortgage crisis, to now, guys like me being treated as though I never made a note payment. It went from almost a *laissez-faire* lending environment to, if you don't have a nail for that one penny, in collateral, you're not getting this loan."

Gordon Douglas says, "In previous meetings, we told them several different ways we thought they could help us make it work, in terms of structuring payments and what he could do. And they would sit here and act like they listened, and then come back with something that was completely different. It was like saying, *'Okay, I can pay you X amount of dollars a month,'* and they would say, *'Okay,'* and then they would come back and say, *'You gotta pay me three times that much.'* I mean, do you not understand? It ain't gonna work that way. And it was such a desperate situation."

That was the biggest problem. Kenney, after taking on all of that debt for them, felt like the bank never treated him like a partner. Instead, they treated him like an enemy, or, again, some dumb kid, some lesser-than who didn't know what he was doing. And maybe they did. Maybe they looked at a guy willing to take on millions in debt he doesn't have to take on, and thought they had a dummy on their hands.

It's hard to say for sure. Multiple attempts were made to contact and interview all parties on the bank's side for this book, and nobody wanted to participate.

Whatever the case, after years of this, Kenney's patience began giving way, and the cracks in his confident mask began to show.

■ ■ ■

In December 2012, Kenney's lawyer, Adam Beaudoin from Ward and Smith, drove to Mount Olive from Wilmington to visit and catch up. It had been about seven months since they'd finalized Hwy 55's new trademark, and he wanted to take Kenney and Neal and whoever else out to lunch and just see how everything was going.

They went to a local steakhouse. Kenney refused to let Beaudoin pick up the bill. "He doesn't ever let me buy lunch for him," Beaudoin says.

"That's just part of what we do, too," Kenney says. "It doesn't matter where we go, what we do, we pay. I've watched people and companies expect Pepsi to give them free tickets to a concert, or expect their attorney to pay if they're going to lunch or whatever. It's just not who we are. I appreciate how hard Adam worked for us. Now, I know I paid him, but I also know that it was personal to him almost as much as it was to me. And it's just another way for me to say thank-you for our friendship, as well as the work that he's done with us. And you know, I'm sure he has clients that are just the opposite of me, that wouldn't even offer to pick up the check if he took them out to lunch. But that's just not who we are."

After lunch, Kenney and Beaudoin and a few others hung out in Kenney's office. Beaudoin asked if anything else was going on that he should know about, and Kenney made an offhand remark along the lines of, "Oh, just this thing with the bank," and gave Beaudoin a quick overview. "He didn't really go into details about it," Beadoin says, "but I could tell it was bothering him."

And things were about to go from bad to apocalyptic.

■ ■ ■

On Dec. 21, 2012, the day that many paranoid humans believed the Mayans had predicted for the world to end, the bank sent Kenney a terrifying new loan package.

First, they wanted to close the deal by the end of the year. That was way too rushed.

Second, the term lasted just 18 months. That meant that he had to pay them all $6 million within the next year and a half, which was impossible. At that point, they could call his note, put him in default, and take everything they were asking for in collateral.

Third, what they were asking for in collateral seemed excessive, maybe even sinister. They wanted his equipment, which made sense, and his accounts receivable, his franchise fees, which he understood and was okay with — but they also wanted his trademarks and his stock in the company.

In Kenney's mind, that meant that when he hadn't paid off this loan in a year and a half, they could take everything and sell it to someone else on the cheap, make a million bucks or so, and be done with him. That's what it felt like they were trying to do.

"I had a paranoid feeling," Kenney says. "They are taking my trademark, they are taking my stock, they already have all of these other caveats in here, these covenants in here. They wanted the franchise concept. They wanted to put that in there. All my franchisee fees in there as well. And then you look at 18 months and you think, *Are these guys basically looking to call this note on me in 18 months? And then have all of this? When I can't pay five, six million dollars in 18 months? And basically take over my company? And then turn around and sell it to somebody else?* And it's paranoid, but that gives them 18 months to find a buyer to give them $6 million 19 months later. Because they'll have all the documents. They'll know what the business is doing."

Kenney's brother, Keith — who had returned to the company not long after leaving, his upstart law firm having failed — looked over the documents. The more they looked at them, the less Kenney liked the terms. Keith tried convincing Kenney that they weren't that bad, they weren't that scary, and he tried showing him their lawyers' side of things. Kenney wasn't having it. "I don't like it," Kenney said. "Sorry, Keith, but I just don't like this deal."

After some more arguing Kenney said, "Dude, you are *my* attorney. Be on *my side.*"

Keith kept arguing, so Kenney called Beaudoin. "Hey, are you in the office?"

"Yeah, I'm in the office, man," Beaudoin said.

"I'm coming down to see you," Kenney said.

"What's going on?" Beaudoin said.

"I'll tell you when I get there."

This worried Beaudoin. "This has never happened before," he says. "Kenney has never called me and said, *'I'm coming to see you right now'* or *'I need you up here right now.'* Usually most of this stuff is planned out, or *'You get on that and I'll do this and you do this and we'll do it over the phone,'* or email or whatever."

A little more than an hour later, Kenney — and Keith — walked into Beaudoin's office carrying a stack of documents.

"The terms were very aggressive," Beaudoin says. "Just at first blush, flipping through, giving an hour to look at these documents, the terms were much more aggressive than what he previously had."

"We caught all these new covenants that they wanted," Kenney says. "They didn't discuss the covenants with me, they just threw the covenants out at me."

Beaudoin told Kenney, "I close business deals all the time. And this is a good-sized deal. But I've closed bigger ones and not seen this level of securitization that they want." Beaudion says now, "I never thought they were going to try to take his business, but they were trying to leverage him and create uncertainty based on the term. It would've been different if they'd said, 'Yeah, we want all this, and we're giving you 10 years.' But there was no trust."

Kenney agrees, saying, "If they had come in here and said, 'Kenney, we have a collateral hole. You are $1.5 million, $2 million short on our new collateral regulations that have been forced upon us. We'd like to take your stock, we'd like to take this here, but don't worry, we appreciate what you've done, you've been a great client' — if that would've been the conversation, I would've been okay with it. But I was not approached that way, in any way, shape, or form. It was all about force."

After reviewing the new loan package, Beaudoin said, "Quite honestly, it's pretty unreasonable for the bank to expect you to have your lawyer, during the holidays, review something like this."

Beaudoin called and spoke with one of the bank's attorneys and said, "Look. You just dropped these loan documents on my guy."

They told Beaudoin, "Well, we've been trying to get this worked out for months with him, and he's been delaying."

"This is total crap," says Kenney. "The actual original loan actually ran out *in September*. They were supposed to give me an extension, and *they delayed* on that. And I *continued to make payments even when I didn't have a loan*."

Beaudoin told the lawyer, "Look. I don't know you, you don't know me, but as one professional to another, I'm gonna tell you right now, I've got two young kids at home, and I want to spend some time with them over the holidays. Can you give me some grace for us to review these documents and work on something?"

Says Beaudoin now, "To her credit, she went and checked with them, came back, and long story short, thereabouts, they did a note modification."

The modification allowed Kenney to wait and start making payments on January 9, and they would meet on January 11 to discuss the loan further. "Basically," Beaudoin says, "this gave him about 45 days. Kenney had no intention of working with [the bank] during those 45 days. But that's what was sold to them. We're going to take this 45 days, give us some breathing room, look at these documents, let our client get comfortable with it, we'll see what we can do."

What they set out to do was find a new bank to give Kenney a $6 million loan so that he could pay off his debt with the first bank and be rid of them.

As the January 11 meeting neared and Kenney lined up

interviews with banks, everyone was finally feeling a little better about everything. "I'm not worried about it," says Beaudoin. "January 9 has come. He's made his payment. The foot is off the gas pedal, because he's feeling good. We've got people on it, we were working on this through December, and getting these bankers lined up, and everybody's excited in the banking industry after the new year starts because they've got to make first quarter. And this is an attractive business, and Kenney's never put himself in the position where he needs everything. He hardly pays himself anything compared to what he could. That's how he stays lean and can keep growing. He probably could have a salary of five hundred grand if he wanted it. Easily. For a business of this size. And then dividends in addition to that."

But he doesn't take anywhere near that much, because, he says, "I don't need it."

Kenney doesn't want his salary made public, but here's a good way to put it in context: In 2013, the average CEO made 354 times more money than the average worker, who earned about $35,000 in 2013. By contrast, in 1983, the average CEO made only 46 times the pay of the average worker. "CEOs switched from asking the question 'How much is enough?' to 'How much can I get?'" Roger Martin, dean of the University of Toronto's Rotman School of Management, told Bloomberg.

According to various studies, Walmart's CEO earns 1,034 times that of the company's median worker. Target's CEO salary is 597 times that of its median workers, and Disney's is 557 times larger. Studies have also found that CEO pay is growing at three times the rate of everybody else's, and that CEO pay grew 127 times faster than worker pay over the past 30 years.

Kenney's 2013 salary was *less than 20 times* that of *the*

federal minimum wage. Not less than 20 times that of the average worker — *minimum wage.*

"I reinvest in keeping us growing," he says. "To keep us moving."

"If you're a bank, you want Hwy 55," Beaudoin says. "This business will make you money if you're a lender, because it cash flows, and in a big way."

20

MORE THAN A BUSINESS
Growth of Andy's, Part 6

A big reason why Hwy 55 cash flowed in a big way goes back to the early 2000s, when Kenney brought on Lacoe and Cottle and more of their ilk. They showed Kenney the true potential for his company. By 2003, Kenney had opened 63 Andy's restaurants all over North Carolina.

He could've rested. He could've taken it easy, coasted, made good money and lived out his days in comfort. But instead, he took new risks and dreamed new dreams.

He wanted to create his own construction, restaurant equipment, and food distribution companies under the Andy's umbrella. He saw 100 stores in North Carolina. He saw Andy's selling stores to franchisees, and then building the stores themselves, and then filling them with their own equipment. He saw a hydroponics building and processing plant that would enable them to grow and distribute their own fresh food. And all of this not for his own sake, or to make himself richer, or for some sort of legacy, but rather so he could better make other people successful, as many people as possible. The other businesses would help him to do that, help him sell all these goods and services to his franchisees for prices much lower than anybody else could.

Kenney moved the corporate office from Kinston to a new building he had custom designed and built in Mount Olive, about 20 miles down North Carolina Highway 55 East, back to where he and Karen had moved in 1995. This brought their lives full circle in a way.

The new office sat on a large stretch of flatland maybe a mile from the Mount Olive Pickle Company headquarters and plant. The building had a sprawling two stories with about three dozen offices, a nursery, a gym, a playground, and a warehouse. In the middle of nowhere, surrounded by the flatlands of rural North Carolina, Mount Olive seemed the perfect place to grow his new businesses.

With the new office came new characters.

Amy Lancaster, a smiley preacher's wife with bright eyes and curly brown hair, was working three jobs back in 2003 — in the mornings from 4 to 11 as a school bus driver, then as a teacher assistant, in the afternoons and evenings as an Andy's waitress, and on the weekends for the Red Cross. And she was only 21 years old.

While working one night at a new Andy's, Amy met a woman who worked in the Andy's corporate office. This prompted Amy to tell her bosses, the store's owners, that if there were ever a job at corporate, she'd love to work there. They told Amy that as it turned out, there was an opening right then — this was when Carrie was leaving to be a stay-at-home mom. They said they'd get Amy an interview.

The truth was, Neal and Kenney thought they already knew who they were going to hire, and Neal met with Amy to be polite to the owners.

"So how did you hear about this job?" he asked Amy.

She said, "God."

"I'm sorry, what?"

Amy nodded. "It's God's will that I get this job. If you don't hire me, then you are out of his will."

Earlier that week, her church had gathered around her and prayed that God would send her one job to cover her three. Amy was a prototypical small town Southern Christian girl, and as true and pure a believer as you'll find. Getting this interview made it *obvious* to Amy *who* was responsible.

Neal said, "Alllll rightee then," and sent her on her way.

But she made such a strong impression Neal told Kenney, "You've got to meet with this girl Amy."

So he did. A couple of days later, sitting in the same conference room at the same table, Kenney asked her the same question: *How'd you hear about this job?*

God. It's God's will.

She got the job. Not because Kenney believed *it was God's will*, but because she was motivated, she wanted the job, and she seemed like someone who would work hard and learn well. He also appreciated her boldness, so openly saying she should have the job because God wanted her to, even if, of course, he also teased her about it for years.

Amy had to learn how to deal with Kenney, though, and how to be a Christian without being a jerk. When Kenney dropped f-bombs and lost his temper, Amy furrowed her eyebrows and rolled her eyes and shot him looks, and she made sure he and everyone else saw her do it. After several weeks, Neal called her into his office and told her, "Amy, look — he is a good guy. He's very generous, and he's very spiritual, probably more than you in a lot of the ways he takes care of other people. And besides that, you're not being a true *Christian* if you're always wearing judgment on your face. So leave him alone. Get off his back."

Now, Amy says, "That really spoke to me. I had to grow a lot. Because, you just gotta love people."

She took up that old adage, *Preach the gospel every day; use words only when necessary.* And she'd learn from no one better than Kenney himself. Neal wasn't just saying it when he said Kenney took care of people. He'd seen it himself.

■ ■ ■

Even as Kenney worked to expand the Andy's empire, after having four great, healthy kids, he decided he wanted to do more to help the world, particularly children.

In 2000, Kenney put together a charity golf tournament to raise money for the Make-A-Wish Foundation. His goal was to get 60 teams of two. He had a hard time getting that many, and some guys showed up having never even played golf before. The ragtag group played at a nice country club in New Bern, with some of the guys wearing jeans and t-shirts and brogan boots. Very Happy Gilmore. Kenney's kind of people, in other words.

One of the course pros went to Kenney and said, "Uh, Kenney, they really shouldn't have brogans on those bent-grass greens."

Kenney said, "Hey fellas! Come on up here! You get another gift! I'm buying you some shoes!" He bought a pair of golf shoes for whoever needed them.

At the end of the tournament's last day, they held a party and a silent auction. And that's where Kenney met Jesse.

Jesse was 10 years old and had multiple sclerosis and a plethora of other medical problems, and he had to be wheeled around on a cart. "And Jesse came in and just won every-body's heart riding around on that little cart," Neal says. "He was popping wheelies, and that type of thing, just having a great time."

Jesse was a passionate kid who wanted to do something good and meaningful with his life. He wanted to touch people, impact the world, inspire humanity to be a little better. When Kenney stood in front of everyone to speak and announce the auction winners, he couldn't help but talk about Jesse, and then he started crying. "It wasn't because I felt sorry for him," he says now. "I just got overwhelmed by — *we've gotta help kids like this.* I just got absolutely overwhelmed." Afterward, Kenney says, "You saw these guys who'd been drinking beer all day long on the golf course go outside and get on their cell phones, *'Tell the kids that I love them,'* just blubbering. It was amazing. It was a really emotional day."

One man, Drew D'Angelo, came up to Kenney afterwards and asked him how short he was of his fundraising goal.

"Ten thousand," Kenney said. He'd wanted to raise $25,000.

"It's done," D'Angelo man said. "My wife and I are going to write a check."

Kenney was so moved that he made the golf tournament an annual event, the Andy's Golf Classic.

Kenney and Jesse were friends until Jesse died. Jesse told Kenney he wanted to work for him when he graduated from college, but, much to Kenney's heartbreak, that never happened: Jesse died soon after finishing high school.

However, Jesse made the lasting impact he'd always wanted. In 2006, Kenney expanded the tournament into the Andy's Charitable Foundation, which has since raised $1.5 million for charities of all types, its primary focus the Miracle League of the Triangle, a baseball league for special needs kids that's based in the Raleigh-Durham-Chapel Hill area.

But Jesse's impact on Kenney's went even deeper than

inspiring the Andy's Foundation. He's literally added years to Kenney's life. A few days after meeting Jesse at that first tournament, Kenney and Neal took one of their countless smoke breaks on the sidewalk outside the Kinston office. Kenney lit his cigarette and took a pull, then he held the cigarette out and gave it a long look. "Neal," he said, "what would Jesse do to have my body for one day? What would he do, for one day, to feel what grass feels like between a pair of bare feet? What would he do to be able to run on it? Would he pollute it with a cigarette? I don't think so."

Kenney dropped the cigarette and stepped on it.

He hasn't had one since.

"And I've had numerous triggers," he says. "Before they made you stop smoking in bars [in North Carolina], I'd be in a bar, and I'd sit at a table with five other people who were lighting up and drinking beer, and normally that's a true trigger for me. I mean, there were times I woke up with a cigarette hangover, not an alcohol hangover. It was amazing. It's like something came over me. No desire at all. Coffee in the morning used to be a trigger for me. No desire. I still dip a little Copenhagen now and then, and I chew Nicorette." He laughs. "I chew Nicorette like a madman. I'm addicted to it now. I was told by a doctor that what could come from Nicorette is, I could end up with sore joints and stuff like that later in life, for some reason, and it could be painful. But as far as health-wise, it's nothing like the tar going into your lungs and all of that. It is what it is. But my lungs feel good. I have absolutely no desire to pollute my lungs anymore."

■ ■ ■

In 2008, the Andy's Foundation, specifically the Andy's Golf Classic, even made pop culture history. In September of that year, *Billboard* magazine named Chubby Checker's hit "The Twist" the number one single of the past 50 years. And as it worked out, the weekend after that announcement, Chubby Checker himself was at the Andy's Golf Classic as part of a promotional contract he'd signed with Andy's.

The night after the tournament, they had a big party. They had a band. People drank, danced, had a good time. Chubby Checker took pictures and signed autographs. Kenney went up to Chubby and said, "Chubby, we are trying to raise a lot of money for the kids. I bet if you got up there and did 'The Twist' tonight, I bet people would run up there and give us tons of money." He'd told the band to learn the song, knowing Chubby would be there.

Chubby said, "No, I'm not performing that tonight."

Kenney shrugged like it was no big deal and said, "Well, the kids would appreciate it." Then he walked away.

Five minutes later, Chubby Checker was on stage and holding a microphone, saying, "Bring me some money, people." And then, for the first time after "The Twist" was named the number one single of the past half century, Chubby Checker performed it live at the Andy's Golf Classic party in little old Mount Olive.

As the Andy's Foundation grew, Kenney funneled its focus and funds into local charities, all of which helped kids. He goes to Miracle League games whenever he can, and he loves those kids to death and melts into puddles out there with them. Parents call and write all the time, fathers blubbering on the phone, thanking him. These days, the golf tournament fills up almost immediately upon being opened and raises around $125,000 every year.

But Kenney didn't do nice things because they were tax deductible and made his company look good. He stayed invested, perhaps too invested, in his employees' personal lives, too.

Here are some stories Kenney would never tell anyone, but stories that others in his life made sure made it into this book.

One year, LeAnne, a waitress and single mother of a three-year-old daughter, got in a car accident that left her paralyzed from the neck down. When waitresses companywide pooled $10,000 from their tips to give to LeAnne, Kenney matched it with ten grand of his own.

Another woman, Charity, worked in the corporate office and once let it slip that she was embarrassed about her family coming to see her on Christmas Eve because she didn't have furniture in her living room. Kenney and some of the office staff went to a furniture store, bought her a full living room set, and delivered it themselves.

Another girl in the office, Jerri, suffered the sudden death of her father, who lived up in Pennsylvania. As soon as Kenney heard, he bought her plane tickets.

One year during a hurricane, an office employee's living room was flooded. Kenney paid for a crew to clean it up.

Another year, an employee's air conditioner went out during a brutally hot summer. Kenney bought the family a new HVAC.

Franchisees Jeremy and Sandra Bond were young when they got married, bought their own Andy's around the same time, and *then* they had two children in two years, which caused all kinds of stress. They struggled for awhile. Kenney helped them through it. He went to their house often, helped them talk through issues, and, Jeremy says, played a huge role in keeping them from splitting up. "He gave so much of himself," Jeremy says.

One guy stole $14,000 from an Andy's that Kenney owned.

Kenney learned that he'd been smoking and injecting it all, addicted to heroin. Instead of having the guy arrested, Kenney spent another $6,000 of his own money to send the guy to rehab. Of course, not every act of kindness has a happy ending: After rehab, the employee stole from Andy's again, and this time Kenney let the legal process work. But he didn't regret that trying to help.

Amy herself benefitted from Kenney's kindness more than once. "We are a close-knit family here," she says. "We will fight like family. But we also love like family."

Amy and her husband, a pastor, had two kids within three years. When Amy thought she might be pregnant the third time, just three months after giving birth to her second child, she went into the bathroom at the office to take a pregnancy test. It read positive. She fell apart. She didn't know how they'd survive with her modest office manager's salary and her husband's even more modest pastor's salary. She walked out of the bathroom in tears, saying, "I'm gonna be a hobo!"

Everyone hugged her, including Jaclyn, who never hugs adults because she thinks adults hugging each other is weird. Kenney gave Amy a raise on the spot. "You're not going to be a hobo," he said. "Never while you're here, anyway."

Not long after having her third kid, money was so tight for Amy's family that she didn't even bring lunch one day. Everyone in the corporate office eats lunch together every day in the conference room upstairs, so they noticed when she worked through that day. Jaclyn came downstairs to Amy's office and said, "Why didn't you eat lunch?"

Amy says, "I struggled with that, because, being a Christian, you don't want to say, 'I didn't have enough money to eat lunch today,' because I should have enough money to eat lunch today, because, you know, *'God will supply all your needs,'* or whatever. But finally, I was like, 'You know what, I do not have money to eat lunch. And by the way, my gas light's on in my car, and I have no idea how I'm gonna get home.'"

Jaclyn stalked off and returned moments later to supply Amy's needs, throwing her debit card at her. "You go get something to eat," she said. "And you fill your car up with gas." And then she walked off before Amy could see her cry. Or try to hug her.

That's how almost everyone in the corporate office is. And they all say it's because of Kenney. Not to keep making this a Kenney-worship-fest — for the sake of balance, feel free to take a moment here to remember how he has failed, failed, failed along the way. And of course, it's easy for a wealthy CEO to throw money at problems and help people that way. But Kenney wanted to do more than that.

He felt this powerful *need* to do all he could for people when he saw some way to help them. During one of Amy's pregnancies, she began having Braxton Hicks contractions — false labor — in the office. Kenney knew that's probably all it was, but Amy was freaking out, so he put her in his Maserati and drove her the half-hour to her house so that her husband could take her to the hospital.

The most ironic thing about Amy's first impression of Kenney, that he was some godless sinner for all of his cussing and swearing and anger, isn't even that he was so generous and charitable — it was that she, along with most other people in Kenney's life, had no idea that all along, as part of his lifelong search for peace, he'd been trying to find God, and with all the same passion he put into everything else.

21

KENNEY GOES
LOOKING FOR GOD

Karen had been a church-going Christian all her life, even taking their kids to First United Methodist in Mount Olive on Sunday mornings while Kenney worked or slept.

But in the mid-to-late-'90s and on into the 2000s, as Andy's became an unquestionable — and lucrative — success, Kenney began to have a crisis.

He had money now. He could even afford to splurge a little. He bought a nice house down in Orlando (although, naturally, he offers it free of charge to whoever wants to stay in it). He bought himself his dream car, a Jaguar. He would later also buy himself a Maserati, and after that, a Tesla. He never owned more than one at once — when he bought the new car, he'd trade in or sell the other. He bought Karen a Mercedes SUV, because according to his research, it was the safest possible vehicle that wasn't also horrible to drive, and he wanted Karen to be able to carry the kids around. But he'd never wanted some exorbitant garage full of cars, and he's no gearhead, but he loved the beauty of a well-crafted car, particularly one that can go fast.

And now he could buy some for himself.

He'd *made it.*

And that was somehow more terrifying than when he'd had nothing.

"I didn't know that I was worthy of it," he says. "Isn't that strange? I was not trying to sabotage myself in any way, but I just didn't know that I was worthy of it."

As he worked through this, part of his process was figuring out how he felt about God. "For assurance that I *was* worthy of it," he says. "And also, a reminder to remain humble about *having it,* and remember that with it came some responsibility."

He also wanted to be a better example for his kids. He wanted them raised in the type of environment most churches — good churches, at least — create for children, one of respecting your neighbor and loving your fellow man and woman, that sort of thing. Karen had always been, by far, the spiritual leader of the household. When they'd moved back to Mount Olive, they went to her old church. She'd started taking her faith in God more seriously around the time their first daughter, Emma, was born, and their marriage had been strained because of the aforementioned misunderstandings between Kenney and female employees.

"I realized I needed a lot more to sustain me than going to church," Karen says. "That came from a long period of time going, *Something doesn't feel right. Something's not quite right. Is it hormones? Is it me? Am I overly jealous? Am I being catty?* And as often happens, that's when you say, *'I can't do this by myself.'* And that was when I realized what I had to have, what I needed, and I started reading the Bible." She chuckles and says, "Just the New Testament. And you know, every day. I started doing that. I started doing the reading. Just stopped being a mental loafer. Just learning more and more about it. I didn't preach anything to Kenney at all. And I wanted to bring the children up the same way. And, you know, over the next three to four years, as I come to understand what it is to be a loving, non-judgmental person, I see that Kenney is a really good person. He treats people by using the Golden Rule pretty much every day. And he always did what was right. When we got a little bit of money in the beginning stages of Andy's having some success, I was like, *'Christmas!'* And he was like, *'Bonus, for Dan. He's been doing this for me the whole time.'* I was like, *'Of course! That's what I meant!'* So he had to go against things like that with me. He always did the right thing.

"I bought him a Bible or a book or something, and I wrote to him, *To the most spiritual person I know. I went to church,* and *he* was the most spiritual person I knew."

So Kenney began going to church with Karen and the kids, and he started going to Sunday School.

But as it turned out, finding God wasn't as simple as walking into a church.

He believed that there was *something* out there, maybe even *Something* with a capital S, and maybe that Something was also Someone. He wanted to find what he could. He knew he could never *know*, because why else would they call it faith? And he wanted to remain humble, and the search alone would do that. How prideful can a man get, trying to answer the unanswerable?

But he wanted to have his belief rooted in something more than emotion, or obligation, or pressure to conform to a community norm. He lived in eastern North Carolina, after all, where it's easier to find an evangelical Christian church than a McDonald's. And although he kept going to church with Karen and his kids, Kenney never considered himself a "Christian," and he found himself drawn elsewhere, too.

"I've never been a kind of guy to accept things just because someone else said so or my parents said so," Kenney says. "I've always had kind of an inquisitive mind, and I always wanted to look. Just because somebody sees something one way, or writes something one way, that doesn't mean you got me. I'm not going to buy everything hook, line, and sinker, for good or for bad. Just like people will read this book, and probably not buy everything hook, line, and sinker. And that's okay. That's *good*."

From the mid-90s until 2004, Kenney explored a number of religions, and he practiced several. He couldn't quite get into atheism or agnosticism, but he explored almost everything: Christianity, Islam, Buddhism, Hinduism, Mormonism, you name it, he tried it. He found differences, yes, but what really struck him were the things that were the same. He found that many religions worshipped and believed similar things, only in different ways.

He got into Buddhism for a while after reading a moving book by a Vietnamese Buddhist monk, Thich Nhat Hanh. For several months, Kenney woke up at 5:30 every morning to meditate for an hour. To this day, he loves yoga, and he still meditates.

Then, in 2000, two Mormon missionaries knocked on his door, and he invited the two young men inside. Kenney tried to respect everybody, to see where they came from, to empathize with them. And in the Mormons, he saw a loving church. "I think sometimes it gets a bum rap," he says. "These missionaries are willing to leave their families and preach their belief for two years while they're young. I think that's pretty astounding. So to me, it was definitely worth my time to sit down with them and have a conversation. They're willing to leave their families for two years — I can give them an hour of my time."

That hour became a weekly meeting for a year. What appealed to him was how family-oriented the religion is. Kenney once had a Mormon manager fall on hard times and need a place to stay. Kenney bought a small house that he rented to the man and his wife for cheap. When the man missed a rent payment, Kenney got a check from the man's church. "That's their sense of community," Kenney says. "They're willing to take care of their own. I think that's how all churches should think. You should take care of your own family first, and then expand your works beyond that into your community. That was very attractive to me."

Karen says, "He wasn't trying to be anti-Christianity or anti-anything. He was just trying to be a better person, and he was really trying to understand. He just had a lot of questions."

After about a year, Kenney's Mormon journey had run its course. "I saw a lot of good," he says, "And I don't think it's fair when people call them a cult. But at the end of the day, I just saw some things I couldn't really get my arms around."

Kenney ended up circling back around to Christianity. "Jesus in particular," he says. "I always came back to his story."

But it's not like it's easy for Kenney to declare an affiliation with the religion. "The beauty of exploring so much was, I came back to understand these other types of religions more, and also seeing the merit in each of them, too," he says. "I love yoga. That's strange. A lot of people don't like yoga. It's painful at times. It's an Eastern exercise. But I come away from that refreshed not only in body, but of mind, when I finish it. Now, I may not do 'ohms.' At the end when I'm laying there in corpse pose, when I'm done and I'm spent, I may actually say a prayer then."

Plus, Kenney doesn't buy all of the church or all of the Bible — there are things about them that he can't get his arms around, either: "I disagree with some of the traditional churches' views on things," he says. "Like, you know, when they get into social issues, a lot of social issues have become very judging of people. I'm not a big fan of that. So I don't know if I could even be called a marvelous Christian. But I do believe in loving your neighbor, and I do believe in extending yourself for your fellow man, regardless of how it feels to you. That's what I do. I try to do it through my actions and my reality moreso than my words. For me to sit here and cite Scripture and this and that, no.

"The Bible is an awfully thick book with an awful lot of lessons in it. But if you love your neighbor, you're not going to covet his wife. If you love your neighbor, you're not going to kill him. You know what I mean? If you keep it down to that, and then frame your viewpoint around that — love your neighbor, love God, man. And then base your frame of reference around that."

By *"love your neighbor, love God, man,"* Kenney is referring to a passage in the Gospel of Mark. The religious leaders of the day are arguing with Jesus, trying to trip him up, trying to get him to subvert himself. They come up with what they think is a brilliant trick question: "What commandment is the most important of all?" Jesus answers, "You shall love the Lord your God with all your heart, and with all your soul, and with all your mind, and with all your strength." Then he adds, "The second is this: You shall love your neighbor as yourself. There is no commandment greater than these."

Kenney says, "And you know what, I don't know if it's enough to get me into heaven or not, but it's the way I believe I should live my life. The Bible doesn't say judge people. It doesn't say tell them what rights they have. I am a firm believer in the good of people. And even the corporations like mine, who have foundations, and give to their community, and whatnot — I'm a firm believer that we will take care of our own. And that the government should be very small. And, look, I am a Christian. I say that unabashedly. But I think there's a lot of good in all of them. You know? It's when they come to loggerheads against each other — 'No, ours is right, and yours is not!' — that's when the whole thing breaks down, and it's caused a lot of death throughout the years. But at the end of the day, there's a lot of good in all of them."

One of the reasons Kenney so loved helping people, was so passionate about it, was because of how well he knew the deep pain of abandonment, and thus he also knew well the power of having someone steady in one's life. He'd loved loving people and helping people long before committing to Christianity, long before all of that. He landed on Christianity *because* of the way *Jesus* loved people — he didn't love *because of* Christianity, because he felt he was *supposed* to. He *wanted* to. He *wanted* to give people a man who could also be a rock for them, as much as he could. He wasn't under any delusion that he could be everyone's father, or even a father figure, but he wanted to love everyone as much as he could. He wanted to give people someone in their life they knew they could count on. He wanted the darkness of his past to contribute to a greater good, like dark strokes in a beautiful painting.

■ ■ ■

As Kenney quickly came to learn, contrary to what the proselytizers would have you believe, finding God didn't automatically mean finding peace. Not only does Christianity come to loggerheads against other religions, but also within itself, and all the time, as churches fight other churches and even amongst themselves. First United was an old, traditional church, the kind that sang out of hymnals and used an organ. Some of the congregation wanted to create a more modern service and bring in some drums and a guitar and some more modern songs. "And there were just quite a few people who had been in that church for a long time that absolutely did not want to see that service succeed," Kenney says. They even tried moving it into the fellowship hall rather than using the main sanctuary, and that didn't work. "I was baptized in that fellowship hall," Kenney says. "My spirit was moved in that fellowship hall. And to know that a lot of the elders of the church were not that comfortable with that service almost made me uncomfortable with wanting to worship. And instead of me making a big wave, I just slipped off and went elsewhere. I could've pushed for the contemporary service, but these were people who had a 30-year connection to that church. Who am I to come in here and try to change things? So I just moved on."

The man who showed Kenney the most about what it meant to really love God and love his neighbor was Pastor Bill Wilson, "a big black guy" from Philadelphia who ran a church called The Lord's Table in Goldsboro. Among other things, Kenney appreciated that Wilson never asked him for money or tried guilting him into tithing to his church, as pastors had in the past. Kenney and Wilson became close friends, often meeting for coffee or meals together. Kenney picked his brain and they both shared deep and earnest thoughts. "Just two men being honest with each other," Kenney says. Kenney told

Wilson about his past, and Wilson told Kenney about his.

He'd been born in 1948 in Philadelphia, and he grew up doing drugs with his mom. An addict by adulthood, when he was 26 years old, Wilson was stabbed, shot, and left for dead. That night, he became a Christian. After some time in prison, he spent the next two decades traveling the world as an evangelist before settling in Goldsboro in the late '90s, just as Kenney began his own search for God.

"He didn't judge you," Kenney says of Wilson. "Because Lord knows, he had enough skeletons in his past, so he wouldn't judge you."

Kenney loved the way Wilson preached. He didn't sound like a *preacher,* but rather like a man excited to tell people about something he loved. "He didn't have to be preachy to get me to understand," Kenney says. Kenney often liked Wilson's sermons so much that he would take his notes from Sunday and repurpose them for his staff and managers' meetings. "Bill had that knack of giving a sermon, and he would read some scripture, but he would get it down where you lived," Kenney says, "He would tell stories, and, they were very, I don't know if 'secular' is the right word. But they were very much in reality of where you lived. And a lot of times that was exactly what the company needed to hear at that time too. I'd take his sermon and secularize it."

April and Neal were going to The Lord's Table at the time, and they would go up to Kenney after meetings and say, "Good meeting tonight. Good message."

"Did it sound familiar?" Kenney would say.

"A little," Neal would say. "Why?"

"That was Sunday's sermon at The Lord's Table. Shows how much you were paying attention in church."

Perhaps the most loving, most God-like part of Wilson

was his honesty. "He shared a lot of personal stuff with me," Kenney says. "We'd pray together. I'd share company issues and get his advice. We talked about politics. Bill Wilson, being a black man, told me, prior to the 2008 election, *'You know, I'm a Christian, I'm a pastor, so I'm anti-abortion, and there are a lot of things I don't agree with Barack Obama about, but I never thought in my lifetime I would ever see a black man with a chance to be president. So I'm torn.'*

"I thought that was so incredibly honest that he would share that with me. He was basically saying, *'He doesn't really stand for a lot of the things that I believe, but, Kenney, if the shoe were on the other foot, and you had never had a white president, wouldn't you have an inkling to vote for one if he could actually win?'* And I thought that was incredibly honest."

Bill Wilson died in 2011 of Hepatitis C that he'd contracted many, many years earlier when sharing a needle with his mom. "That tore me out of frame," Kenney says. "I couldn't even go to the funeral. That shook me more than most anyone even knows. I just couldn't go. I couldn't accept that he was gone."

■ ■ ■

Kenney still reads his Bible, reads devotionals, all that. He studies, he keeps looking for God in new ways, he prays all the time, although he almost never prays for himself. He prays for those he loves, and for his employees, for their lives to be peaceful and good, but he never asks God for favors of his own.

Kenney still has a hard time with church. Even Bill Wilson's church had its problems. The congregation wanted to ban its music director after the man confessed to having an emotional affair. Kenney even stood up in front of the church to defend the music director's right to stay. "My key line was, *'Perfect people need not apply,'*" Kenney says. "We all need to remember that." But the congregation was still upset. "And people still left the church," Kenney says. "I guess they wanted him drawn and quartered. But that's people. And some of them had their own skeletons, too."

It's things like that, and the way he was treated at his church before The Lord's Table, and the stories he hears from other Christians who are treated likewise at other churches, that keep Kenney leery of organized church now. "Church could be wonderful," he says. "But the politics of church and the close-mindedness of church — sometimes I find that disconcerting."

■ ■ ■

After Bill Wilson died, Kenney and Karen went back to First United, which got a new pastor and headed in a more honest direction. And all along, Kenney made sure his children felt free to explore as he had. "We exposed them to the church, and to these different things," he says, "but at the end of the day, when they went off to college or whatever, they're going to form their own ideas. They're navigating their own way with these subjects — religions, politics, you know. I know a lot of young people whose parents have so beat into their heads that, *'This is the way the world works,'* I'm not sure they haven't stunted them. And I wouldn't want to do that. Now, does that mean I've wanted to strangle my little liberal children sometimes? Yeah, absolutely. Do I wish they had a little more Christianity? Absolutely. But in due time. Or maybe never. But at the end of the day, they know it's there. They know we're here. They know where we stand. And hopefully they find their way back. And if they don't, that's fine, and we're going to love them anyway. I never wanted to raise mini-me's. That was never my goal."

※ ※ ※

One of big thing that bothered Kenney was that he couldn't seem to make himself stop cussing and swearing all the time. "I look at older, or elderly, southern gentlemen, and I would like to be one some day," Kenney says. "And not be this quasi-renegade that I am now. I find that appealing. To be that old, nice grand-dad. And it'd be tough if I'm still dropping f-bombs. I'm just too good at it. Too fuzzing good at it. And Bill would be honest, and say, 'You know, sometimes, one slips out of my mouth. It doesn't make you a bad man, Kenney. We're not perfect.'"

Kenney needed to remember that. Finding God doesn't make you faultless. And God as Kenney understood him didn't expect him to be perfect. This was good. Keeping this in mind is one way Kenney survived his guilt over knowing that his personal and even moral failures had brought on the bank situation.

He learned to focus on the good in his life, on how he had done what he'd set out to do more when he started the company. He'd built his empire, and he'd found a true family. Neal and April, along with Jaclyn, Amy, Guy, on and on, all came to feel like brothers and sisters. And Karen came to feel the same. "Like I think most people feel about their husband or wife's family," she says, "that's how I feel about them."

Kenney may have had his demons, but he also had his angels. And with the hell brought by 2008 and the years that followed, he needed them.

22

THE DEVIL ROARS
The Bank Saga, Part 9

A s the bank situation escalated throughout the years after 2008, while Kenney did a good job keeping the company's troubles hidden from his managers and staff, those closest to him saw his stress growing heavier by the day.

Kenney was so furious with the bank because of how they were treating him, and because the way they treated him reminded him so much of the people he'd worked so hard to get away from all his life — but *also* because it reminded him, every day of his great failure, a thorn deep and digging into his side. He was furious with himself for bringing all this on his family and his company by allowing Johnson to stay so long. And he made sure to never make that mistake again, no matter the cost.

When Kenney started trying to bring on new franchisees in 2010, he wasn't *desperate*, but there was a sense of urgency to the whole endeavor. They'd blown fifty grand and nine months on The Franchisers with almost nothing to show for it. They were deep into franchising now, and they wanted it up and running and getting attention and making money.

And even still, they made sure to weed out candidates who didn't seem to share their values, even those with lots of money and experience. Kenney remembered Johnson and the bad seed he'd sown all too well. The bank reminded him every day.

"We had one from the Florida area come in here," Kenney says, "and I mean, this guy already owned 20 restaurants. And he was looking at our concept to go with his 20 restaurants that he had, and as a matter of fact he reminded me of Johnson so much over the course of Discovery Day that when we walked in my office when it ended, I thanked him profusely for coming, told him to be very careful going back, and when my group walked him to the door here, we all shook our heads and went, no way. He had the same attitude. The same tonality. The same know-it-all swagger. I believe after 22 years, I've earned the right, if I'm talking to you, that you listen to me, that you not sit there while I'm talking just thinking of what you're going to say next. And that really disturbs me. And it disturbed me when I watched him do that the whole half hour we talked.

"You can see it in their eyes. Their wheels are turning, they're glancing around, they're not necessarily listening to what you have to say. They're thinking about what their comeback is, or how their company does it better. And look, I'm all for getting better, but don't demean me while you're in my house. And don't demean me or my concept. And I was getting that from this guy. This guy actually went into one of our stores with a pair of glasses on with a camera, filming it, and as he saw something that he thought might be bad, he would do this condescending talking about what was going on. And of course I watched the video later on, and everything was fine. It was just his attitude. And this was a guy who could probably have opened 10, 20 stores. No desire for his money. Or to have him in the family. We've learned that lesson. We've been there once. We're not going back."

■ ■ ■

After five sleepless, stressed-out years, in January 2013, after getting the loan modification and the 45-day extension from the bank, and after scheduling some interviews for the next several weeks with new banks, Kenney was starting to feel okay. And then everything exploded. Adam Beaudoin says, "Kenney had a plan. He lined up all his interviews with these banks, and he had more coming, and then the [first bank] team shows up. I call it 'Black Friday.'"

On Friday, Jan. 11, 2013, Kenney met in the Hwy 55 corporate conference room with the bankers, and Neal Dennis, and Keith, and Butch Talbot. Gordon Douglas couldn't make it, and Kenney didn't think he'd need Beaudoin. They were going to work on getting a better deal on the new loan moving forward. Coming from the bank were Mr. Western North Carolina and some new banker — yes, yet another new banker — being brought onto the account.

Kenney had never met the new banker, never spoken to him on the phone, never even emailed with him. They shook hands, and the man said, "Look, I'm from New York. I understand this has been a tough relationship, and that you're tough to deal with, but I'm from New York, and I'm tough, too."

Kenney thought, *Whoop-dee-damn-doo. I'm from North Carolina, and I can whup your ass, too.*

Mr. I'm Tough Too continued, "You need to understand something. Things are going to happen today that you don't like. Let's just see what we can do about it."

Kenney couldn't believe it. He couldn't believe the bank. He couldn't believe *this guy*. First time they've met, and *that's* what he says?

"This was the first comment out of his mouth," Kenney says now. "Once again, if the tact had been, *'Hey Kenney, look man, our file looks thin collateral-wise. Could you help us? If you could pick up this piece, when we redo this note, it sure would make us look better.'* I would've been like, *'Sure. Here you go. What else do you need?'* But to come in and treat me like that?"

Kenney wanted to hit the guy in the mouth, and he wasn't the only one. Butch Talbot is so mellow and mild-mannered that Kenney calls him Eeyore, after the donkey in *Winnie the Pooh*, and even Talbot was infuriated. "I've just never seen bankers act the way they acted," he says in a thick, rolling, molasses-like Southern drawl. "They were just so arrogant toward someone that had been a good customer for 20 years. There's no telling how many fees and how much interest and all that Kenney had paid them over the years. Millions of dollars. And it was like *they just did not care*. They were as unprofessional and as un-bank-like people as I have ever dealt with. I wanted to hit them, too."

The meeting lasted 10 minutes, if that.

They reviewed the loan documents and Kenney raised his concerns with them, and as usual, the bankers continued to rebuff everything he was trying to accomplish.

Neal Dennis says, "I've got notes where you sit there and explain to [the bank] what happened. That you'd been paying everybody else's notes, trying to get them on the phone, and it was like nobody paid any attention to you. Nobody gave you any credit for any of that. They were just like, 'Well, here's what it is now.' And to them, it was like it didn't matter."

Talbot says, "It would've been different if it would've been the other way around. If [the bank] had been calling here trying to get something done, and Kenney's ignoring them, avoiding them, not answering the phone — but that's not the way it was. We were trying to do the right thing. Whereas, I know bankers are chasing people they can never get on the phone. And that's not the way it was."

After a few minutes of tense conversation and more unrelenting condescension, Kenney said, "Guys, once again, here you go again. You're doing it to me again. This is what I've been dealing with. And I've never missed a payment. I saved your asses, and you've never once come in here and told me 'thank you.'"

Mr. Western North Carolina looked at Kenney and said, "Well, you had culpability in this."

Kenney froze. He leaned back in his chair. His eyes went wide. Fire-eyes, everyone calls them. "I have *culpability*? What *the fuzz* are you *talking about?*"

"Well, you were the franchisor. You sold him the franchise."

Kenney snapped. By his recollection, "That's when the *'fuzzin' fuzzety fuzz fuzzes'* came out of me. Because I was like, *are you KIDDING me?* I sell you a house, a bank finances you, you quit paying — and *I* have *culpability* because I sold you the house? That's the dumbest thing I've ever heard. That is absolutely insane."

For *years* he had been *trying* to pay them. He had taken on loan notes that he didn't have to take, made payments he didn't have to make. Even *now,* he wasn't trying to walk away from any of the responsibility. He was *still trying to pay them.* And yet they come in here trying to strong-arm him? Trying to take his trademarks and his stock? For two decades he had built Hwy 55. He had sweat and bled and wept over it.

Through it he had touched the world. Through it he had come to know God.

And now they were doing this to him? If he agreed to their terms, and then if something happened in the next 18 months — if he missed a payment, if he looked at them crooked — they could take his company. And true or not, that's what it felt like they were trying to do. Take it and flip it and make the bank an easy million bucks and forget all about him.

In that moment, years of feeling demeaned, of feeling like he'd been treated as though worthless, treated like a child, erupted out of Kenney.

He said, "All you've got is a bunch of stores full of old restaurant equipment. I'll throw it out on the street and let you pick it up. And by the way, I own an equipment company, and I can roll in some brand new stuff the day after you pull yours out. And I'm closed for two days, we clean it up and paint it, and we reopen, and it's our spring cleaning. And you'll get a warehouse full of used stuff that, guess what, I'm probably gonna go buy at ten cents on the dollar." Then he roared, *"Get. The. Fuzz. OUT."*

Kenney stormed out of the conference room and slammed the door behind him. Everyone in the building heard it.

Looking at the doorframe years later, Talbot is amazed that it's still standing. "We need to figure out who built this," he says.

Kenney headed down the hallway toward his office and slammed down into his chair. He heard the bankers open the conference room door and go down the stairs toward the lobby, talking loudly. Kenney charged back out of his office, ripping off his jacket, fire eyes at full blaze. Watching him move, Neal said to himself, "Oh, fuzz. This is not going to be good."

"And by the way," Kenney barked, stalking after them, *"shut* the *fuzz* up. There's nothing you have to say that we need to hear."

Neal and Keith and Butch managed to slow Kenney down, trying to talk him down, trying to get him to let them go, long enough for the bankers to scramble through the lobby and out of the office. By the time Kenney reached the lobby, they were in their car and racing away.

"Kenney was headed to the parking lot," says Talbot. "He mighta hit somebody if he'd got out there. He mighta hit somebody. And we were trying to tell him, *'You don't need an assault and battery charge.'"*

"It wasn't pretty," Kenney says. "But you have to understand — it was three, four, however many years that came out of me in that one burst. And I think what got me more than anything was their attitude towards the company. You don't like me? I can deal with that. I really want everybody to like me, but if you don't, hey, that's fine. But to demean my company, that's to demean the people I work with, and that's demeaning my family, man."

Kenney called Karen, who was in the car with the kids, on their way to Florida for vacation. Emma, who'd started college at St. Andrews in Scotland, was flying down to meet them. Kenney told Karen that there was no way he could go.

"For all we knew they were going to call the note and we were gonna lose everything," Karen says. "That's where we were. Driving to Florida, *'Hey, this is fun!'* I was thinking, *We're gonna lose everything.* But you know, I really felt like this would've happened regardless of whether Kenney got mad or not. This had been building and building and building with them. I didn't blame Kenney at all. It wasn't like, *'Well, if you'd held your temper a little, we wouldn't be in this'* — it wasn't that way at all. Because why would I expect him to be somebody that he's not? It's just stupid at this point to expect him to be somebody that he's not."

Kenney says now it probably would have been better if he *had* kept his temper, though. "If I had it to do all over again, I wouldn't have gotten so upset," he says. "It would've saved me a lot of gray hair."

■ ■ ■

Adam Beaudoin spent most of January 11, 2013, in a marketing conference with his firm. He finished around 5 p.m., and that's the first time he checked his work email and voicemail. He saw an email from one of the bank's attorneys. "And he's saying, basically, *'We're calling the loan,'*" Beaudoin says. "Basically, *'You have breached the agreement, you have done all this, you have done all that, we want immediate payment. When February 9 comes, you're paying us the whole thing, or we're going to release the hounds on you. We're gonna open up the heavens and swallow Kenney Moore.'*"

23

A BREAKDOWN OF
EPIC PROPORTIONS
The Bank Saga, Part 10

After getting the bank's email, Beaudoin picked up his phone to call Kenney, and he saw that he had a voicemail from the bank's lawyer. "And I could tell the nervousness in his voice," Beaudoin says. "He's like *(talking really fast, like he's out of breath, panicked), 'Um, I just sent you a letter, um, you need to call me as soon as you can. Uh, you know, we're calling this note, and, you know, there's been some threats made, and you know, you better tell your client, he's not throwing anything out on the street. And um, you need to assure me that [the bank's] interests are gonna be protected pursuant to the loan documents,'* and all this. Reading between the lines, my impression was that he didn't want to have to file an injunction — he was basically telling me, *'Get control of your client.'"*

Beaudoin called Kenney. "Man, what *happened?*"

"Man, these fuzzers came in ..."

"He was ticked off," Beaudoin says. "And I mean, not in a frustrated way that I've seen him ticked off during the franchise process, but in like a really, angry, angry way. And he did say at the time, *'I know I shouldn't have done it. I lost my cool. But these smug SOBs come in here …*' Keith got on the conference call, and he was getting all ticked off too. It was really bad.

"But what it told me was that [the bank] really thought that during that extension period they were going to have a workout with Kenney. But it seemed to me that the workout that they had in mind was to strong-arm him into accepting their terms. There was to be no negotiation. They were going to come in, and they were going to tell Kenney Moore, in his own office, in his own building, what he was going to do, and how he was going to do it. That tells me you don't know Kenney Moore, because you don't do that to a business owner who basically created this from nothing. That tells me that you haven't given the time to know the man. No one reacts well to bad news in general, but you don't come in and disrespect somebody where they live. If you're coming in to meet with somebody in their own place of business, that they have grown, you've got to have appreciation for that. And they didn't. That's basically what happened."

Kenney told Beaudoin that he wasn't going to throw their collateral out onto the street or anything like that. He'd just gotten caught up in the moment and said some things in his blind rage that he didn't mean.

Beaudoin called the lawyer back, and best he remembers, the lawyer said something to the effect of, "My guys were mistreated worse than they were ever mistreated in their lives. I mean, they feared for their lives! I don't know *what* kind of people you represent, but — "

"Whoa, whoa, whoa," Beaudoin said. "We're not going to make this personal. They came in, they had an agenda, my client didn't like their agenda. They left. We're not going to get into the details, because it doesn't matter. He didn't punch anybody. He didn't shoot anybody. He didn't do anything. He's a private property owner. He's allowed to ask people to leave, and in whatever way he sees fit. It just may have been a little more aggressive than your guys might have liked."

Beaudoin says now, "Had I been there, I would've been like, *'Can you give me a moment with my client, please?'* Because I would've started to see the red. Because he probably wasn't happy that they were there, but I know Kenney well enough to know that he's got composure and restraint. He's a businessman. You can't do that. It's just that he had had enough. But you also have to remember, and to come to Kenney's defense, you have to know the climate where he was mentally. He was feeling good. He was feeling a lot of love, because he had a bunch of appointments set up with a bunch of different banks, so he was feeling pretty confident."

And for good reason. Not only did Kenney have appointments set with several banks, but Hwy 55's franchising had taken an explosive leap forward.

They were going international.

■ ■ ■

In the spring of 2012, at the height of college basketball's March Madness, Hwy 55 entered the BurgersBusiness.com March Madness bracket for the Country's Best Burger as a 16 seed. (For comparison: In 2014, Wahlburgers, founded and long operated by Paul Wahlberg, brother of the actor Mark Wahlberg, entered the competition as a 16 seed, and riding publicity from an A&E reality TV show in which Mark also starred, to boot — and Wahlburgers didn't make it past the first round.) Hwy 55's competition included McDonald's, Burger King, Wendy's, Hardee's/Carl's Jr., Five Guys, Krystal,

White Castle, and more, including California cult favorite In-N-Out. And Hwy 55 *won the whole thing.*

This caught the attention of Khamis Al Rumaithy, a 28-year-old businessman from Abu Dhabi, the capital of the United Arab Emirates, located in the southeastern corner of the Persian Gulf, due south of Iran. Al Rumaithy is in charge of the food and beverage side of his family's business. His father, who passed away a few years ago, had been Abu Dhabi's Minister of Economic Development. Al Rumaithy has several brothers, all of them in charge of some part of the family business, all of them wealthy. He is worth $150 million.

Al Rumaithy saw the bracket, and he looked Hwy 55 up, and he thought their food and their concept was great — but what he loved most was what Hwy 55 used to serve its kids meals: a cardstock model of a '57 Chevy that held the food in its seats.

Al Rumaithy had his executive assistant, Hussein Sefket, contact Hwy 55. Sefket left Guthrie voicemail after voicemail. Guthrie actually ignored him for a little while because Hwy 55 had no plans whatsoever to try going international until they'd gotten a handle on America first. But Sefket was relentless. Guthrie asked Kenney what to do about them, and Kenney said that if they were that interested, it was worth hearing them out. So Guthrie finally called Sefket back.

Sefket was a Muslim raised in London, and he spoke with a soft British accent. "It was a strange phone call," Guthrie says. They exchanged a few emails. Guthrie sent him their franchising information and had Sefket fill out some paperwork. Then Sefket said, "We think we've seen what we need to see. I am coming to America to see you."

Sefket flew the 17 hours to North Carolina and went

through a Discovery Day. He came away impressed. "You could tell he was very intelligent," says Guthrie. "He'd been in the food business for 30-some years. He knew all the questions to ask. And he was very impressed with what we had in place in terms of our back of house system. Our Sysdine."

Sysdine is a computer program for logging employees' hours and, in short, running a company. When Kenney had acquired all of those stores back around 2008, he'd been forced to find a more efficient way to manage so many stores, which led him to Sysdine. He implemented it company-wide, and now has computers in every store that enable managers to access Hwy 55's Sysdine databases anytime. There's nothing particularly special about the program — it's a commercial product — but it was unique for a company as small as Hwy 55 was at the time to use something so sophisticated.

Guthrie says, "[Sefket] said, 'I have not seen a company, your size especially, that has the systems in place to help run a business like you guys do.' That was one of the selling points for him."

Sefket went back to Al Rumaithy and told him they should buy into Hwy 55. After some negotiation, in January 2013 — not two weeks after Black Friday, as a matter of fact — Al Rumaithy signed a master franchising contract to develop 85 stores in the Middle East and North Africa (MENA) region over the next 10 years.

After the deal was made with Al Rumaithy, Hwy 55 was featured in a trade magazine out of Dubai. Some businessmen from Toronto in Dubai, Muslim gentlemen similar in some ways to Al Rumaithy, read the article. They went through almost the same process as Sefket and Al Rumaithy, coming to Mount Olive and going through a Discovery Day. They signed on to develop no less than 10 stores in the Toronto region.

This was a big deal, and another example of Kenney's renegade spirit and his willingness to break stereotypes. There are hundreds if not thousands of churches in eastern North Carolina, the vast majority of them some variation of fundamental evangelical Christianity. And Kenney is the Christian CEO of a major company founded and headquartered in eastern North Carolina, and yet he is partnering with Muslims from the Middle East.

"I lay it all out there from the get-go," Kenney says. "This is what I am, this is what you are. This is what it is. We're not going to play any games. We're not going to hurt each other's feelings. We're going to talk like men. Yes. I am different. I have a different religious philosophy than they do. But once again, our focus is on loving your neighbor. That's what their focus was on. They're good guys. They're smart guys. They're hard workers. And they're guys I'm honored to be in business with. They get up every morning and love their families just like we do. Are there radical factions of what they do? Sure. Are there radical Christians? Absolutely."

Guthrie, also a Christian, went to visit Al Rumaithy in Abu Dhabi when they were working out their deal. "I didn't see that," he says. "I saw a family that was tight. I mean, a close-knit family. You could tell they loved their family. There were playgrounds in the back, there were toys everywhere outside. And I couldn't have been treated any better."

Guthrie spent a week there. They had a car waiting for him at the airport with a driver *and* a guy to carry his bags. When they dropped him off at his hotel and he went to check in, Guthrie pulled out his credit card. "No, no," the receptionist said. "Everything's already been taken care of. Mr. Sefket paid cash earlier in the week."

"Just how much would that be?" Guthrie asked. "Just so I

can know, and send a thank-you?"

It was more than $4,000.

As Guthrie traveled and toured with Al Rumaithy and his people that week, he noticed items in stores — gadgets and clothes and things like that — and say, off-hand, "Oh, wow, we don't have anything like that in America."

Toward the end of his trip, they handed him a few bags full of the things he'd pointed at. They'd bought him all of it. "Except for the new BMW," Guthrie says. "I was like, 'Wow, I have not seen one of those in America!' I did not get one."

▪ ▪ ▪

So, yeah, Kenney was feeling good. "It was a little premature, probably, to pull the band-aid off with [the first bank]," Beaudoin says, "but it was going to come off anyway, and it was going to sting no matter what. It just would've been nice had he given me a little more rope to work with."

After Kenney went off on the bankers, Beaudoin says, "It became pretty clear to me that at this point, the bankers made it personal. They were almost acting with this mentality of, *'We want to hurt him. We want to cause pain.'* And that was apparent. It already was personal to Kenney, but it became personal for these gentlemen."

Beaudoin was able to calm the lawyer down and talk with him and their other lawyer in more rational terms. "What can we do about this?" he said. "Because it's ridiculously unrealistic to think my client's going to be able to come up with almost $6 million within the next 28 days. Because, here's the deal: He doesn't want to refinance with you. He's never wanted to since this process started. We've got lots of irons in the fire. I think if you'll just work with us, it'll be a win-win. You don't want his business anymore. He doesn't want to do business with you. We don't need to talk about who shot John. Let's just make it happen."

Beaudoin says now, "They didn't believe me. And to say they didn't believe me is to say they didn't believe Kenney. So they started requiring a list of financial institutions he's meeting with, when he's meeting with them, when he's meeting with private investors. And we gave it all to them, by the way. I mean, Kenney cooperated fully. But the problem was that, as we met with more and more, and we started to peel back the layers of the onions, we knew it wasn't going to be that easy. The loan was undersecuritized, and the banking climate had changed.

"And so long story short, we're back and forth with them. We're buying time, he's having to submit financial records, because they are going to require him to do a business valuation. It seemed to me that, in order to keep his loan, internally at [the bank], from going to a bad place, the bank had to at least create the appearance that it was being refinanced. So even though they knew it wasn't gonna be, internally they did whatever they did to keep negotiations alive.

"And I don't know that this for fact, but my gut tells me that some of these people were trying to save their jobs. They needed this book of business not going from troubled to really bad, not to look like it was not performing, for whoever they reported to within the bank. And so they made him provide personal tax returns, financial statements for all of the entities, all kinds of stuff — everything that he owns personally, for this process.

"And by the way, he gets to pay for it all."

▓ ▓ ▓

After Black Friday, Kenney met with more than a dozen different banks and private investors, trying to find the $6 million he needed to get out of his deal with the nightmare bank. And he felt the pressure, like a big moment in an important baseball game, except with real, life-altering consequences. Every time he met with a new bank, he had to be prepared, and he had to manage the pressure and cope with it. He felt more empty by the week.

And he was brutally honest with the bankers. "Just saying, 'There's no point in hiding the ball on this stuff,'" Beaudoin says. "'We don't need to go into the exact verbiage he used with these guys, but basically, he said, *The relationship deteriorated, and I'm trying to find a new home.*'"

"But I also couldn't sound desperate," Kenney says. "It's that balance between cockiness, confidence, and the desperation. You know, it's like, the girl will never go out with you if you act desperate. If you act like you don't care, she probably will. It was playing down the middle."

And Hwy 55 had a lot to offer the new bankers. Franchising was going well, and the company was poised to explode. On top of his international dealings, every week, Guy Guthrie fielded dozens of requests for master franchising information.

But as far as the banks were concerned, it was like none of that mattered. "I was in here doing the dog and pony show for bank after bank," Kenney says. "And I was getting nothing but '*no.*' They'd go, '*Oh yeah, we'd love to!*' Next day: '*Sorry, we can't do it. Click.*' The banking environment was tough. My God, it was tough. I was calling friends and business acquaintances, and anybody that knew somebody in the banking business, going, *Please, put them in front of me, put them in front of me.*"

A couple of weeks into this, with the February 9 deadline creeping up, the bankers and Kenney were all getting nervous. "The last thing anybody wanted was to go back on their hands and knees to [the first bank]," Beaudoin says.

The banks and investors all loved the international expansion and projected growth, but the instant they saw that $2 million collateral gap in Kenney's loan, they said no. To put it frankly, they were all scared — except one: Fifth Third Bank, a regional bank headquartered in Ohio and new to North Carolina.

Kenney's contact with the bank, Martin Green, came to Mount Olive to meet with Kenney and tour his office and learn all about his business. Where everyone else balked at the $2 million collateral gap, Green looked at Kenney's projections and his franchising plans and saw gold. He told Kenney they would make it happen.

"This was a group that was saying, 'We are going to move heaven and earth if we have to, to make this thing happen for you'," Kenney says. "And I believed them and I trusted them."

Problem was, there was no way Fifth Third could make it happen by February 9.

Beaudoin says, "I told [the first bank's attorney] point-blank, 'My guy doesn't have that money to pay this off. I wish he did. He wishes he did. But the way he set this up, the way he's growing things, this year is not a good year for this to happen.'"

The bankers were furious. They hinted at lawsuits and foreclosure and all kinds of things. Beaudoin went back at them, just short of threatening in return, saying, "Look, you know what your client has in this. You know you're under-securitized. And yeah, you can sue, and there may be some personal guarantees and some other things that you can do, and you can make life hell for everybody, but at the end of the day, the bank's gonna lose its shirt. It's gonna lose a lot more than Kenney Moore's gonna lose."

Beaudoin told the bankers, in essence, "Look, we'll give you anything you want document-wise, information-wise, who we're meeting with, to show you that we're not full of it. We literally are trying every angle — we're *meeting with private equity investors* — to get this paid off." Beaudoin says, "It seemed to me that the bankers didn't believe that Kenney was actually doing due diligence. And I told them, 'Look, he is *breathing* getting away from you. Every breath he takes involves getting away from you. I can promise you, his focus is all on this.'"

If there was any relief to be found, it was that even though the bankers seemed unable to grasp the nuance of the situation, their lawyers did. They convinced the bankers to be at peace if Kenney could show them a Letter of Intent from another bank. That is, Kenney needed another Fifth Third to put in writing that they were going to work out a $6 million loan so that he could pay them off. That would help settle everything.

Kenney says, "The last thing I really wanted was to say, '*Okay, come get your equipment, I'll roll some trucks in here, put some new equipment in, and we'll go bankrupt, and we'll figure it out later.*' That's the last thing I wanted to do. That goes against who I am. I am not the type of person that wants to stick anybody. Contrary to what those two guys might've thought when they left here [Black Friday]. So, temper? Yes. Lack of character? No. Every penny that I said I'd pay, I want to pay."

But of course, as with everything else those days, that wasn't going to be simple. "You talk about how many times missiles were almost fired between the U.S. and the Soviet Union during the Cold War?" Beaudoin says. "This was a very tenuous piece. Like, somebody blink first. What's gonna happen?"

The first bank breathed down their neck every day, and every day, Kenney and Beaudoin called Fifth Third asking when the Letter of Intent would be ready. Every time, Fifth Third told them, "You'll have it tomorrow," or "You'll have it soon."

Finally Beaudoin had to say, "Listen, here's the deal: The trust we have with [the first bank] is very small. Don't give me B.S. deadlines. Tell me something real, because this is undercutting everything we're trying to do."

Beaudoin was working overtime to keep the first bank convinced that Kenney was honest, that he was doing everything they wanted him to do, and that Fifth Third really was trying to help him get away from them. Beaudoin says, "I think [the first bank] never believed that anybody else would want to deal with Kenney."

Fifth Third finally had a commitment letter and the loan terms document ready on Feb. 22. Kenney signed it right away, and he and Beaudoin and Karen and Neal and everyone were all excited. It was a couple weeks late, but they had it.

The first bank said it wasn't good enough.

The bankers fussed over whatever they could, including the fact that Kenney and Beaudoin redacted the interest rate and monthly payments that Fifth Third was offering from the banker's version of the letter. "We *need* to know," they told Kenney.

"No you fuzzing don't," Kenney replied. "You just need to know that they're giving me a loan and you're gonna get paid."

In addition, Fifth Third's commitment to the loan depended on approval from the Small Business Association to fulfill part of it with them, but they hadn't gotten an SBA commitment letter yet. In other words, the deal between Fifth

Third and Kenney, the salvation of Kenney's company from the bad bankers, all depended on Kenney's old nemesis, the government. The bankers didn't like that, either.

Martin Green at Fifth Third told Kenney and Beaudoin to tell the first bank that he was certain that the SBA approval would come through. It was just a matter of time. He even offered to speak directly to the bankers, but they didn't want to, preferring to keep everything between lawyers. And Green's guarantees did nothing for the bankers.

Everyone on Kenney's side went to work on getting SBA approval.

Beaudoin says, "That was the most nervous I've ever seen Kenney. The most stressed out."

"When things get tough, don't go stick your head in the sand," Kenney says now. "*Fight.* This was 20 years of my life that could've, not necessarily gone down the tubes, but could've gone to somebody else. And how does that protect my people in here, too? If [the bank] sells it to another group based somewhere else, this place shuts down and all my people lose their jobs. And the big company takes over and they roll on with the big concept we had all our blood, sweat, and tears invested in. That just wasn't gonna happen."

Waiting to hear if they got SBA approval seemed to take forever, and the process was laborious and expensive, costing Kenney upwards of $100,000. "You wouldn't believe the stuff we had to put together for the SBA," Kenney says. "The conversation Fifth Third was getting from the SBA was all positive. It's just, again, the government. The government wheels are very slow turning."

The first bank put a deadline on Fifth Third getting SBA approval, and in the meantime, they needed to polish up their loan, because things on their end looked dicey to their superiors. Kenney hadn't made any payments since December. "They hadn't asked for it, by the way, either," says Beaudoin. "That's the other side of it. He offered to pay them, too, but they didn't want the payment."

"They didn't want me to be able to say, '*Well you accepted my payments when I didn't have a loan*,'" Kenney says.

"And I get it," says Beaudoin. "If I were on the other side, I would've done the same thing."

"But they did accept it in September the previous year when I didn't have a loan," Kenney says. "September, October, November, and December."

In mid-March, Beaudoin worked out an extension with the first bank. Kenney would only pay interest, allowing the principle of the loan would stay the same. When applying for an SBA loan, one has to apply for a specific amount, and can't apply for more than is needed. The SBA doesn't want people taking out loans for cash. They couldn't pay down the principle with the first bank because what Kenney owed them needed to stay in line with what Fifth Third was saying they would put up combined with what they were applying for from the SBA. "Otherwise the numbers don't work," Beaudoin says, "and you have to start all over again."

The first bank agreed to that. They gave Kenney until June 10 to close the deal with Fifth Third, and until May 10 to get SBA's letter of commitment. In the meantime, Kenney could make interest-only payments for March through June, and he had to come current on the interest payments for January and February. He also had to pay interest and fees on those because he was paying them late. "Which wasn't right in my mind," Kenney says. "But at this point, I had Fifth Third telling me they were pretty sure we were gonna have a deal, and that they felt really good about the SBA. I was just ready to move on. They'd worn me down. They'd exhausted all the fight in me."

Or so he thought. He was fine with everything, ready to agree to it all, and then Beaudoin told him the kicker. "To secure the deal, you've got to pledge your stock." And not just to Hwy 55, but also to all of Kenney's companies — A & E Vends, Dylan James Equipment, several more. Everything.

If Kenney put up his stock for collateral, and the bank decided to call the note, which still felt too possible, then they owned everything.

On top of that, Kenney felt like the bank asking for his stock wasn't even a business decision. It felt personal. "They knew that would set me off," he says. "That was just one more little knife. Just a little stab."

"Look," Kenney said, "I'll let them secure it with my franchise fees. They can get the proceeds." Kenney had never offered that before. "It's way more than they would need to cover the cash flow. That's how I run things. But I can't give them my stock."

Beaudoin went back to the bank's lawyer and said, "All the terms are great, except we're not giving up the stock. We're just not going to do it."

The lawyer called Beaudoin back the following Monday. "If you do not do this," he said, "then it's done. We're walking away from the table, and whatever happens happens." Kenney's deadline was Friday.

Beaudoin told Kenney what they had said.

"Nope," Kenney said. "There's no way I'm doing it."

Keith was there, too, saying, "Come *on*, Kenney. You need to do this."

Kenney's fire-eyes lit up. "I'm not gonna do it," he said. "Adam, you tell them to fuzz off."

Beaudoin called the lawyer and said, "Sorry, no dice. Our last offer stands. We'll give you anything, but we're not gonna give you that."

"And of course," Kenney says, "we got a little whisper in their ear about bankruptcy, and about unfair and deceptive trade practices, those types of things, just to let them know, *Yeah, you might try to push us, but we're gonna push you back.*"

"What's his *problem?*" the lawyer said. "Why doesn't he want to give it to us?"

"You guys don't trust him," Beaudoin said. "He doesn't trust you. This is his business. This is what he's grown. This stock represents control."

■ ■ ■

Kenney spent the rest of the afternoon thinking about it. He knew he was rolling the dice. Big-time. But he was used to that. He'd been rolling dice and risking everything all his life. And Karen, and his family, even with them, he was willing to take risks, because he knew he would find a way to take care of his family. "Bless her heart," he says. "Karen married in."

But then he started thinking about everyone else who worked for him. "That is a whole different story," he says. "This company employs so many people, and provides for their livelihood, provides food for their table, for their babies. It's a whole other thing to roll the dice with them. And that hit me that night."

He called Beaudoin around 7 p.m. "I'm gonna do it," he said.

"I could tell he was defeated," Beaudoin says. "You could hear the brokenness in his voice."

Beaudoin asked, "What changed?"

Kenney said, "It's one thing to play chicken with my own

life. And that's what I've been doing. I've been playing a serious game of chicken with a major bank. But I can't do it to all the people that work for Hwy 55, not just in my office, but everywhere. I can't play chicken with their lives."

He kept hearing that same little voice in the back of his head, the one that had been echoing for decades now, always reminding him, "It's not about you."

■ ■ ■

On Wednesday, March 27, 2013, Kenney went to Raleigh, an hour's drive from Mount Olive. Karen went with him. Beaudoin went to the Ward and Smith office in Greenville to get Kenney's stock certificates from their vault, then met up with him and Karen.

Sitting in a boardroom with them, Kenney had to excuse himself. Bathroom. To catch his breath.

While they sat there alone, Beaudoin told Karen, "I want you to know that I don't take any of this lightly. I have conferred with different people. I'm not trying to do this on my own."

"The effect that Kenney has on people amazes me," Karen says now. "Adam was just letting me know that he had done every single thing he felt like needed to be done. And he got emotional. He was physically upset that Kenney was having to go through that. He had tears in his eyes."

Kenney came back in. He could not get the paranoia out of his head, the fear out of his chest. "I just don't trust this, Adam," he said. "I just don't trust this."

Beaudoin's words and tears fresh in her mind, Karen said, "Kenney, we are going to trust Adam. He's going to be on both sides of this. He knows what he's doing. He knows what to do. This time, right now, the eleventh hour, we are not going to pull out. This is it. We have to do this. And you know we have to do this."

"If Adam hadn't done that, hadn't said that, I probably wouldn't have been that sure of it," Karen says now. "I maybe would've just not said anything, because Kenney's judgment is sound. Very sound. He doesn't need me to tell him what to do for him. Maybe to eat. Or, you know, be quiet. Don't be so mad."

Kenney signed what he needed to sign. Beaudoin took the stock to another room. He didn't want the exchange to happen in front of Kenney. He gave the documents and the stock certificates to the bank's two lawyers. "The lawyers were obviously happy," he says now, "but they were also relieved in a lot of ways, too. I don't think they wanted to have the fight. We had come so far, and done so much good in terms of building up and getting a win-win for everybody."

Beaudoin remembers asking the lawyers, "Why are you guys doing this to him? Why did you push this?" And he remembers them telling him that the bankers wanted it because "they wanted to make sure Kenney was serious about Fifth Third."

Beaudoin says now, "That's not good business. But see, the lawyers can't tell you that. They were doing their jobs, doing what their client required. At the time, it's negotiating. But the stock is equal to the same amount as the cash flow. They already had the equipment. They already had the inventory. They could have taken the cash flow instead of the stock. What did the stock give them? Nothing. It was symbolic."

"It was totally symbolic," Kenney says. "And they knew that bothered me."

"The lawyers knew they didn't have to have it to get the deal done," Beaudoin says. "That was one of the worst days

I've had as a practicing lawyer. I mean, just not wanting to do that, and having to go with Kenney, somebody I have a lot of respect for, and for him to have to do that, to fall on his own sword over something that didn't need to happen — it hurt me."

■ ■ ■

After the meeting, Kenney, Karen, and Beaudoin went to lunch at the Hwy 55 in the Crabtree Valley Mall in Raleigh. Beaudoin ordered something off-menu that he'd ordered at other Hwy 55s before: Two Andy's cheeseburgers, no bun, smothered with cheesesteak. "The Beaudoin Special," Kenney calls it. The waitress was young and new, and she didn't know Kenney, and she got flustered. "I gotta go check and see if you can do that," she said and then scurried away.

Even then, on one of the worst days of his life, Kenney wasn't insulted by the fact that a waitress in one of his stores didn't recognize him, Founder and President and Grand Whatever of Hwy 55. He just laughed. "Don't worry," he told Adam. "We'll make sure you get that."

Beaudoin got his Beaudoin Special.

And as always, Kenney picked up the check.

■ ■ ■

From that day, March 27, until the June 10 deadline to close the deal with Fifth Third, there was much sitting around and waiting and stressing, and not much sleeping. The deadline for SBA's commitment, May 10, came and went. Beaudoin stayed on the phone with the first bank, convincing them to relax, to trust them to get this done.

Kenney stayed in constant contact with Martin Green and the Fifth Third team. They worked on his loan and almost nothing else for the better part of a month. "Restaurant equipment is not the most fabulous collateral," Kenney says. "It really isn't. It has very limited use beyond the restaurant. So they had to do a lot of arm-twisting."

At one point, Kenney couldn't stand the suspense any longer, and he called Green at home on a Saturday night. He could hear his little kids playing in the background. "Martin, just tell me," Kenney said. "In your heart of hearts, in your gut, on a scale of zero to one hundred percent, how positive are you the SBA is gonna do this?"

"Ninety-nine percent."

▩ ▩ ▩

The SBA commitment letter arrived on June 5. Now, with some of the steps involved after — getting real estate deeds of trust in place once SBA approval was secured, and other boring, tedious details not worth getting into — all parties involved knew that there was no way to close on the deal on June 10. But everyone was excited. Even the first bank felt comfortable at that point. Everyone knew the loan was going to happen. Kenney was going to get the first bank out of his life and start with a new bank, Fifth Third, that knew him and believed in him and his vision. Kenney bought a few big, expensive bottles of Camus wine that he planned to crack open whenever they closed the deal.

And then the first bank sent over their term sheet on June 10.

They said everything was fine, and they would only keep charging interest — but then Beaudoin noticed something else: a $50,000 default waiver fee, out of nowhere.

Beaudoin says now, "It's not rooted in anything legal. It's not in any of the loan documents. It was blood money."

Beaudoin called Kenney. "Over the past seven months, I've

asked you to eat a lot of crow," he said. "But this time — no. Do not pay this."

Keith was on the call, and he said, "But it's only $50,000."

"It doesn't matter," Beaudoin said. "There's no way that I, as your lawyer, can tell you to pay this money. This is just one last kick at you on the way out the door."

"That's exactly how it feels," Kenney said. "There's no way I'm paying it. Absolutely no way. Do what you gotta do. Tell 'em to shove it."

Beaudoin called the bank's lawyers. "We are not paying this," he said.

"Or what? The loan's not gonna close."

"Well," Beaudoin said, "then the loan's not gonna close."

The lawyers didn't have the authority to get rid of the $50,000, so they told Beaudoin that they would have to talk to Misters Washington, Western North Carolina, and I'm Tough Too. Meanwhile, Beaudoin and Kenney went back through their correspondence with the first bank, and Beaudoin dropped a few new emails their way. "I didn't want to spoil the deal," he says. "I didn't want to do that to Kenney. But at the same time, I was threatening in a very subtle way. I wanted to let them know, *we haven't forgotten about these other things that you've done, which may or may not have been above-board, which may or may not help you if things go south.* And you know, just put the little whisper of bankruptcy in their ear. Nobody wants to deal with that. He could've rolled on. He could've done personal and corporate bankruptcy, and rolled on."

It would've been a mess to sort out. But Kenney still had the leases on a hundred stores, and he had commitments from franchisees for another 600, and now he knew that he had Fifth Third and the SBA ready to loan him whatever he needed. If the first bank tried to take over and sell his company, he would fight like crazy in court, where he believed he would win, and while they fought, he would keep on running Hwy 55.

"At this point, too," Kenney says now, "after this entire gyration, I'd already put it in my head, *you know what, if I go bankrupt, what are the worst case scenarios?* Worst case scenario is, I may not sell another state. People might come in here and go, 'I don't want to do business with this guy, because he has a bankruptcy on there.' I can explain it to them, and hopefully they'll join on. But if I don't, I've sold the rights to over 600 restaurants right now. We'll just build *that* out. And that'll still be a good company. And I won't have any debt. So I had made that break. *'That's fine. Let's get it on.'* But really, I knew that if they walked away from $5 million over $50,000, they were idiots. But I was willing to let them be idiots."

The bank's lawyer called back two days later, on June 12. "We're sorry," the lawyer said, "but we can't budge on that."

"Okay," Beaudoin said. "Well, I'm really sorry, and this is gonna be a real shame. But I think you oughta go above the head of whoever you're talking to. Whoever that person is who's holding the line on the fifty grand, you need to get to their boss."

The lawyer came back to Beaudoin later that day and said that the bankers said there was no way Kenney was walking away from the deal. Beaudoin says, "They reminded us the bank had his stock, his franchise fees, all of his real estate, basically everything. It was like they were saying, *'Really? He's going to give all of that up over fifty grand?'*"

Beaudoin replied, "Guys. Who are we talking about here? This is Kenney Moore. And I'm telling you, Kenney Moore is crazy enough to tell you to shove this deal and go bankrupt on you."

The lawyer went back to the bankers, passed along the message.

Months later, Beaudoin had a chance to talk with the lawyer as a peer and not an adversary, and that day came up. The lawyer said that the three bankers had all been in a conference room working on Kenney's deal together. When Kenney refused to pay the $50,000, two of the bankers relented, but one of them — you can probably guess who — wouldn't give it up, saying something to the effect of, "That's gonna be my footprint on his butt, and I'm gonna make it hurt."

The others told him to let it go — if he let it go, the loan was gone, and the psycho was gone, and none of them had to be threatened to have their asses kicked in Mount Olive, North Carolina anymore.

Two days later, the bank sent Kenney a new term sheet. The fifty grand was gone.

The deal was going to close.

■ ■ ■

On June 27, everything was squared away for Kenney to close his deal with Fifth Third. Beaudoin went to the Hwy 55 corporate office to review everything with Kenney and the staff. They went through every document, page by page. "Martin Green, and those guys at Fifth Third, they really showed why they got Kenney's business," Beaudoin says. "At the end of the day, they may have been the only ones that gave a good, legitimate deal."

Green told Kenney that, coming down the stretch, they had a dozen people working on the loan as hard as they could.

Also worth noting: For the money to be wired into Kenney's trust account, he needed all of his accounts moved over to

Fifth Third, and he needed automatic debit set up, and he had to iron out several more details, and he didn't have any of it yet — and Fifth Third gave him zero grief for it. Kenney says, "It was, '*Here, catch your breath. Go run your company. We'll leave you alone. Yes, there are quarterly things that we need to see to make sure that our money is well taken care of.*' Perfectly understandable. '*But go run your company. That's what you do.*'"

Fifth Third also gave him a break on starting his loan payments. For the first six months, they told him only to pay interest, and pay off $250,000, and then don't worry about anything else. "They were very flexible," Beaudoin says. "Because they knew that when the clock struck midnight on 2013 and we moved into 2014, he's going to have more stores open, and Kenney's cash flow would boom, and he would be able to continue to grow the business, and not have the loan cripple him."

In other words, they trusted Kenney, and more than that, where nobody else had, Fifth Third looked at Kenney's and Hwy 55's futures, and they believed in them.

▪ ▪ ▪

Kenney signed everything that needed to be signed, and then he called Neal and April Dennis and Guy Guthrie, along with Dave Thompson, his Chief Business Development Officer, and Bobby Parker, his Marketing Director, and some other employees into the Hwy 55 conference room. He broke out his bottles of Camus wine. He offered Beaudoin a glass, but Beaudoin doesn't drink red wine, and besides, he had a drive to Raleigh to make and loan documents to deliver.

Kenney and everyone else sat around in the conference room drinking and reflecting. Looking back, Kenney saw things more clearly. "You have to understand, when all of this was happening to me, the banks were under incredible scrutiny from the federal government at the same time," he says. "Dodd Frank was passed. Our president said he was going to clean up the banking industry at that time. All of the banks got lumped under this new legislation and regulation. And so banks changed their relationship with their customers. And I got caught in that. It was a perfect storm. I got caught right in the middle of it. Relationships didn't matter anymore. And that's kind of where it went."

He adds, "If I had it to do all over again, the only thing I would've done different, I think, is, I would've held my million dollars. I wouldn't have made a payment. I would've said, *'Come here, let's talk.'* That would've put me in more of a strength position. I could've said, *'Look. We have some bad franchisees here. I'm willing to take it all on. But here are my terms.'* I kind of set a precedent that year by making the payments. I kind of was at their mercy a little bit. But at the very beginning, I should have said, *'Oh boys, you gotta mess on your hands here! But here's how I can help.'* That's what I would've done differently. That's the difference.

"I had bankers on a certain level as business people, and I still do with the ones I deal with today, but I also found out that a lot of times, people wear really nice suits but they're not as smart as they like to act and think they are. I came away with that. I had them intellectually at a certain level, and I learned some of them just aren't that smart.

"And I've come away less trusting. That's a lesson I've learned from all of this. You just can't trust people. Or at least, you have to be very careful of the people you trust.

"I've come away a little bit harder, too, as far as, I'm not going to take everybody's problems, either. I don't do that as much as I used to. I will help to a certain level, but I'm not going to take everybody's problems in the future. I didn't create them. Especially if you don't follow the processes and the game plan we put in front of you. You don't do that, and you get in trouble, what do you want me to do? If you had followed everything hook, line, and sinker, I may be willing to help you, but if you've got your own vision of what being a restaurant owner is, or what being a manager is, or whatever, and you don't follow our plan, then why do you want me to help you? So I've gotten a little bit tougher. I've learned some good life lessons. Some good, very expensive life lessons."

■ ■ ■

After a couple of hours of drinking and celebrating, Kenney's phone rang. It was Beaudoin. He was in his car on his way back to Wilmington. While he was delivering the loan documents in Raleigh, Beaudoin picked up something, too.

"I've got your stock," he said. "I just want to let you know. I've got it in my hands."

"Thank you, brother," Kenney said.

He hung up. Took another sip of wine. And then Kenney cried.

And cried.

And cried.

And he kept crying, harder and harder.

He put down his wine glass and pushed his chair back and leaned forward, bawling, holding his face in his hands with tears spilling through his fingers.

"And I'm a man's man," he says now. "I'm a tough guy, I can handle anything, and that — I just *broke*."

Some of the people in the room had known him for two decades, and they'd never seen him like this. Someone at some point called Karen, and soon she was there to tell him she loved him and to hold him.

"It just came out of me," he says. "It finally came out of me. I had been carrying all this stuff, and it finally melted off. I disintegrated. I turned into jelly."

He cried for half an hour, right there in front of his executive staff, broken before everyone, before he looked up.

And when he looked up, he saw that everyone was still in the room, everyone had stayed, and they were all crying with him.

24

A PRAYER THE LIKES OF WHICH
KENNEY NEVER PRAYED BEFORE

By the end of 2013, Hwy 55 sold the rights to 600 stores. Kenney could realistically predict for them to go from a $50 million company to at *least* a $250 million company within 10 years.

Toward the end of the year, the *Franchise Business Review* put out a list ranking the 40 top food franchises in the country, a list that included Auntie Anne's Pretzels (№ 7) and Hardee's (№ 9). Hwy 55 was ranked № 6, barely behind Firehouse Subs (№ 3) and Checkers/Rally's (№ 5).

But for all the wonderful new franchisees and master franchisees Hwy 55 was bringing in, the company still felt squeezed. They were still working through their debt. They'd spent a ton of money over the past few years dealing with the bad franchisees and the bank, as well as building up franchising beyond North Carolina. Plus, January was a down month, as usual for the restaurant business. Hwy 55 was poised to do some great things in the future, but in the present, money was tight.

"There was a lot of gearing up and bringing up new personnel and a lot of new things that had to happen to support the franchising outside of the state of North Carolina," Kenney says. "That cost a lot of money. But we had to invest in the future. And also, as part of the Affordable Care Act along with the wanting to support people, I had to downsize the amount of corporate stores I had. Every time you close a store on the first of the month, the bills continue to come in for the previous month, but the cash flow has ceased. So *that* cost a lot of money."

And then Kenney had to handle some problems he'd been having with a franchisee. For all the great growth and amazing things happening with his company, Kenney still couldn't help but get personally involved.

Like many the franchisee of the past, "Rick" made life miserable for everyone at Hwy 55. He was a former minimum wage employee to whom Kenney gave an enormous and gracious opportunity. Rick was 33 years old in 2011, a former convict who had served jail time, but he sat in Kenney's office with tears in his eyes and told him he'd turned his life around. Kenney believed him.

Several people in the office told Kenney not to sell Rick the restaurant, but Rick had been a great employee for several years, and Kenney loves to take chances on people who've done wrong but are trying to make right, so Kenney sold him a store. And for a year and a half, Rick was phenomenal. He did great work, gathered a good core of workers underneath him, and the store did its best numbers ever. Things went so well that Rick bought another store about half an hour from his first one.

But in mid-2013, around the time that Kenney resolved everything with the bank and signed his loan with Fifth Third, Rick hired people to run his stores who ended up stealing from them, and then he started slacking off, and in no time, Rick was $175,000 in debt and behind on all his bills. "Worse than I was in Year One," Kenney says.

Both his stores were struggling, while Rick worked 10 hours a week, if that. Rick's food distributor cut him off for not paying bills. Customers were calling the corporate office, saying. Rick's store didn't have fries or even cups. "Some people," Kenney says, "for some reason, just self-implode."

■ ■ ■

Between his own financial strain, and Rick, and everything else, Kenney was stressed out all over again that January, so stressed that he did something he had never, ever done before, something he'd never been comfortable doing.

He prayed to God for help.

Remember, he's always prayed, even back before he knew what he believed. He would thank God for his blessings, he would pray for protection for his children and his family, but he never prayed for himself.

Well, that January, he prayed for himself. Not for a lot. "Just for a little help," he says. "I guess I was looking for some kind of help, some kind of sign, that all of this was going the direction it needed to be going."

■ ■ ■

On January 1, Kenney and Neal met with Rick. Kenney said, if Rick wanted, he'd take over Rick's first store so that Rick wouldn't get buried, and he'd take Rick's debt for overdue bills, missed rent, and more — some $140,000 — *and* he would eat his royalty fee. That left Rick with $35,000 in debt instead of $175,000, and free to run his second store and get his act together. Rick agreed to everything.

In the first week after that, Kenney paid Rick's manager for missed paychecks, came current on the rent payments to Rick's landlord, bought new uniforms for all the staff, cleaned up the restaurant, and stocked the kitchen full of fresh food.

On Jan. 7, Rick texted Neal, saying, in essence, that he'd changed his mind, and that if they didn't give him back his stores, "it's showtime." It was as irrational and nonsensical a threat as Kenney had ever heard. "I said, fine," Kenney says. "We'll reset him. Now he's right back to where he was. Which means he's three months behind on his rents. He's going to get eviction letters from them. His royalty payments bounced in December, so he's going to get a default letter from me. Oh, and by the way, our food distributor, they're cutting him off, too. So now he's buried himself. I try to help him, and then we get those texts, which make no sense, and which are threatening me."

Not so long ago, Kenney probably would have raged about it all, but now, "after 22 years, I'm finally getting less shocked by human beings," he says. "There was a time I would've ranted and raved and stomped around this office and called him every name in the book. 'What an ingrate,' on and on. But now I can just take it as it is. And say hey, you know, maybe he's still that guy who grew up in that rough atmosphere and that's just coming back to haunt him now. The sad part is, he's done it to himself — but the *scary* part is that he's trying to blame it on everybody else. Nobody got him in debt. Nobody made him not pay his bills. Nobody made him not go to work.

"It seems to be a common theme with some of our younger owners: They can't take any responsibility for where they put themselves. And instead of going and saying *'Okay, I've gotten myself into a bind, I'm going to work twice as hard to come out of that bind,'* they hide. They stick their head in the sand, and think it'll all go away, or somebody will come save them.

"When I started this company, the first year I was in business, I managed to finance four stores and get four stores open, and three of them were losing money, and I was $35,000 behind on my food bills. The last thing in the world I wanted to do was hide. I worked open to close. I told myself, *'If this doesn't work, I will not have any regrets whatsoever.'* There was going to be no regrets. I would've worked every hour that I could have. I would've saved as much labor cost as I could have by doing the work and cleaning the restaurant up by myself. Getting over that initial hump was pure work ethic, pure going-and-getting-after-it, every single day. And then, this past year when I had all my issues with the bank, the same thing. It was, work. *Fight.* It wasn't run and hide.

"Evander Holyfield was sitting on his stool in the late rounds of a fight with Riddick Bowe. He was beaten and battered by the bigger man, and he thought of his mom. He remembered back to his her putting welfare papers back in the mailbox, saying, 'We don't need this.' And she worked two jobs. And he said now, how tough is it to get back up and fight this man right now? See? That was the voice that resonated in his head.

"And what resonates in Rick's head is the message of, *it's everybody else's fault.*

"If he had kept showing up to the managers' meetings every single month, my little 20-minute talk would change that. Would leave him out of here fired up. *I can be somebody. I can do this.* But he quit plugging in. You gotta stay plugged in. He hadn't been to a meeting in at least four months. You want to be successful? You stay around successful people."

■ ■ ■

So Kenney reset Rick. And within a couple of weeks, Rick was evicted. Kenney heard rumors that Rick and his girlfriend had a substance abuse problem, which pretty well explained everything.

They needed to get Rick's first store back in shape. And even though the company was exploding, going international and riding high, Kenney and his corporate staff still handled it same as they had in the early days. Kenney got into his black $100,000 Tesla Model S and drove to Rick's store, and Keith, Neal, April, and a couple more people from the corporate office rode with and followed him.

Kenney wore brown loafers, slacks, a nice polo shirt. Same for Neal and some of the other men. Keith wore a suit and tie. April wore a pantsuit. They put a sign on the door saying "RE-OPENING SOON. SPRING CLEANING. UNDER NEW MANAGEMENT." And they literally rolled up their sleeves and got to work. They cleaned the fryers, they re-painted everything. Keith rolled walls in pink paint without ever taking off his jacket. They spent the entire day there. Kenney joked with one of the store's cooks, who came in to help, saying, "How many CEOs of companies worth what our company's worth do you think are cleaning and painting restaurants right now?" The guy laughed and says, "None." And after two more days of cleaning and landscaping, the place looked brand new.

"I really do have a wonderful, wonderful group of people," Kenney says. "They're all passionate about what we do, which was proven when we all converged upon a store and went old school. And you know, it was kind of fun to just work on a store, and get it right, and have some conversations with staff, and get out of the office a little bit and do that again."

Kenney held onto that to ease his stress, to keep him hopeful. He still had his family, and they still worked with blue-collar hearts. It wasn't the visible hand of God writing *"You are going to be okay"* on the wall, but it was *something.*

He had no idea what was coming next.

25

TEN CRAZY DAYS IN JANUARY
Or, The Prayer is Answered

On January 20, 2014, two men flew from Texas to Wilmington, North Carolina, to meet with their investing partner, Rex Stephens, a small, energetic 73-year-old man with glasses and whispy white hair who had made a killing in real estate development. They all went to church the next morning, and then they drove north on Highway 117, on their way to an ATV park that they were considering developing in Texas.

After about an hour, they wanted lunch. They passed through a small town named Calypso and couldn't find anything, followed a sign to the next small town of Faison (population 300), and found nothing there, either. They stopped at a grocery store, where the manager old them that right around the corner, there was a little restaurant, Southern Exposure, that had great food. But it was too fancy for their taste, so they got back on the highway and rode until they got to Mount Olive. Stephens said, "There has to be an Andy's around here somewhere." He'd been eating at Andy's — a lot of people in North Carolina continue to call it that

— since Kenney opened his first one in 1991, and he ate at the Hwy 55 in Wilmington all the time. "You guys are going to *love* this food," Stephens said.

They found the restaurant around noon. The place was packed. They managed to get a table. A waitress took their drink orders and then disappeared. Another waitress came up. "Hey," she said. "What can I get you guys?" She was young, mid-twenties or so, with brown eyes and brown hair and a nice smile.

"Oh, someone's already gotten our drink," Stephens said.

"Don't worry about it," the girl said. "I'll take care of you the rest of the day."

She took their order, and they got their drinks and then their food — and they were blown away. They devoured their burger, they guzzled their orangeade, they thought it was everything Stephens had promised and more.

"I wonder if they're franchising?" said John from Texas.

"I think they are," Stephens said.

Stephens called their waitress over. "Do you know anything about the franchising that's going on with Hwy 55?"

■ ■ ■

At the Hwy 55 corporate office, there appears to be a '57 Chevy parked in the lobby. The Chevy is authentic, but it's only the front of the car: The rest has been converted into a desk used by the corporate receptionist, who greet visitors saying, "Welcome to Hwy 55. My name is Amber. How can I help you?"

Amber works at the office fulltime, and she's trying to save money, so she also often works another 10 to 20 hours a week as a waitress at the Mount Olive Hwy 55. And when Rex Stephens and his investor friends ended up in that Hwy 55 that Sunday, Amber was his waitress.

■ ■ ■

"As a matter of fact, I work at the corporate office," she told him. "What do you need to know?"

She answered several of their questions, and she gave them a card and wrote Guy Guthrie's personal cell phone number on it. They were on their way.

Monday morning, Guthrie got a phone call from John in Texas. They talked for 45 minutes, Guthrie answering question after question.

"Okay," John said. "We're going to send you a deposit check for the state of Texas."

Hwy 55's master franchising is structured so that each store serves an area of about 100,000 people. This helps prevent overcrowding. In Texas, with a population of 26.5 million people, that means 265 locations.

Nobody had *ever* sent in a deposit check for an entire state.

■ ■ ■

Guthrie went to Kenney's office to fill him in. "And I'm not excited," Kenney says. "I'm like, okay. Sure. It's not that I'm jaded. Or cynical. It's just, we don't *know* this guy."

John told Guthrie that they were going to send him a copy of the check by email, and that he would get the actual check by mail soon, and in the meantime, he should look for a letter from the bank on behalf of Rex Stephens.

The next day, Guthrie got the letter, which verified that Stephens had more than adequate liquidity and assets to back up the deposit. Guthrie showed Kenney the letter. "I think this is serious," he said.

"All right, let's invite him to a Discovery Day," Kenney

said. "And make it whatever day he wants to do it. I know we normally do it on Wednesday, but hey, if they're this eager, we'll set one up this week."

Guthrie called Stephens, who said that he could meet on Thursday morning. Guthrie said great, and he told Stephens to meet them in Newton Grove, a little town between Raleigh, Wilmington, and Mount Olive, and they'd drive him the rest of the way to the Crabtree Valley Mall in Raleigh, where they always do the restaurant portion of their Discovery Days. Then they could all drive back to Mount Olive for Stephens to get to know their corporate office.

Guthrie reported back to Kenney, who had a sudden *feeling* that they should move Discovery Day to Guthrie's store in Kenansville. It was closer to Wilmington and Mount Olive, and Kenney knew that Guthrie had just remodeled it. "Let's just take him to Kenansville," he said. He had no idea why. They had never done a Discovery Day anywhere other than Raleigh. Again, it came down to *feel,* and *It's Not About You* — this would make things easier on Stephens.

Guthrie called Stephens back and told him to meet them at the Kenansville store at 10 a.m. on Thursday.

The deposit check arrived Wednesday.

On Thursday, Stephens arrived in Kenansville at 9:40.

Stephens had always liked the Andy's/Hwy 55 concept, and he liked how it had evolved over the years. But one thing he never did like was how bland the interiors always seemed. For a long time they were just walls of mirrors. The bathrooms were also boring, nothing more than plain white walls.

Guthrie's store was not boring. He had the walls covered with period memorabilia — vinyl records large and small, paintings of Marilyn Monroe and Elvis, and everything was fun and colorful. Even the bathrooms looked good.

Stephens walked in and said, "This place looks amazing. It's not like any of your other locations. Is this a new look?"

"Kenney's always lenient on the interiors," Guthrie said. "You can do pretty much whatever you want to do to design it as long as it has the '50s flair and the same color scheme."

One of the area operators they brought in for the Discovery Day was Kachina, who'd never done a Discovery Day before, and usually didn't even work in Kenansville.

As Neal and April were talking with Stephens, Kachina came up to Guthrie and said, "I think I know him. He's from Wilmington, right?"

"Yeah, Rex Stephens."

"Yep. He and I have met."

Kachina and Stephens started talking, and she told him that five years before, when she was 19 years old and had just started running a store near Wilmington, he had come in and given her his business card and spoken with her like a true professional. He was the first person in her life to do that, she said, and he'd inspired her. She ran out to her car and grabbed his business card, having saved it all those years. "I even change card portfolios over the years," she said, "and I would make sure to pull your card out and put it in the new one."

As they ate lunch in Kenansville, "He keeps saying these one-liner quotes that Kenney always says," says Guthrie now. "I mean, they're saying the same things. And these guys have never met each other."

Then they go back to Mount Olive to meet Kenney, who had a 24-hour virus and almost missed Discovery Day. Karen convinced him to sleep in that morning, so by now, he was feeling better. He elbow-bumped Stephens instead of shaking his hand, and then they proceeded with the grand tour.

Stephens had no idea how organized Hwy 55 was. Like Khamis Al Rumaithy and Hussein Sefket, Stephens loved the Sysdine system, and he was impressed by how they ran their office and everything else. He told them, "I've been studying ya'll for a long time. I've wanted stores since back when you weren't franchising. I really wanted one of these. But now that you've done this new look and you guys have really come a long way, I definitely, definitely want to do this. I was a 9 on a scale of 10, but now I'm a 14. And to tell you the truth, I feel as though God led me right to you. Where do I sign?"

They all laughed and then groaned — Guthrie still had to give Stephens the franchise disclosure documents, and federal law required Stephens to wait two weeks after receiving them before he could sign.

Stephens called his investment partners in Texas and said, "This is a done deal. I would've written them a check today if they would've let me."

It didn't end there.

A few days after his Discovery Day, Stephens called Guthrie. "Hey, I've got a buddy down in Charleston," he said. "Whatever I do, he wanted to be involved, and whatever he does, I'm involved. Is the state of Georgia available?"

"Yes sir, it is," Guthrie said.

"It is, all right?" Stephens said. "We want Georgia, then. Put us down for Georgia."

Guthrie fired off the franchise disclosure documents.

It didn't end there, either.

The next day, Guthrie got a phone call from John in Texas, who had a few quick questions. As they wrapped up, John said, "You know, I've got some buddies in Charlotte that run an investment group. I was talking to them yesterday, and they asked me what I was up to, and I said, '*Well, actually, we're investigating doing this burger concept in Texas.'* And the next thing out of the guy's mouth was, *'Hwy 55 Burgers?'* I said, *'Yeah, you know about them?'* The guy goes, *'Yeah, we were checking them out not too long ago. See if Georgia's available. See if Tennessee's available. And see if Virginia's available.'"*

"I think Georgia's been spoken for," said Guy, not believing any of this was happening, "but Tennessee's available, and I've got the western part of Virginia."

"Okay," said John. "I'll let them know."

It still did not end there.

A few days after that, Guthrie got a call from Stephens, who said, "You know what, Guy? I've been up all night. I've been studying. I've been looking at the maps. And there's that Dallas to Oklahoma City corridor that is just fantastic. There's so much traffic on there, and there's so much oil in Oklahoma. Is Oklahoma available?"

"Yes sir. Let me look real quick and see what the population is."

"It's 3.8 million people," Stephens said. "That's 38 stores."

"It sure is."

"Yeah, I gotta have that," Stephens said. "I gotta have Texas and Oklahoma. They're together. And I gotta have that corridor. Put me down for Oklahoma."

"Okay," Guthrie said. "Do you want me to just wrap that into your original agreement?"

"Can you do that?" Stephens said. "And if you do that, can you separate later between Oklahoma and Texas?"

"Sir," Guthrie said, "I'll do whatever you want me to do."

Nor did it end *there.*

A couple of days after *that,* the man from Charleston called. He wanted to talk about the Georgia deal and get all of that squared away — and then he said, "I've been talking with my dad, and he wants to know if Kentucky's available."

■ ■ ■

This all happens in a week and a half.

■ ■ ■

After the Kentucky call, Guthrie went to talk to Kenney.

In astonishment, Kenney told him about the prayer he'd prayed not two weeks earlier, asking God for a little help.

Guthrie said, "Are you serious?"

"Yeah?"

"I did the same exact thing," Guthrie said. "About two weeks ago, I said, 'God, just send me somebody. Send me one person right now. I need a little help.'

Guthrie has to sell franchises in order to maintain the lifestyle that he had when he owned stores, and it had been tough. He says, "It's just eerie how this all fell together."

"It's not eerie," Kenney says. "It's spiritual. Let's summarize: A sincere prayer, times two. They're in Calypso, North Carolina. Can't find anything to eat. Decide to not sit down at a restaurant in Faison and eat. Go past the one, two other restaurants that would've been quick and good. They decide on Hwy 55. And who waits on them? Somebody from the corporate office who can answer their questions, who happens to be working there part-time, for just a little extra cash. All right? And then, switching to *Kenansville*, of all places. I had not even *seen* the store at that point. I just assumed Guy would do a first-class job with it, which he did. I loved it. And then, Kachina, of all people, who *never* does Discovery Day, we bring her in just because we want to have a couple old-timers in there to make sure we handle it properly.

"So then I start talking about our servant leader philosophy, I start talking about all that, and he loves it. And it's just an incredible match. And I have a 73-year-old man that is just a kindred spirit. I'd like to grow up to be like him. Not necessarily his wealth or whatever, but I'd like to be that kind of 73-year-old man — a nice Southern gentleman, and still have that fire in my belly."

Kenney laughs and throws out his hands. "This was a gamechanger. This was an amazing series of events. You're looking at the rights to 400 stores being sold in 10 days. Four *hundred*. In *10 days*. It's *crazy*. It's almost a doubling of the company. It takes us to basically the rights to over 1,000 locations. This takes us well toward becoming a billion-dollar company."

■ ■ ■

In the following months, Hwy 55 opened new stores that set company sales records one week after another. One of their stores in Georgetown, in April 2014, made $53,478 in sales in its first week. Kenney couldn't help but laugh at that — it had taken him six years from starting the company before he had a story make $50,000 in a *month*.

Through the spring and summer of 2014, Hwy 55's corporate office fielded so many franchising information requests that they could barely keep up. Whatever worries Kenney ever had about the fate of the company were long gone. Now his biggest problem was figuring out how to manage their growth and make sure they grew well.

As they grew in size, they also matured. Many of their old stores underwent design updates to incorporate the '50s theme. Bobby Parker, Hwy 55's Vice President of Marketing, says that they are trying to make their design, and their whole brand, more unique compared to other fast-casual restaurants such as Five Guys, Zaxby's, and the like. "What has so many people on, say, the Apple bandwagon, isn't just the functionality and the way Apple products operate," Parker says. "It's the art behind it. If you're buying an Apple product, you're not just buying the product and the things it does for you. You're buying the art that Apple infuses all of their work with. And that's what we want to be. We're going to become the Apple of the fast-casual dining industry."

■ ■ ■

In the late spring of 2014, Kenney joined state business leaders at a big round-table meeting with North Carolina Secretary of Commerce Sharon Decker. She was intrigued by Hwy 55's growth, particularly in Abu Dhabi. "I reminded her, whatever you do, just think long-term," Kenney says. "Is what you're doing going to be a help or a hindrance? I said, I'm feeling a tick up right now in everything. The best thing you can do is not mess that up."

26

THE END AND THE BEGINNING

One day in May 2014, two doors down the hall from Kenney's office, a new nameplate went up on an office door: THE ORIGINAL ANDY.

Andy Moore, son of a man who almost didn't hack it at a two-year college, graduated from Duke University in 2012. He majored in political science, but he also worked for The Chronicle, Duke's student newspaper, as sports editor, and he interned with a Washington, D.C. media firm specializing in digital communication for high profile clients. After Andy graduated, Kenney offered him a job with Hwy 55, but Andy didn't take it. Like most millennials, he wanted to strike out on his own, blaze his own path and make his mark and find himself.

That's not to say they have a bad relationship. They are close, but different people. They think differently about politics and religion, and where Kenney is impulsive and emotional and makes decisions based off feel, Andy is more calculating and analytical, thinking through every side of everything. But they don't let these differences bruise their hearts. They know where each other stands, and they might have debates, but they won't fight. They play golf together and love each other like friends.

And Kenney always thought that once Andy grew up and grew older and struck out on his own, he'd want to be known as Andrew or Drew or something else, so he wouldn't be so identifiable as Son of Kenney, but he remained Andy.

And Andy is definitely Kenney's son in some ways, namely his passion for whatever he decides to do. He started playing baseball as a kid and heard a million stories about how great a ballplayer Kenney was back in his day. He switched to golf by high school, which he liked better and still plays a lot today. But like most sons, Andy wanted an identity different from his father's, so he threw himself into academics. He stopped homeschooling in middle school, and he won tons of academic awards in the regular school system, never making lower than an A throughout high school.

After graduating from Duke, when Andy decided to go somewhere else, he really went somewhere else. He went to New York City, where in 2012 he took a job with Woven Digital as an associate editor for one of its websites, where he helped increase readership from 2.4 million to 6.3 million per month by 2014.

But he wearied of that world, of doing work he wasn't sure would have any real or lasting impact, and when he looked at what his dad was doing back home, he knew what he wanted to do. The millennial had looked upon his father's work, and he saw that it was good.

He saw a place to build his own little empire, but more than that, he wanted to be part of what his dad and Hwy 55 had going on. He wanted to be part of something that was growing, something that was changing people's lives. "And not just the charity work they do," Andy says. "It's really empowering how their business model enables people to work up to owning their own business."

So he called his father and he said, "I would love to come home." Andy's apartment lease in New York was due to expire in June, and when it did, he wanted to be working for Hwy 55. He'd already mentally broken from his job and from New York City, and he was reading books on the restaurant industry. He also insisted that his hiring not be nepotism, something that Andy's always been sensitive about, and he sent over a resume and a letter detailing everything he had to offer.

Kenney gave him the job — Director of Communications — and told him to come on home. He'd even pay his June rent.

Andy started by taking over Hwy 55's social media, which had never been utilized particularly well, and he made plans to do much more. "They're doing some pretty special things here," he says, "and I want to help. I mean, it's somewhere I don't feel like a spin doctor. All I'm doing is getting the word out about what they're doing."

■ ■ ■

All of this, everything from 2014, Kenney says, "It's divine. And I never say things like that. I don't think of the world in those terms, that God is involved in everything. But I've been sitting here thinking about what the catalyst has been, and it has to be that prayer. If I had to pick one moment — that's when things started to shift. I just said, 'God, help me.' It's almost like he looked at me and said, 'I've been waiting for you to ask.' If I had lost my way a little bit in the last five years, trust me, God didn't just give me a sign. He hit me over the head with a two-by-four. And he continues to hit me with it."

There is, of course, the question of *Why?* Why would God

respond to people like Kenney, for whom, all things considered, life is pretty amazing, with so much going bad around the world, human beings suffering horrible things?

Given this question, Kenney thinks for a minute, then says, "Maybe this is a reason: When I get up in front of a store and do that staff meeting, I always say, 'I'm not your preacher, I'm not your teacher, I'm not your mom, I'm not your dad. This is what worked for me.' Without fire and brimstone or without telling them, 'Or else!' like parents do — without making them feel forced, or blackmailed, or like criminals. I just say, 'Hey, look, I'm rough around the edges, I am what I am, but this is what's worked for me — this is what took me from $500 to now doing potentially a billion dollars, and this is the discussion I had internally that night with God.'

"Now, once again, I'm not a preacher. You want to sit here and discuss the Bible with me, and ask me what Philippians whatever is? I'll have no idea what you're talking about. But I know what has happened to me and why I believe it has happened. It all leads back to the only thing that really matters. Whether you call him Allah, or you call him God, or you call him Buddha, or whatever — it doesn't matter, because the tenet that comes out of that is always going to be the same, and the message is the same, and that is: Love."

■ ■ ■

Speaking of love.

Everything was going well, too well, and then there was another spark that everyone in the office thought would wake the demons up again, make the volcano in Kenney's chest erupt again. And it fell right onto his office desk, where Keith, his kid half-brother, left a ranting eight-page letter when he quit, on the very same day that the nameplate went up on

Andy's door.

Kenney and Keith had a big disagreement a couple of weeks earlier, and the disagreement turned into a fight, and then Keith started fighting with others in the office, even exploding on Neal, but the details aren't all that important. Keith leaving is almost not even worth bringing up, except for one thing.

Keith's letter thoroughly disparaged the vision for the company Kenney had been killing himself to bring to fruition and some of the people working for Kenney, whom Kenney considers family. And you know Kenney by now. You don't like him? He can deal with that. He really wants everybody to like him, but if you don't, hey, that's fine. But to demean his company — that's to demean the people he works with, and that's demeaning his family, man.

Of all the people to leave him, and of all the ways for them to do it, this may be the nastiest. Kenney's own blood hadn't merely abandoned him, but had also, in a sense, betrayed him.

If ever something could provoke Kenney's old familiar demons, if ever something could make him rant and rave and rage and break things and scare people, this was it. Everyone in the office braced. Nobody knew who or what would be collateral damage. No, there already was damage — their hearts hurt for him. Someone made a card that said "We love you Kenney!" They all signed it, framed it, gave it to him as a group, reminding him, *We are your family, too.*

He smiled and thanked them, saying, it's nice, no, it's wonderful. It reminded him of the afternoon in the conference room with the wine and all the tears.

But they needn't have worried.

When Kenney read his brother's letter, he didn't even

flinch. He read the letter and then he tossed it aside, and then he turned in his chair and faced the big window in his office, overlooking acres and acres of gold and amber fields.

He didn't know it at the time, but within the next year, he would sell even *more* franchises all over the world, putting his total well over a thousand and his company's projected growth well over a billion dollars. Nor did he know that in January 2015, *Franchise Business Review* would name Hwy 55 as *the* single best food and dining franchise in the United States.

Even still, the volcano in Kenney's chest was dormant, the demons silent, his heart at peace. He didn't dwell on how he may have just been wronged. He thought instead about all the far, far better things there were to think about. He thought about his son coming home, about the empire he had built and how it was growing, about how he'd just survived the last few years. He thought about all the ground still left for Hwy 55 to cover, about all the many people he had to serve.

EPILOGUE
Or, What Kenney Says You
Should Learn From All This

Kenney and a writer sit in his office in Mount Olive in early 2014. Kenney wears jeans and a navy v-neck t-shirt and brown loafers with flecks of pink paint.

They talk for a long time, now and again and again, countless hundreds of hours over the next year, about chasing the American Dream, and how hard it is for some people to just work hard, and all of those hours Kenney spent slaving away at Andy's the Restaurant while Andy the Son was at home growing up, and about turning minimum wage employees into business owners, and about dealing with the likes of Johnson and Arthur and Rick, and of course, the bank saga, and a million other things.

The writer also goes to the mountains of Virginia, where the highways become two unmarked lanes that then become gravel that turns into nothing but dirt as he drives and drives and drives, until he's so far up, and so deep in the forest, that his phone doesn't work, because he wanted to find Kenney's parents, who live as far from civilization as possible. The writer talks with them and he talks with more than 300 other people over more than a thousand hours, talks and talks and talks, about how a broke, tobacco-armed boy from Newport goes from that to building a billion-dollar international company. They talk about taking dozens of broken and broke minimum wage people and helping them build their own little empires.

But today, in one of their first meetings, the writer is just curious: "What do you think this book should be about? What's the heart of it, in your mind?"

Kenney scratches at his goatee. "I think this book should be the best business book ever," he says with laugh and a big smile. He thinks a moment longer, then his big blue eyes go wide and he says, "I don't want people to read this and think, *Oh, man, he's so awesome.*"

He knows a book telling his story will hold many lessons. He spent a lifetime finding peace, and learning how to control his universe, and giving other people control of theirs. But how to boil it all down? There are countless lessons he's learned, countless things that he wants others to believe.

A moment later, he's got it. Jesus had one simple commandment under which all others fall: *Love.* Kenney boils all of his lessons down into one, too: "People should look at me and go, *Well, if THAT guy can do it, then I can do it.*"

ACKNOWLEDGEMENTS

BRANDON SNEED

I've been eating Hwy 55 burgers and cheesesteaks since I was nine years old, back when the joint was called Andy's and there were just a few of them scattered around eastern North Carolina. To get to know the Andy's/Hwy 55 creator, much less write a book about him, has been surreal, and a blast.

Kenney Moore — I can't thank you enough for agreeing to this project, and for how generous and honest you were with your story. People like you, and stories like yours, are why I do this. I'll always be grateful to know you.

Not to mention all of that crazy crew you have over at Hwy 55. It's been refreshing to be around people who seem to truly want to serve others. Thank you so much.

I don't have room here to thank the hundreds who were gracious enough to spend hours and hours of their time talking with me about Kenney and his story, especially when the questions sometimes became uncomfortable. Thank you all, so much.

Eric Lupfer, my agent at William Morris Endeavor, thank you for your feedback and your guidance.

Thank you to everyone who helped to edit and proofread

the book. Albert, Susie, Logan, Heidi, Kara — your excitement to read whatever I write is astounding but also so appreciated. And you are amazing readers — your notes always make my writing better. I'm so grateful for your help.

Also, shout-outs to others who read and gave feedback — Dad, Webb, Rick.

Glenn, thanks for your insight and advice.

Louis Dail, thank you so much for driving that beautiful car of yours to Mount Olive and letting us use it for our cover photo shoot.

Jonah! You showed up right when this process began and you hung out all along the way, first in your mom's belly and then in meetings with me, and then in my lap and by my side while I wrote and wrote and wrote, so curious about what that glowing thing was Dad was always staring at. You make life crazy and amazing, like a whacky, fun dream. You're an awesome little kid.

And of course, there is my wife, Katie. Not to make whoever's reading this part queasy from cheesiness, but I'm so glad you're my wife, and I love you so freaking much. I'm still amazed you married me, even now, going on six years later, and I'm so glad to be living this life and working on these projects and raising our son, together.

KENNEY MOORE

My thanks first and foremost to the woman I dedicated this book to, my wife Karen, who's stuck by me longer than anybody else ever could. Without you, I'm not sure I would have ever done anything worth putting into a book. Thank you.

And of course, I have to thank the rest of my family, particularly my kids, for their patience all these years, and for growing up to find their own ways to be servants themselves. You inspire me to do better constantly.

I have to thank my co-author, Brandon Sneed for the countless, seemingly thousands of hours spent talking with me — it was like therapy, man. You really fuzzing dragged those demons out of me — and I think I became a better man for it throughout this whole process. I could not have asked a better writer to tackle my story, and you captured it perfectly. This is an amazing book, and I think people are going to enjoy it immensely.

Also, thank you, Katie, for being Brandon's loving and patient and understanding wife, and thank both of you for your tireless efforts on bringing this book to the finish line and putting it out into the world, even while going through a pregnancy and raising your firstborn. You're both studs.

Thank you, also, to the many hundreds of you who participated in this book, allowing Brandon to interview you for hours on end.

And last but not least, thank you to my Hwy 55 and Andy's family for all of your hard work and passion, and for sharing our philosophy of Love Your Neighbor. You amaze me with your spirit.